Checkpoint, Temple, Church and Mosque

Anthropology, Culture and Society

Series Editors:
Professor Vered Amit, Concordia University
and
Professor Christina Garsten, Stockholm University

Recent titles:

Checkpoint, Temple, Church and Mosque

A Collaborative Ethnography of War and Peace

Jonathan Spencer, Jonathan Goodhand,
Shahul Hasbullah, Bart Klem,
Benedikt Korf and Kalinga Tudor Silva

PlutoPress
www.plutobooks.com

First published 2015 by Pluto Press
345 Archway Road, London N6 5AA

www.plutobooks.com

British Library Cataloguing in Publication Data
A catalogue record for this book is available from the British Library

ISBN   978 0 7453 3122 5   Hardback
ISBN   978 0 7453 3121 8   Paperback
ISBN   978 1 7837 1214 4   PDF eBook
ISBN   978 1 7837 1216 8   Kindle eBook
ISBN   978 1 7837 1215 1   EPUB eBook

Library of Congress Cataloging in Publication Data applied for

This book is printed on paper suitable for recycling and made from fully managed and sustained forest sources. Logging, pulping and manufacturing processes are expected to conform to the environmental standards of the country of origin.

10   9   8   7   6   5   4   3   2   1

Typeset by Stanford DTP Services, Northampton, England
Text design by Melanie Patrick
Simultaneously printed digitally by CPI Antony Rowe, Chippenham, UK
and Edwards Bros in the United States of America

Contents

List of Illustrations

Figures

Maps

Composed by *Shahul Hasbullah, Bart Klem and Marc Vis, using field observation and open sources (Google Earth, Open Street Map)*

Tables

Series Preface

Anthropology is a discipline based upon in-depth ethnographic works that deal with wider theoretical issues in the context of particular, local conditions – to paraphrase an important volume from the series: *large issues* explored in *small places*. This series has a particular mission: to publish work that moves away from an old-style descriptive ethnography that is strongly area-studies oriented, and offer genuine theoretical arguments that are of interest to a much wider readership, but which are nevertheless located and grounded in solid ethnographic research. If anthropology is to argue itself a place in the contemporary intellectual world, then it must surely be through such research.

We start from the question: 'What can this ethnographic material tell us about the bigger theoretical issues that concern the social sciences?' rather than 'What can these theoretical ideas tell us about the ethnographic context?' Put this way round, such work becomes *about* large issues, *set in* a (relatively) small place, rather than detailed description of a small place for its own sake. As Clifford Geertz once said, 'Anthropologists don't study villages; they study *in* villages.'

By place, we mean not only geographical locale, but also other types of 'place' – within political, economic, religious or other social systems. We therefore publish work based on ethnography within political and religious movements, occupational or class groups, among youth, development agencies, and nationalist movements; but also work that is more thematically based – on kinship, landscape, the state, violence, corruption, the self. The series publishes four kinds of volume: ethnographic monographs; comparative texts; edited collections; and shorter, polemical essays.

We publish work from all traditions of anthropology, and all parts of the world, which combines theoretical debate with empirical evidence to demonstrate anthropology's unique position in contemporary scholarship and the contemporary world.

Professor Vered Amit
Professor Christina Garsten

Acknowledgements

The research for this book was funded by the Economic and Social Research Council (award RES-155-25-0096), as part of its Non-Governmental Public Action (NGPA) programme. Subsequent work on analysing the field material and writing has been greatly facilitated by an International Partnership award funded by the Economic and Social Research Council (ESRC) and the British Academy (award IP090196) as well as by two grants of the Swiss National Science Foundation (awards PDFMP1 123181 and 100017_140728). Preliminary work was supported by a series of small collaborative awards from the British Council in Colombo. We are especially grateful to Jude Howell, Director of the NGPA programme, who has been an enthusiastic supporter of our work throughout. Our own universities – Edinburgh, Peradeniya, Zurich and the School of Oriental and African Studies – have provided us with the time and facilities we needed, not just for the fieldwork but for the countless meetings that are one of the pleasures of collaboration of this sort.

In Sri Lanka, we accrued many debts. At Peradeniya University: Mr W.M.K.B. Wickramasinghe, Mr Kamalaratna Thusara, Revd Pahamune Sri Sumangala, P. Malini, Mufizal Aboobucker, John Nigel, S. Satheesmohan, A.G. Fathima Shifani, N. Pushparajah. At Eastern University: Kanesh Suresh, who played a key role in supporting and helping conduct the field research; the late S. Ravindranath, Jeyapraba Suresh, Sivakolunthu Ponniah, M.B. Fowzul, A.L.M. Mujahid, Sinnah Maunaguru, Sitralega Maunaguru, Dominic Saminathan. At Southeastern University: the late Faleel Haq, S. Gunapalan, A.N. Ahmed. In Ampara: Revd Kirindiwela Somaratna, Poddiwela Chandraratna, Revd Girambe Mangala, Mr Sunil Kannangara, Mr A.A. Bawa; in Akkaraipattu: Devadasan, Eardley Bathasar, I. Riswan and A.M. Jaufar; in Kattankudy A.R. Jesmil; in Batticaloa, Ananda Galappatti and Sarola Emmanuel, Amara and Sorna, were especially hospitable, as were the staff at the Riviera guesthouse. Academic colleagues with their own long engagement in eastern Sri Lanka were enormously generous with their time and suggestions: Harini Amarasuriya, Timmo Gaaasbeek, Dennis McGilvray, Luke Heslop, Patricia Lawrence, Sidharthan Maunaguru, Neena Mahadev, Ariel Sanchez

Meertens, Kanchana Ruwanpura, Yuvi Thangarajah, Rajesh Venugopal, Rebecca Walker, Oliver Walton and Mark Whitaker. Maarten Bavinck gave us permission to use the photograph taken by his father with which we start the book.

Some of this material has been presented at seminars in Zurich, Oxford, Tufts, Johns Hopkins, Bielefeld, Lund and Fudan University. We are grateful to our hosts and interlocutors on those occasions. Early analyses were presented at the Development Studies Association annual meeting in 2008, at the Association of Asian Studies meetings in Chicago in 2009 and at the Toronto Tamil Studies conference the same year. We organized two memorable workshops at the very end of the research in 2009, one at the Hotel Topaz in Kandy, the other in Edinburgh. The participants at both provided exactly the right combination of warm encouragement and searching questions, and much of the argument of this book has been shaped by the discussions on those occasions.

Marc Vis at the University of Zurich helped us in producing the maps in the book and David Christie provided excellent editing at the very end. We are especially grateful to the University of Zurich for its support for these final stages of the process. Wolfram Lacher, then at SOAS, prepared an excellent literature review for us in the early days of the project, which we have drawn on in the opening chapters of this book. Jessica Spencer stepped in to prepare the index at the very end.

Finally we have to thank those members of our own families who have had to put up with sudden disappearances for fieldwork purposes, unexpected visitors, and the background noise of skype conversations over the years, but also meeting funny characters speaking in strange languages: Janet Carsten and Jessica Spencer, Rachel van der Kolk, Christine Schenk with Johanna and Rafael Korf, Suatha, Jafar Sadiq, Safna, Hasna, Tanya Kaiser, Danny and Lara, and Susila.

Glossary and Acronyms

bhikkhu	Buddhist monk
CBSM	Confidence-Building and Stabilisation Measures
CFA	Ceasefire Agreement, 2002 agreement between the Government of Sri Lanka and the LTTE, brokered by Norwegian mediators
CHA	Consortium for Humanitarian Agencies
Dry Zone	area of northern and eastern Sri Lanka, which receives rain from the north-east monsoon only
DS	Divisional Secretary
EHED	Eastern Human Economic Development
EPRLF	Eelam People's Revolutionary Liberation Front, Tamil separatist group active in the east in the early and mid 1980s
ESRC	Economic and Social Research Council
FCE	Federation for Coexistence
Gal Oya	river in Eastern Province which was the site of the first big post-independence irrigation project, the Gal Oya Scheme
grease *yaka*	lit. 'grease demon', a man who covers his near-naked body in grease to evade capture, and is believed to prey on unprotected women
hartal	protest strike, usually involving the closing of all shops and public businesses
ICRC	International Committee of the Red Cross
IDPs	internally displaced persons
INGO	international non-governmental organisation
IPKF	Indian Peace-Keeping Force, deployed to police the 1987 Indo-Sri Lankan Accord and eventually withdrawn in 1990
IROP	Inter Religious Organisation for Peace, Batticaloa-based inter-faith group
JHU	Jathika Hela Urumaya, hardline Sinhala nationalist party formed in 2004

JRS	Jesuit Relief Services
JVP	Janatha Vimukthi Peramuna, left-wing, and for much of its life hardline nationalist, Sinhala party behind anti-government insurrections in 1971 and 1987–90
KKS	Kankesanthurai, a port in the Jaffna peninsula
kovil	Hindu temple
LTTE	Liberation Tigers of Tamil Eelam, Tamil militant group formed in the 1970s, and dominant from the mid 1980s onwards in the Tamil opposition to the Sri Lankan government, before its final defeat in May 2009
madrasa	Islamic school
Mahavamsa	Great Chronicle, history of the island written by Buddhist monks. The first part was composed in the fifth century CE, with subsequent updates continuing into the twentieth century
Mahaveli, Mahaweli	river that runs from the central hills to Trincomalee Bay. In the 1970s and 1980s, it was the centre of the government's biggest development project, the Accelerated Mahaveli Development Scheme, which combined plans for an expansion of irrigated agriculture with new hydroelectric capacity
MIRJE	Movement for Inter-Racial Justice and Equality
NCA	Norwegian Church Aid
NCC	National Council of Churches
NGO	non-governmental organisation
nikaya	major division within the *sangha*
NPC	National Peace Council
NVPF	Non-Violent Peace Force
OBA	Old Boys Association
OMI	Oblates of Mary Immaculate
PA	People's Alliance, coalition led by Chandrika Kumaratunga which came to power in 1994
PAFFREL	People's Action for Free and Fair Elections
PLOTE	People's Liberation Organization of Tamil Eelam, Tamil militant group with strong Marxist leanings, active in the east until the late 1980s
poya day	Buddhist lunar holy day, the full-moon *poya* is a public holiday each month

P-TOMS	Post-Tsunami Operational Management Structure, controversial proposals for sharing of post-tsunami resources and administration between the government and the LTTE, struck down as unconstitutional by the Supreme Court in 2005
sangha	order of Buddhist monks
Sarvodaya	one of Sri Lanka's oldest and biggest NGOs, founded in 1958 by A.R. Ariyaratne
SEDEC	Social and Economic and Development Centre
SLA	Sri Lankan Army
SLFP	Sri Lanka Freedom Party
SLMC	Sri Lanka Muslim Congress, Muslim political party founded in 1980s
STF	Special Task Force, paramilitary unit of the Sri Lankan police, frequently accused of human rights violations during the war
Tablighi Jamaat	transnational Muslim reform movement, started in India in the 1920s
tawhid, also *tawheed*	lit. 'oneness', term used to cover a range of Muslim reform groups in eastern Sri Lanka
TMVP	Tamil Makkal Viduthalai Pulikal, political party formed from the faction of the LTTE that split off under the leadership of the eastern commander, Colonel Karuna in 2004
TNA	Tamil National Alliance, coalition of Tamil parties, originally formed before the 2001 elections
TULF	Tamil United Liberation Front
TVA	Tennessee Valley Authority
UPFA	United People's Freedom Alliance, alliance of parties led by Mahinda Rajapaksa's Sri Lanka Freedom Party (SLFP)
UNHCR	United Nations Human Rights Council
UNICEF	United Nations Children's Fund
UNOCHA	United Nations Office for the Coordination of Humanitarian Affairs
UNP	United National Party, right-of-centre political party, in power from 1977 to 1994, and winner of 2001 parliamentary elections

Vanni	remote hinterland area in northern Sri Lanka, which served as the centre of LTTE activity from the mid 1990s onwards
Vidyalankara Declaration	1946 declaration asserting the right of monks to participate in modern political life
Wet Zone	densely populated area of southern and western Sri Lanka, which receives rain from both the north-eastern and the south-western monsoons

1

Introduction

The photograph is a puzzling one. It appears to be taken from high up on a boat, with a calm sea stretching to the background horizon. Two incomplete figures frame the central image. On the left, a man's arm hangs down from a white short-sleeved shirt. On the right, lower down, we see the legs and torso of a man in shorts and a white shirt. In between there is what looks very much like a cage, hanging from cables. In the cage is a small group of obviously Christian clergymen, dressed in white robes. One wears a reddish-purple sash around his waist.

The picture was taken in 1993 at the port of Kankesanthurai (KKS) in Sri Lanka's northern Jaffna peninsula. The photographer was a Dutchman,

Figure 1.1   Priests boarding a transport ship, Kankesanthurai, 1992 (photo by Ben Bavinck).

Ben Bavinck, at the time employed by a consortium of Christian non-governmental organisations (NGOs) in Sri Lanka. This was the midpoint in the long civil war in Sri Lanka, which had started with sporadic skirmishes in and around Jaffna in the late 1970s, and would end with the definitive defeat of the rebel Liberation Tigers of Tamil Eelam (LTTE) in May 2009. Bavinck first came to Sri Lanka in the 1950s, working as a missionary-teacher at Jaffna College. He retired to the Netherlands in 1972, but returned to Sri Lanka in the late 1980s. In his new role as an NGO coordinator, he travelled back and forth across the island, delivering supplies for Christian projects and recording what he saw and heard in a meticulous diary (Bavinck 2011), selections from which have now been edited and translated from the Dutch (a choice of language which Bavinck, quite rightly, thought as good an encryption tool as any). At the point when the picture was taken, Jaffna was almost unreachable by land routes, and those few civilians trying to get in – rather than out – had to negotiate passes and permissions from the defence headquarters in Colombo.

The picture provides a striking visual metaphor for one central argument of this book. It is a picture that combines capacities and constraint, movement and boundaries. Priests are able to travel across the boundaries thrown up by the war, very often with a freedom afforded to almost no other civilians, but their means of travel, at this point at least, is a cage. The cage confines them and allows them to move. This is a book about religion and conflict, and it is a book that explores the paradox that combines capacities and constraints, borders and transgressions. It is a book researched in the last days of a long and brutal war, and written in the first years of what is turning out to be a troubling and unsettled peace. It is written by a group of researchers with their own differing histories and engagements in Sri Lanka.

In 2006, the authors started work together on a project focused on the role of 'religious organisations' in 'the conflict' in Sri Lanka's Eastern Province. This was an area that had suffered some of the worst of the civil war, but it had also been badly hit by the December 2004 Indian Ocean tsunami, and by the 'second tsunami' of humanitarian organisations that flooded the coastline, seeking partners and projects to absorb the huge amounts of money raised around the world in response to the disaster (Korf 2005; Stirrat 2006; Korf et al. 2010; McGilvray and Gamburd 2010). Our assumption was that faith-based NGOs, such as World Vision and Islamic Relief would occupy much of our attention in our research, and we assumed that the civil war between the government and the LTTE was the only conflict we would need to consider. Instead we found ourselves concentrating on rather more obvious religious organisations – the temples, mosques and churches of our title – and, in so doing, discovered there was no shortage of conflict within and between religious organisations, conflict which sometimes aligned with the deep currents of the war and ethnic polarisation, but at other times operated at a tangent to them.

Conflict

We start, though, with '*the* conflict', the war between the government and the Tamil secessionist LTTE. Sri Lanka is a relatively small island, about 450 km from north to south, and 200 km wide at its broadest. Its population of 20 million is divided by language, religion, and what until recently was routinely referred to as 'race'. The last is now more politely called 'ethnicity'. The population divides relatively neatly on linguistic lines, with Sinhala the first language of just over 70 per cent, and Tamil the first language of nearly all the rest. The oddities of history and politics have combined to pull the classification one way and then another – Tamils are Tamil-speakers, but so too are Muslims, who are not considered 'ethnically' Tamil. Muslims constitute an 'ethnic' category, as well as a 'religious' category; Hindus, though, are a 'religious' group but not an 'ethnic' group. Malays are religiously 'Muslim', but 'ethnically' not Muslim. Almost all Buddhists are Sinhala, but not all Sinhala are Buddhists. Academics have not helped clarify the taxonomic landscape, as they tack back and forth between constructivist arguments, in which everything was invented in the nineteenth century, and primordialist counter-arguments in which all has been as it is now for thousands of years (Spencer 1990a; Rogers 1994).

Much has been written about the war and its causes. Many accounts start with the moment in July 1983 when the LTTE pulled off its most spectacular operation to date, killing 13 government soldiers in an ambush on the edge of Jaffna town. This was immediately followed by retaliatory violence against Tamils and their property in the south of the island. No credible official death toll was ever announced, but it is certain that hundreds, probably thousands, died in the week that followed the Jaffna ambush. It is also now widely agreed that much of the violence was orchestrated by ruling party politicians and carried out by party workers, with the active assistance in some cases of the police and security forces (Manor 1984; Spencer 1990b; Hoole 2001). All was changed. Many Tamil families started to leave the island, joining family and friends in Britain, Australia, the USA and Canada. Young Tamil men, though, slipped away to join the different paramilitary groups fighting the Sri Lankan government. Paramilitary activity quickly spread beyond the immediate surroundings of Jaffna town, to Tamil-speaking areas along the east coast. By 1984, what had been a geographically contained situation was now something very like a war, with an embattled state confronting increasingly organised and disciplined resistance across a wide stretch of the north and east.

The 1983 narrative provides a conveniently clear chronology for the war, a moment of beginning to join the unusually clearly demarcated end in 2009. But it inevitably obscures the rising level of conflict in the decade before that, a back-and-forth of provocation and repression between the government and radical youth in Jaffna, parallel in some ways to the youth insurrection and repression in the south in 1971. The obvious similarities are demographic and political. In 1971, a group called the Janatha Vimukthi Peramuna (JVP) launched an audacious attempt to seize state power, attacking police stations and other targets in the south. The insurgents were young Sinhala men (and sometimes women), mostly rural, mostly educated, often un- or under-employed. The JVP itself was a leftist group, with roots in earlier small Maoist groups and, mostly unnoticed at the time, a braiding of Marxist and nationalist rhetorical strands in its propaganda (Moore 1993).[1] The early volunteers for the different Tamil groups that sprang up in the late 1970s, were from similar backgrounds, and were also motivated by varying combinations of Marxist and nationalist appeal.

If we view the war as something that stretched from 1983 to 2009, the story lends itself to a purely military interpretation, an account of insurgency and counter-insurgency, interrupted by a succession of more or less unsuccessful attempts to broker a political solution. If we move back to the 1970s, we have instead a story of the political aspirations of educated but under-employed youth. If we start the story of conflict even earlier, in the years after independence in 1948, our account shifts out of the demographic-economic register and back into something more recognisably political. In 1956, a patrician politician with a demagogic streak, S.W.R.D. Bandaranaike, won a landslide election victory on a populist platform dominated by the demand to make Sinhala the national language. His campaign was supported by members of the Buddhist *sangha* (order of monks), just as his later attempts to resolve Tamil complaints about the new language policies were successfully opposed by the *sangha* (Manor 1989; Spencer 2008). Here, in the 1950s, we find a tangled mixture of religion and politics at the very moment when the faultlines between

Tamil and Sinhala dramatically deepened. Not surprisingly then, the writing on religion and politics in Sri Lanka is dominated by analyses of the role of Buddhist monks, and the political fortunes of Sinhala Buddhist nationalism. We review some of this writing elsewhere in this book, but our introductory experiment in reverse chronology helps make it clear that the conflict is not just about the claims of Buddhist nationalism – it has specifically political, economic, demographic and military dimensions, and a proper analysis must take all of these into account.

Whatever the political and other antecedents, the war that gathered force in the mid-1980s increasingly took on a dynamic of its own. At this point, the LTTE eliminated other Tamil militant groups, and attacked moderate Tamil politicians, declaring itself the 'sole voice' of the Tamil nation. Indian attempts to impose a solution in 1987 ended disastrously, with the troops of the Indian Peace-Keeping Force (IPKF) bogged down in an unsuccessful confrontation with the LTTE, while the Sri Lankan government faced a second insurrection from the JVP. The new government of Chandrika Kumaratunga was elected in 1994 on the promise of peace but, after a very brief window of optimism, found itself mired again in a draining military stalemate with the LTTE. In the late 1990s, Norway began to emerge as a potential third-party peace broker. With a new Prime Minister in place, and with promises of hefty external aid for post-war reconstruction on the table, a formal ceasefire was agreed between the government and the LTTE in 2002. Despite escalating infringements on both sides, and a return to open warfare in 2006, the ceasefire was only formally abandoned in January 2008, a little more than a year before the end of the war (Goodhand et al. 2011).

Our project was conceived in what was officially a period of peace, but soon enough war broke out again. The period of the Norwegian-brokered ceasefire was certainly less violent than the years that preceded it, if only in terms of body-count, but it was not free from all moments of violence, especially after a split between the northern and eastern leaderships destabilised the LTTE in 2004. The election of Mahinda Rajapaksa as President the following year was followed by a steep rise in ceasefire violations on both sides and, pretty soon, a return to open war. This time the war was different. The government had a decisive advantage in artillery and airpower, and at first the LTTE conceded territory rather than risk its own cadres and equipment in extended confrontations. Within a year, the Eastern Province was declared a liberated zone, while the final phase of the war was fought out in the northern badlands known as the Vanni. Here the LTTE leadership, the surviving cadres, and several hundred thousand civilians they had taken with them, were bombed into submission in May 2009. Although the war officially ended at a very precise point in time, this does not mean our story ends quite so abruptly, and in Chapter 7 we sketch in some of the more obvious religious and political developments that followed the LTTE's final defeat in 2009.

Religion

This book is about religion and conflict. Public discussion of this topic is often heated and rarely edifying. For the so-called New Atheists – figures such as Richard Dawkins and Christopher Hitchens – religion is always and everywhere not merely a source of intellectual error and confusion, it is also a cause of most of the world's more intractable conflicts. In these imaginations, religion ignites fundamentalism, violence, divisions between different social groups and political collectives. As well as the obvious case of Islamist violence associated with groups like Al-Qaeda, such visions also find confirmation in violent religious conflict in South Asia. Hindu–Muslim violence in India is the best-known example, but Sri Lanka, where ethnicity is closely tied to religious identifications, would seem to offer further support. A starkly different vision continues to insist that religions, and religious leaders in particular, *should* be active advocates of peace and harmony: any departure from this expectation – and there are many, as there have always been – becomes an occasion for lamentation and surprise.

These competing perspectives gloss over the ambivalences and nuances of religious public action in spaces of violent confrontation, and the hybrid role that religious agents perform. In Edward Said's terms, sometimes they may act as 'potentates' working to reinforce political boundaries, and sometimes as 'travellers' able to transgress the same boundaries (Said 1994). Looking at the complicated ordinary work and acts of some 'extraordinary' figures, such as the Catholic priests who continued to travel back and forth over dangerously contested terrain, but also at less publicly visible religious figures and their work, allows us to paint a more complex picture of the relations between religion, politics and conflict. This presents a rather different image of religion in the postcolonial world, one in which religion is not only a problem but also a force with the potential to act at the margins of the political field to make life a little more bearable in otherwise terrible circumstances. This potential draws upon the work that religious leaders can perform as brokers crossing political boundaries, whether simply because they are religious leaders or because of some inner source of ethical conviction based in their religious life.

And yet, religion can also be a source of trouble, tension and conflict. In Sri Lanka, the most obvious issue is Buddhist nationalism, in which religious attachment and ethnic nationalism combine in a claim to the island as a Sinhala Buddhist space. Such claims are not mere abstractions; they have material force in the demarcation of sacred Buddhist spaces, and the movement of populations in conscious emulation of Buddhist kingdoms of the pre-colonial past. In one of the most famous passages in the island's Buddhist chronicles, the warrior king Dutugämunu is filled with remorse at the deaths he has been party to on the battlefield. He is visited by a group of Buddhist monks who tell him there are only one and a half for whom he should feel sorrow – one who had taken the Three Refuges (in Buddha, *dharma*, and *sangha*) and one who had taken the Five Precepts (Mahavamsa XV. 109–11; cf. Obeyesekere 1988). The deaths of non-Buddhists are of no karmic consequence. However, the entanglement of religion and violence is again complex. Religious zeal can be directed to outsiders, but also to insiders who fall short of the ideal. Peter Sloterdijk excavates this double-edged sword of religious zeal in the biblical story of the Jewish people in the Sinai. After Moses found the Israelites dancing around the golden calf, he not only ordered the destruction of the artefact but also the killing of all those who did not express their faith in God: brothers and friends, dearest and nearest, there was no mercy, no pardon, just killing (Exodus 32: 27; Sloterdijk 2013: 31f.). We find a similar story of internally directed violence – on a much smaller scale, of course – in Chapter 4, where those seen to have departed from the pillars of Islam find their buildings attacked and the body of their dead leader exhumed and stolen by fellow Muslims.

We need a further qualification: in this book, 'religion' is always in the plural. First, the cast of Sri Lanka is a complex religious field, with Hindus, Muslims, Christians and Buddhists living in a tapestry of communities and settlements. Second, each 'religion' is plural in itself: we find Sinhala Buddhist monks who are strong advocates of a militant Sinhala Buddhist nationalism, but we also find those who distance themselves from this and engage in projects of inter-ethnic coexistence. We find different competing movements within the Muslim community, struggling for influence, believers and public space. Furthermore, there is a wide range of Christian denominations, from so-called 'mainline' ones like the Catholics and Methodists, to more controversial recent arrivals such as the many Pentecostal churches. Within the Catholic clergy, there are those driven by the social message of Vatican II and the influence of Liberation Theology, and there are those who are less enthusiastic about these new roles for the priesthood. Talking about 'religion' as a single set of practices is as futile as talking about 'Muslims' or 'Buddhists' in general, rather than the actions and statements of particular Buddhists or particular Muslims in particular circumstances. As Veena Das has recently put it: 'religious pluralism is the normal condition in which religious subjectivities are formed' (2013: 82).

This raises an issue of definition. Our project was part of a wider research programme on Non-Governmental Public Action, and the specific focus came in response to a call for work on conflict and on religion. However, 'religion' is not a self-evidently neutral term, so before we go any further, a little conceptual clarification is called for. Religion would seem to pose a problem in a number of slightly different contexts: it has become a problem for social scientists in general (somewhat less so for anthropologists than others), for liberal commentators, and possibly also for politicians. After many decades of neglect and indifference, mainstream social science rediscovered religion at some point in the late 1980s or early 1990s. The unexpected role of religious leaders in the 1979 Iranian Revolution and the rise of the religious right in the US were two obvious reasons for liberal social scientists to wake up to a possible issue. Alongside these troubling departures from liberal expectation, were more obviously progressive religious initiatives like the rise of Liberation Theology in Latin America and the role of the Church in opposition to Soviet hegemony in the Polish Solidarity movement. Theoretically, for social scientists there had been few advances on the path-breaking work of Weber and Durkheim in the early twentieth century, while empirically any manifestation of religion in public argument carried a sense of anachronism.

Academic sociology developed Weber's legacy into what has now become known as the 'secularisation thesis', the presumption that religion would inevitably decline as a feature of modern, and modernising, societies. In his illuminating comparative study, *Public Religion in the Modern World*, Jose Casanova (1994) subjected the secularisation thesis to a forensic critique, while providing a strong argument for the continuing value of a more or less Weberian approach to understanding the role of what he calls 'public religion'. Empirically, outside Western Europe, it is simply not the case that religious engagement has declined steadily since the nineteenth century. Although alive in terms of individual participation, religion has not retreated into the realm of private conscience: the cases of Iran and Poland show quite clearly that this is not the case. What Casanova does rescue from the empirical wreckage of the secularisation thesis is a very specific part of Weber's vision of the modern: the necessary 'differentiation' of religion from 'secular spheres', something that can happen without any presumption of religion's decline or retreat from the public arena. Differentiation implies the construction of bounded areas of life – the economy, politics, religion – which in turn requires the construction and maintenance of boundaries. What is the boundary-work that seeks to mark off religion from other areas of life? Are boundaries purely a matter of constraint, or do they have productive consequences in certain circumstances? The issue this raises is the status of 'differentiation' itself – is this institutional or rhetorical, normative or empirical? To some extent, this book is an exercise in thinking through these questions and their implications.

Anthropology, as we have already noted, deserves a degree of exemption from the charge of indifference levelled at the other social sciences. British social anthropology and American cultural anthropology have both taken religion very seriously indeed for many years. One powerful and highly influential argument in recent anthropology would seem to close down this question of the setting of boundaries around religion before we have even started to address it. In a sustained critique of an early essay by Clifford Geertz, Talal Asad (1993) argues that the very idea of 'religion' as a separate, definable object of study is founded on a set of assumptions grounded in the history of European Christianity and inexorably tied to a set of liberal assumptions separating the private inner world of religious conviction from the public world of power and political argument. In an analysis heavily influenced by Asad, and by his protégé, David Scott, Ananda Abeysekera (2002) traces the recent history of arguments about Buddhism and politics in Sri Lanka, from the 1930s to the 1980s. Abeysekera is concerned to avoid obvious definitional issues: the concern is not what 'religion' is or ought to be, the question is how or why certain kinds of questions – like the relationship between 'religion' and 'politics' – come to get asked in certain academic contexts at certain times. The results of his enquiry are somewhat inconclusive, although much can be learnt from the concrete examples he deploys on the way, but he seems curiously uninterested in the most obvious theme that emerges: that Sri Lankan Buddhists have been arguing, often fiercely, about these terms and their relationship for decades. Sri Lankans seem – unlike Asad and his followers – quite relaxed about detaching the category 'religion' from the bigger package of post-Enlightenment liberalism in which it is supposedly embedded. In Brubaker's terms, both 'religion' *and* 'politics' are categories of practice, employed within our social field, rather more than they are categories of analysis (Brubaker 1994; cf. Curtis and Spencer 2012).

We will return to the question of secularism in our closing chapter, but our point of departure is a little different. As our evidence is ethnographic rather than theoretical or normative, we are left with the observation that people in Sri Lanka make frequent use of the categories 'religion' and 'politics' as two key terms in their practical journeys through the world of war. They also infuse these categories with their own normative implications, trying to separate a religious sphere from the dirty sphere of politics and its divisive arenas of struggle. This attempt at separation and at purification – the attempt to step outside of the political into a different place called 'religion' – also tells us a lot about the political, including the subtle ways in which some actors engage in politics while pretending not to. So, rather than settle on unnecessarily tight definitions from the outset, our approach to the language of analysis is pragmatic: what work does the idea of 'religion' do in different contexts? And what possibilities do people see – or not see – in what they take to be 'politics.'

Non-Governmental Public Action

This book is a product of two stimuli. One was a specific moment in the history of the war in Sri Lanka, and especially in the history of the space of the non-governmental in Sri Lanka. The other was the Economic and Social Research Council (ESRC) research programme on Non-Governmental Public Action led by Jude Howell from the LSE (London School of Economics). The 2002 Ceasefire Agreement (CFA) brokered by Norway, was accompanied by a great deal of external aid, much of it directed to conflict-related projects and much of it routed through NGOs, both international and Sri Lankan (Orjuela 2004; Walton 2008). Norway itself contributed around $360 million between 1997 and the end of the war in 2007 (Goodhand et al. 2011). A network of local projects and initiatives sprang up in the shadow of the ceasefire, a small-scale peace industry, with local and international NGOs in a complex skein of partnerships, all driven by external funding. Then the tsunami hit. On 26 December 2004, a huge wave, triggered by an earthquake off the coast of Sumatra, hit shoreline communities across the Indian Ocean. The east coast of Sri Lanka, flat but densely populated, was particularly badly affected: 10,436 were killed in Ampara District, and a further 2,975 in Batticaloa. The global response to the disaster was extraordinary, with record levels of donations in Europe and America, triggering a so-called 'second tsunami' as international organisations jostled for space in an increasingly crowded and dysfunctional humanitarian response (Stirrat 2006; Korf et al. 2010). Urban centres like Batticaloa and Ampara experienced a short-lived real estate boom as international non-governmental organisations (INGOs) looked for suitable accommodation for their teams of experts, while air-conditioned 4-wheel-drive vehicles, sporting the flags of a sponsoring INGO, and often a towering radio mast, became a familiar sight on the road running up and down the coast.

By the time we started our main fieldwork in 2007, this wave was rapidly receding. Many organisations that had arrived in early 2005 had completed their projects and moved on, and others were scaling back their activities. The political consequences of all this activity were more long lasting. NGOs had been the target of intermittent attack from politicians and journalists from the very beginnings of the war: in 1983 the Norwegian organisation Redd Barna was accused of covertly aiding Tamil separatists and, in the early 1990s, President Premadasa launched an official commission to investigate NGOs, apparently in an extension of his personal feud with A.T. Ariyaratne, leader of Sri Lanka's biggest domestic NGO, Sarvodaya. During the war years, external humanitarian aid was, not surprisingly, focused on areas most affected by the war, many of which were under the control of the LTTE, and INGOs proved a useful conduit to ensure that funds reached those displaced by the war. For hard-liners, though, this only cemented the assumption that foreign agencies were pro-LTTE and therefore, in their chosen phrase, 'anti-national' (e.g. Goonatilake 2006). To cap it all, some of the more high-profile INGOs involved in the tsunami response, most obviously World Vision, were explicitly Christian organisations. Tales of 'unethical' conversion by Christian NGOs, offering housing or money in return for religious allegiance, started to circulate alongside rumours of covert aid to the LTTE under the guise of humanitarian relief (Goodhand et al. 2009; Korf, et al. 2010). The only-too-visible excesses of the international response to the tsunami reinforced this growing anti-NGO sentiment (and conveniently allowed the government to divert attention from the shortcomings of its own response to the disaster). And, finally, the election of Rajapaksa as President in 2005 was swiftly followed by the abandonment of all but the flimsiest commitment to the official ceasefire: 'peace' became a dirty word in official circles, and local beneficiaries of the post-ceasefire funding boom had to engage in a process of emergency rebranding (Walton and Saravanamuttu 2011).

So the situation in which we started our fieldwork was a very particular one. The peace process and the tsunami had created an unprecedented boom for local NGOs, most of whom worked in partnership with bigger INGOs, but that boom had already receded by the time we started our work. As well as the scaling down of post-tsunami aid, a return to overt war left NGOs vulnerable to ever more strident political attack. By the end of our research in 2009, those attacks were having quite tangible effects, as visas became harder to obtain for expatriate INGO staff, and organisations seeking to work in the north, and to some extent the east, were forced to enter into delicate negotiations with the Ministry of Defence for the permissions they needed for access.

The Non-Governmental Public Action programme provided a perfect institutional setting for our work. The programme was multidisciplinary and comparative, with a strong emphasis on encouraging collaboration on two axes – between researchers in the global north and the global south, and between academic researchers and practitioners. Although to some extent founded in development studies, with NGOs the most obvious focus for many of the projects, the programme's title quite effectively forced participants to think about the 'non-governmental' in ways that went beyond the more obvious equation of 'non-governmental' with 'non-governmental organisation' (cf. Feher 2007). When the programme put out a call for a second round of projects in early 2006 – with special emphasis on violence, on religion and on legitimacy – it seemed an obvious place us for us to find a home.

In literature on peace-building and reconciliation, for example the work on local capacities for peace (Miall et al. 1999; Reimann 2004; for Sri Lanka, Orjuela 2004), non-governmental public action is often seen as an alternative path to peace-building, as opposed to formal negotiation between the combatant parties or top-down initiatives from the state. Faith-based organisations with specific values of peace or non-violence are often assumed to be important contributors to local capacities for peace (Lederach 1997). As organisations like the World Bank shifted attention to 'social capital' and institutional factors after 2000, so-called 'faith-based' organisations started to emerge as increasingly legitimate partners for development efforts in general (Marshall 2005; Clarke 2006). Here the ESRC programme's emphasis on 'public action' over 'organisations' proved invaluable for the shape of our work. Although we fully expected much of our time to be spent on conventional NGOs with a religious orientation, the circumstances in which our work was carried out – the retreat of INGOs under growing political challenge – meant that we concentrated much more on a range of extremely important organisations not usually thought of as NGOs proper, again the temples, mosques and churches of our title. Our own intellectual background, as well as the political circumstances, also meant that the political dimension of what we were observing – especially issues of sovereignty and the limits of state capacity – was never far from our minds.

Collaboration

This book is also an experiment in collaboration, a collaboration that was warmly encouraged by the programme of which we were part – between researchers based in the global north and researchers based in the south, and between academic researchers and local practitioners. The book is co-authored by a group of six, drawn from different disciplinary (and religious) backgrounds, one anthropologist, two geographers, a sociologist, and two conflict specialists with backgrounds in development studies. Two of us are British, two Sri Lankan, one German and one Dutch. The seeds of our project lie in some very old academic friendships and long engagements with Sri Lanka. Spencer and Silva first met in the early 1980s, when Spencer was a doctoral student carrying out fieldwork in southern Sri Lanka and Silva a young lecturer in sociology at Peradeniya University. Hasbullah was then teaching geography at Peradeniya, and he and Silva had been friends and collaborators for many years. Korf had come to Sri Lanka, originally as a consultant for German development cooperation, but reoriented himself with a PhD based on research on war-affected livelihoods carried out while still working as a development practitioner. He started to write and publish with Hasbullah and Silva while still a PhD student. Goodhand also first encountered Sri Lanka while working for a British NGO in Jaffna in the early 1990s, returning for research that fed into his PhD at Manchester. Klem was the last to join the team. He had first worked in Sri Lanka as a student carrying out fieldwork in and around Trincomalee in the late 1990s, and had subsequently worked with diplomats and policy-makers, including a collaboration with Goodhand on a major report on aid and conflict in Sri Lanka (Goodhand and Klem 2005).

To some extent, the commitment to collaborate preceded the idea of the project itself. Hasbullah and Silva had been heavily involved in attempts to repair the damage the long years of war had caused to the Sri Lankan university system. Where the war had divided academics, an older history had the potential to unite them. In the east, two relatively new universities, Eastern University, with its main campus outside Batticaloa, and Southeastern University, based at Oluvil about 50 km to the south, were divided on ethnic and religious lines. Eastern had been founded in the early 1980s, just as the political situation started to disintegrate. In the violence that followed the withdrawal of the IPKF and the restarting of the war in 1990, over 150 refugees were taken from the university campus where they had been sheltered, and it is believed, massacred by the security forces. Around this time, over 100 Muslims were massacred by the LTTE at prayers in various mosques in Kattankudy, and there were counter-massacres of Tamil civilians in the weeks that followed. The early 1990s were difficult years for Muslim–Tamil relations in the east, and in 1995 a new university was set up at Oluvil for Muslim students and faculty from Eastern, under the patronage of M.H.M. Ashraff, the founder of the Sri Lanka Muslim Congress (see Chapter 2). But if the war had divided the universities along ethnic lines, older staff at all the institutions carried shared memories of their time together as students at Peradeniya. The positive memories of a pre-war world of shared student experience provided the inspiration for a new research consortium linking Eastern, Peradeniya and Southeastern universities. The consortium was based in the social sciences and had the explicit aim of training a new generation of researchers across the ethnic faultlines. For Spencer, who was looking for a way to divert some small trickle of the post-tsunami funding into building research capacity in the local universities, the consortium seemed an ideal framework. All that was needed was some practical research to conduct within its structure. Therefore, if the consortium provided us with a framework for our project, and the east – where all members of the team had some previous research experience – provided a location, the Non-Governmental Public Action programme supplied the spark for the project itself.

The research that followed was multi-sited. Fieldwork was concentrated in and around the towns of Ampara, Akkaraipattu and Batticaloa. Different members of the team were more or less involved in different locations: Goodhand was able to draw on his previous experience in Batticaloa and took the lead for work there, in which Catholic priests and the Catholic NGO EHED emerged as key themes. Klem worked in Akkaraipattu, with time also in Batticaloa and Kattankudy. Hasbullah concentrated on Kattankudy, a dense Muslim enclave immediately south of Batticaloa itself, and documented the emergence of the new mosque federations across the region. Silva, with his experienced assistant Mr W.M.K.B Wickremesinghe, concentrated on Buddhist temples and

Buddhist organisations around the town of Ampara. Silva and Hasbullah joined forces for research on the contested site of Dighavapi, between Ampara and the coast. Spencer coordinated the different components of the fieldwork and spent time in all the sites alongside the members of the team working there. Korf's fieldwork involvement was constrained by the contractual demands of a new position in Zurich – Klem was engaged as his de facto replacement for the fieldwork – but he remained engaged throughout, contributing to meetings of the team, and playing a key role in the writing that slowly followed the fieldwork. In each of our fieldwork sites, we worked with junior colleagues from local universities, and both Eastern and Southeastern provided us with excellent opportunities to share and check the picture that was emerging from our field research.

What did we gain by virtue of collaboration? First and foremost, collaboration allowed us to escape the kind of low-order 'methodological nationalism' that bedevils the study of conflicted places like Sri Lanka. We did not write an account of the war as seen from a Tamil, or a Muslim, or a Buddhist point of view. Methodologically we started from the fact of plurality and built this into the very structure of the project, starting with the research team itself. The composition of the team provided a unique combination of privileged access (especially through the mediation of the Sri Lankan partners) together with equally privileged opportunities for detachment. And it allowed us to attempt an ethnographic understanding of a very large and complex religious and political field (even as it also created occasional anxieties about the inevitable trade-off between breadth and ethnographic depth). It allowed us to carry out research in the final months of a long war without endangering either the researchers or the people who helped with the research.

Nevertheless, the space of collaboration is not a completely neutral space. It does not provide what the philosopher Thomas Nagel calls the 'view from nowhere'. Rather it provides the view from a rather complex but still limited 'somewhere'. This book is always based on a view from somewhere in particular, and always at some quite specific time, and we have tried to be as clear and explicit as possible about exactly where and when the things we talked about happened. Attempts to take this one stage further in the drafting and make it clear exactly who was listening to what at every point in the text ('He replied to Goodhand …', 'Hasbullah asked …') foundered in a morass of clunky syntax, so we have opted instead for a more familiar authorial 'we' in most of what follows. Our study is still necessarily uneven. It is a study in the main of what Casanova calls '*public* religion', stronger on visible leaders and strong institutions, weaker on the ephemeral and the work that goes on 'below the radar'; stronger on Catholics than on Pentecostals, better on Muslims and Buddhists than on Hindus. Some of these known biases derive from who we are, and some derive from the way we worked and the particular moment in which we carried out the work. Insofar as public spaces are often male spaces, and insofar as the core team did not include women, it is undoubtedly weaker on the kind of phenomena documented so brilliantly by other ethnographers of the region like Patricia Lawrence (1997) and Rebecca Walker (2013). Our work must be read alongside – not instead of – theirs. In many cases we have supplemented our own evidence with material from other researchers working in the region, but in other cases we can simply indicate the limits of our knowledge and call for more work in the future.

Sites and Stories

In terms of politics and geography, Sri Lanka presents something of a contradiction. As an island located off the tip of southern India, Sri Lanka has been a place of transit and trade for thousands of years. As a modern nation-state, the island often presents itself as distinctive and entirely separate from its neighbours, despite its dense cultural and economic ties, not merely with the Indian mainland but also with Southeast Asia and the Gulf. This paradox plays itself out in interesting ways in the island's east where this book is located. Until relatively recently, this was a pre-eminently isolated zone, ill-served by the transport and communication technology set up by the colonial government. But even in the early days of British rule, it was a site of agricultural improvement: although the roads and railways of the high colonial era threaded up from Colombo in the west to the coffee and tea estates of the central mountains, the surplus harvest from restored paddy land in the east was either shipped along the coast to the Jaffna peninsula, or slowly hauled up into the same estates by pack-animals on rocky paths. The two chapters that follow are intended to introduce the region, first in terms of religion (Chapter 2), then in terms of political economy (Chapter 3). They tell a tale of unity and division. In Chapter 2, we make a case for going beyond the manifold surface differences between religious groups, and ask what happens if we try to treat the region as a single, albeit divided, religious field. In Chapter 3, we trace a double movement, as state-driven improvements create a distinctive and singular political economy, based on the fertile rice land

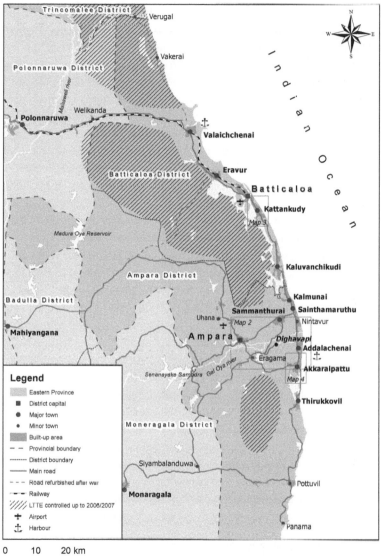

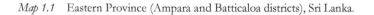

Map 1.1   Eastern Province (Ampara and Batticaloa districts), Sri Lanka.

inland from the lagoon, even as post-Independence political structures encourage increasingly ethnicised claims on resources.

Our fieldwork focused on four sites – three on the coast itself, and one a short way inland: Batticaloa and Kattankudy in Batticaloa District, Akkaraipattu and Ampara in Ampara District. Batticaloa is a hub for communication and government, and a major regional centre of education. The town has a substantial Catholic population, and Catholic priests have been prominent in many local peace and human rights initiatives (see Chapter 6). Kattankudy, which adjoins Batticaloa, is a densely populated Muslim town, the scene of a famous massacre in 1990 when LTTE gunmen killed over 100 Muslims at prayers. More recently, it has become known for the intensity of conflict between different Muslim groups (Chapter 5). Akkaraipattu is a mixed Tamil and Muslim town some 50 km to the south, its economy dominated by the paddy fields that fill the landscape all the way to Ampara, some 20 km away. Ampara is an overwhelmingly Sinhala town, the hub of the post-Independence colonisation schemes, and now a major centre for government security forces. In Chapter 4, we pick up the different registers of division in the two preceding chapters. In particular we take a case study of apparent religious difference – the contested area around Dighavapi, midway between Akkaraipattu and Ampara – to show the way in which conflict can be at once expressed in terms of religious division from one side, while being felt as more straightforwardly economic from the other. In Chapter 5, we further complicate the idea of 'conflict', this time through a comparison between religious conflict *within* the Muslim community in Kattankudy, and the apparent absence of similar levels of conflict amongst Akkaraipattu's Muslims. Chapter 6 opens with a moment of transgression, the assassination of the town's MP while attending midnight mass on Christmas Eve 2005 in Batticaloa. The chapter then explores the changing role of the Catholic priesthood in the years of war, and the role played by religious leaders in mediating moments of extreme danger. Chapter 7 draws on fieldwork we have carried out in the years since the original project on which this book is based. On the one hand, it provides some sense of what has happened since the end of the civil war itself. But its theme – of a growing culture of insecurity and perceived moral danger – is shared by all religious and ethnic groups alike, in a paradoxical reaffirmation of our opening argument for the need to think of the region as a single political and religious field.

As a point of departure, we should emphasise the striking resilience of religious institutions in the face of sustained violent conflict, and their possible importance as overlooked resources for peace. In this part of

Sri Lanka, 'religion' not only provided a place of retreat and consolation (outside the dirty world of the political), but also provided institutions and leaders which have played an important role in local attempts to mediate between warring parties. Religion has also played a role in providing an alternative space for public action in the midst of political disorder and violent contestation. And yet we will also show that the very same leaders and institutions can, in certain situations, be a source of new conflict. Even the ability to act beyond their own communal boundaries – to communicate across contested borders, to mediate or negotiate during delicate political events – may often be grounded in much more hardline gestures in other circumstances.

Two important questions therefore run through this book. One concerns the extent to which different religious traditions contain their own distinctive sets of constraint and opportunity within them, often shaped by the particular institutional structures within which they are embedded at particular historical moments. And, of course, in a world of glib generalisations about these matters, we must always stress historical specificity. The second concerns the source of particular dynamics in the religious field: is a particular change or development the product of forces within a particular religious tradition, is it a reaction to changes in other neighbouring religions, or is it a local manifestation of some much wider, global trend within the particular religion?

This in turn raises the question of the source of change itself, and thus of the relationship between 'religion' and 'conflict'. If religion is as embedded in all areas of life, as we argue it is for most people in this area, then abstracting it and giving it a discrete causal force vis-à-vis other areas of life, begs too many questions, for this to be an entirely useful approach. Religions can respond to political and social changes, but they can also remake the social worlds within which ideas of the political are configured, and reshape people's ideas of what is politically and socially possible or desirable. Despite their own strenuous efforts to portray themselves as sources of order and harmony, religious traditions contain their own, often bitter, conflicts, making it difficult to decide whether conscious efforts to build a stronger sense of religious community are responses to internal or external sources of conflict and threat. Examples of all these processes can be found in the pages that follow.

2

The East as a Complex Religious Field

The East

Sri Lanka's Eastern Province is the most ethnically and religiously diverse part of the island. In 1981, before the civil war between the government and the LTTE, its population of just under 1 million people was divided between Hindus (38 per cent), Muslims (33 per cent), Buddhists (24 per cent) and Christians (5 per cent). In Sri Lanka's categories of ethnicity, Tamils made up 40 per cent of the population, 'Moors' – as Muslims are officially known – 38 per cent, and Sinhala 25 per cent. Many people have come and gone since the war reached the east in the early 1980s, but the region remains as religiously diverse as ever.

During the period of our fieldwork, there were two routes we routinely took into Batticaloa and Ampara. From the north-west, the road passes

Figure 2.1   Kovil, Kokkadichcholai, 2010 (photo by Jonathan Spencer).

the old capital of Polonnaruwa, with its gleaming stupas, irrigation tanks, sprawling archaeological sites – and huge army bases. Then, after miles of bleak, thinly inhabited landscape, broken up by army posts which drivers had to skirt on badly maintained dirt roads, we would reach a very different kind of settlement, one in which mosques, churches and *kovils* (Hindu temples) replace the Buddhist monuments of Polonnaruwa. Approaching from further south, the contrast in religious landscape is even more stark. The road runs through Ampara town, a planned settlement established as the hub of the Gal Oya irrigation scheme in the 1950s, but now home to the Special Task Force and other military units. Signs of an assertive Buddhist presence are everywhere in the town itself. Then there is nothing for a few miles but apparently endless paddy fields stretching on both sides of the road. The next settlement, Sammanthurai, is almost entirely Muslim. A few miles further, at Karaitivu junction (by and large a Tamil village), we would join the coast road which runs from Batticaloa in the north to Akkaraipattu and Pottuvil to the south. Along this densely populated peri-urban strip, with the Indian Ocean on one side and a sea of paddy on the other, signs of religious diversity are everywhere. In town centres, new 'Iranian'-style mosques rub shoulders with Hindu *kovils*, established Catholic churches look across at small Pentecostal chapels; but, if there is one generalisation shared by insiders and outsiders alike, it is this: the signs of religious activity are undiminished by the years of war. Temples have been built and rebuilt, new churches set up, and surprisingly, many of them look to be freshly painted, whatever the condition of the surrounding houses and shops.

In conceiving of a collaborative ethnography, one of our ideas was to combine viewpoints and perspectives in such a way as to avoid the limitations of more conventional field research. In this particular context, collaboration allowed us to move beyond a set of studies of particular religious traditions, and to start to explore the similarities and differences between those traditions as they have emerged in the 30 years of war in the east. From the start, then, we have attempted as far as possible to try to make sense of the east as constituting a single, complex religious field, albeit a field internally divided between a number of different religious traditions, each with its own cluster of institutions and practices, and to some extent, with its own history. Of course, the very idea of a complex religious field presumes there is something we can identify as 'religious', something which can provide a coherent ground for interpretation and comparison. In light of current academic fashion, in which the colonial and/or Christian provenance of the concept of 'religion' has become part of the received wisdom, this is something of a gamble (Smith 1963; Asad 1993; Scott 1996, 1999). It is though, a heuristic gamble whose worth will only be apparent in what it enables us to bring to light by the end of this study.

The reasons for taking this analytic risk are compelling and, broadly speaking, both sociological and political. In the study of nationalism and ethnicity, a powerful critique has emerged of what has come to be known as 'methodological nationalism' (Wimmer and Glick-Schiller 2002; Brubaker 2004). What concerns the critics of methodological nationalism is not so much the reality or unreality of nations, nation-states or ethnic groups; it is instead the way in which the nation, the nation-state or the ethnic group can be given an unreflective status in the analysis of nationalism and ethnicity. Rather than prefigure the analysis in advance, by making the nation-state the unquestioned object of sociological analysis, we should instead investigate the processes by which the nation-state acquires that taken-for-granted veneer of naturalness as a political-sociological entity. That is the force of the sociological critique. The political correlate of the sociological critique is the argument that critical analysis necessarily has to challenge the assumed naturalness of a person's identification with his or her ethnicity or national group. Treating such groups as natural and self-evident closes off that critical option before the analysis has even started.

So, as a point of departure we start with the premise that the religious field in eastern Sri Lanka is not 'naturally' divided into separate incommensurable religious traditions. There are obviously profound divisions, but if these were simply given in the order of things, why would so many people invest so much in efforts to *make* the different traditions bounded and separate? We will give more examples of this boundary-making in later chapters. At the same time, we acknowledge the potential absurdity of simply denying the specificity and historical weight of those traditions we do encounter. People in the east of Sri Lanka do not swim in a genial soup of blurred or hybrid religiosity, disturbed only by the rude arrival of modernist reformers eager to pit religion against religion. That particular fantasy has remarkable staying power in other polemics about religion and identity in South Asia (e.g. Nandy 1990), but it is problematic at best. We also add a second premise: that the shared experiences of war and political crisis, not to mention rapid economic and demographic change, should in theory create certain shared religious predicaments. In some cases, the result of these predicaments may be new areas of shared practice that cut across the boundaries of the different traditions. In other cases, shared predicaments generate divergent responses as people draw creatively on the rather different resources available within their own particular tradition. In yet other cases, the traditions themselves are differently located in the terrain of the conflict itself, either because one faction pursues the war in the name of their religious community, or because another finds itself targeted and victimised because of its religious affiliation. In these cases, the dynamic of the conflict itself blocks off some of the opportunities for common religious responses.

The Problem of the Plural

In 1954, Edmund Leach demolished the impossibly particular tribes-and-cultures approach of colonial ethnologists in his brilliant analysis of highland Burma. Leach showed how certain structural features of social organisation could explain an apparently bafflingly diverse setting. The point which in part inspires this section of our study is Leach's truistic observation that ostensibly different people living in more or less the same place 'are likely to have relations with each other' (Leach 1954: 17). Our different religious traditions are not sealed off from each other once and for all: their adherents live in the same world as each other, sometimes go to the same schools, vote when they can in the same elections, often struggle to make a living in the same fields and workplaces (cf. Das 2013).

Leach's larger argument is based on the premise that 'structure' and 'culture' are more or less completely independent of each other, an argument which may be just about defensible as part of a polemic aimed at late colonial ethnic taxonomies in Burma. It is less helpful when confronted with the Catholic Church or the Buddhist *sangha* in Sri Lanka, or even a relatively recent phenomenon like the Muslim reform movement Tablighi Jamaat. All of these entities combine religious ideology, histories of debate and contestation, structures of leadership, and quite particular institutional forms. In these examples, seeking some foundational 'structure' that is isolable from the messy stuff of cultural content is no easy matter. A somewhat better model is offered by Gerd Baumann's (1996) analysis of the ways in which different immigrant groups in London's Southall self-consciously use the concepts of 'culture' and 'community' as a means to negotiate their way across a contested political landscape. Baumann's analysis differentiates the sense of culture as an essentialised property of a bounded group of people – a concept found in what he calls the 'dominant discourse' of official multiculturalism and also, some of the time, in people's own 'demotic discourse' – from a more anthropological

sense of culture as a field of shared understandings. This kind of culture –
in which people from different official 'communities' converge on similar
political projects or share similar anxieties about the implications of
change – can emerge from the very processes that explicitly seek to divide
people into discrete 'communities', each with its own unique 'culture'.

In this context, though, recent trends in the anthropology of religion,
which emphasise particularity and difference, are not as helpful as
we might expect. Even new efforts at comparison, seem to premise
themselves on difference. For example, in the past decade much of
the intellectual running in this area has been made by writers eager to
establish the anthropology of Christianity as a special sub-field with its
distinctive problems and issues (Robbins 2003; Cannell 2006). Exceptions
to this trend are few and far between. Brian Larkin and Birgit Meyer have
initiated a debate on religious change in West Africa, and specifically on
the similarities that may be thought to underlie the apparently opposed
and hostile projects of Pentecostal Christians and Muslim reformers.
Their point of departure is important:

> [Instead] of taking for granted the oppositions between reformist Islam
> and Pentecostalism, [we] explore their commonalities, seeing both as
> examples of structural shifts in the way religion articulates relations
> between society, the individual and modernity. Both religions copy from
> one another, thus crossing boundaries and blurring sharp distinctions,
> while at the same time stereotyping and objectifying the other in order
> to generate the energy for 'crusades' or 'jihads'. In this way both are
> doppelgangers, enemies whose actions mirror those of the other, and
> whose fates are intertwined. (Larkin and Meyer 2006: 287)

John Peel (in press), in a magisterial reflection on the anthropology of
world religions, builds on Larkin and Meyer's argument as part of a
broader critique of calls for a distinctive and separate 'anthropology of
Islam' (Asad 1986) or 'anthropology of Christianity':

> It is surely not only a student of the Yoruba or Nigeria or Africa, where
> Islam and Christianity coexist and interact with each other, who must
> believe that a sociology (or anthropology) of the world religions is what
> we need, not a series of discrete sub-specialisms for each religion. (Peel,
> in press)

Where Larkin and Meyer look for structural similarities, and moments of overt engagement across religious boundaries, Peel is also concerned to bring out the distinctive resources different religions bring to any particular historical moment. Understanding the linked but distinctive histories of Islam and Christianity in West Africa, Peel argues, is necessarily a *comparative* exercise, in which the work of comparison is tempered by attention to shared history and shared context. Therefore, Peel's fuller analysis of the recent history of the two religions in Nigeria devotes as much attention to the differences between them, as it does to moments of symmetry or confluence, as he traces the intersection of distinctive traditions with new contexts.

In talking of Christianity and Islam as 'traditions', Peel is self-consciously building on Talal Asad's argument in his influential 1986 lecture on an anthropology of Islam (Asad 1986). Asad himself takes the term 'tradition' from the philosopher Alasdair MacIntyre who, in *After Virtue* (1981), presented a version of 'tradition' which emphasised continuity of argument rather than fixed content, something that allowed Asad to deftly evade the problem of essentialism in identifying the subject matter of his putative anthropology of Islam. But Asad's sense of 'tradition' is, in his own terms, that of a 'discursive' rather than an institutional tradition, relatively indifferent to the distinctive vehicles of Islamic history, which, Peel argues, surely have some bearing on the ways in which that tradition adapts to or shapes new contexts: 'the Koran, ancillary media such as *hadith*, *tafsir*, legal texts and so forth, to say nothing of the ritual practices (such as those involved in the *Hajj*) which evoke the past to shape behaviour in the present' (Peel, in press). Peel in contrast is as concerned with the institutional features of particular religious traditions as with the more purely discursive content of the tradition: 'Why is it impossible to imagine Islam as having monasteries, or Christianity Sufi brotherhoods?' (Peel, in press). Peel's question is strikingly germane to the problems that concern us in this chapter, and throughout our book. Institutional structures like the Buddhist *sangha*, with its property, its authority structures, and its elegantly choreographed relations with the laity, to some extent constitute their own structures of possibility when confronted with exogenous change. An organisation like the Society of Jesus, to take another example, provides transnational support networks and a repertoire for leadership that is not obviously replicated in, say the administrative order of a large Tamil Hindu temple (cf. Mosse 2012: 38).

In the chapters that follow, we will use this modified sense of 'tradition' to characterise the different religious strands that ravel and unravel through the recent history of eastern Sri Lanka. Three decades of war provide a powerful shared contextual factor which should be able to hold together what might otherwise be an unruly and unbounded story; but as the case study of reform and dispute in two Muslim towns in Chapter 5 demonstrates, even the idea of 'conflict' is itself potentially plural, with serious conflict happening *within* particular religious traditions alongside the overarching dynamic provided by 'the' conflict between the government of Sri Lanka and the LTTE, which we examine in more detail in the next chapter. Before we turn to this, however, we must first take stock of what we already know about the religious traditions we encountered in the east, and especially about the ways in which they may or may not have been caught up in the decades of conflict. In this chapter, we draw on previous writing about religious change and religious conflict in Sri Lanka in order to provide a sharper frame for our own field material. That previous writing is almost all presented in terms of the view from one particular religious tradition – Buddhism and conflict, Catholics and conflict, and so on. The task is to find a way to knit those perspectives into a single coherent narrative, without overly distorting the real differences between the trajectories of our different traditions in the years of war in the east.

The east is not the normal point of departure for analyses of Sri Lankan politics and religion, but this in itself might give its ethnographers certain advantages. As the religious life of the east is relatively undocumented, we have a degree of freedom in choosing to adopt or ignore conventional accounts of religion in Sri Lanka; but, because those accounts are in many cases so rich and insightful, we can begin to see more clearly what is distinctive about the particular setting in which we worked. The religious tradition that is best documented in Sri Lanka is, not surprisingly, Buddhism, and there are enough books on Buddhism and conflict or Buddhism and war, to fill a small shelf of their own. However, because Buddhists are a numerical minority in the districts in which we worked, we are allowed to start our argument elsewhere, in east coast Hinduism, and only turn to Buddhism last of all in our survey of what we know already about religion and conflict in the east. This small gesture of displacement already allows us to escape the 'obvious' story of the conflict, which treats Sinhala Buddhist nationalism as a prime causal force in the island's history, with other communities and their histories relegated to a zone of effect and reaction. Empirically, the east defies that too-easy take on religion and conflict.

A Place 'Outside' the Conflict

In 1991, an American graduate student called Patricia Lawrence arrived in Batticaloa with a plan to carry out fieldwork in Tamil villages. Over the years that followed, she managed to complete a remarkable study of everyday life under conditions of extreme violence. The early 1990s were desperate years in the area immediately around Batticaloa. In 1990, as the IPKF withdrew from the country, the LTTE slipped in to take control of the villages on the land side of the Batticaloa lagoon. Batticaloa town, and areas on the sea side of the lagoon, were in the hands of government forces, including groups like the police paramilitaries, the Special Task Force, who arrived fresh from a brutal but ultimately successful counter-insurgency operation against the Sinhala rebels of the JVP in the south of the island. From June 1990, the sides exchanged massacres and atrocities; from August, Muslims were drawn into the violence. The figures alone are terrifying: 600 Sinhala police officers detained and disappeared in June, over 100 Muslims killed in Kattankudy in August, 184 Tamil villagers in Sathurukondan in September. And so on and so on.

Lawrence's 1997 PhD thesis tells two kinds of story. One concerns the way in which local people, especially women, took to village temples – especially temples devoted to the mother goddess Amman – as a source of solace and healing amidst the turmoil of the war. The other documents the incidents and atrocities that punctuated her long stay in the field, trying as far as possible to establish exactly who was responsible, what exactly happened, and what kinds of follow-up occurred. The combination remains one of the most vivid and compelling ethnographic accounts of people getting by in often quite extreme situations of fear and uncertainty. Families seeking news of the lost and disappeared come to see women like Saktirani who, through possession and the agency of the goddess, are able to bring a sort of a solace to those afflicted by the war:

> The creative collages through which Saktirani begs, borrows and steals what she can from traditional narratives and popular cultural practices create a place in which to speak of abductions, arrests by the state, and conscription by militant organizations. She often attempts to create moments which interrupt political silencing. Sometimes, moral dilemmas that arise from political fragmentation may be resolved in these moments. She creates confidence about relationships at a time when relationships are being shattered. In the context of daily reports of killing in the war, she insists on an alternative moral vision in which

family relationships are not sacrificed. Saktirani also attempts to create confidence about maintaining connections with family members in the diaspora, however far away they may be … She helps people overcome trauma and loss, and in this work she does not differentiate herself from the suffering of others. (Lawrence 1997: 322–3)

Saktirani, a woman in her mid 40s at the time of Lawrence's fieldwork, cuts a figure familiar to students of popular religion in Sri Lanka. Like the female ecstatics in Obeyesekere's extraordinary *Medusa's Hair* (1981), she is someone who has transformed her own life, and the lives of the people who come to her, through her intense relationship with her chosen goddess. She found her goddess at a small temple on the edge of Batticaloa town. In those days it was little more than a hut in the middle of a settlement of washermen caste families (many of them Christian); when we visited it in 2008, it had grown into something much more imposing with new buildings, lights, not to mention hints of Sanskrit in the well-attended Friday evening *puja*. The marginal space where marginal figures like Saktirani provided solace in the worst days of the war, had in the intervening years grown into an established religious institution visited by Hindu pilgrims from elsewhere in the east, visitors from the diaspora, not to mention members of the security forces and (so it was whispered) even incognito businessmen from the nearby Muslim town of Kattankudy. We were told that 8,000 devotees had walked the fire-walk in honour of the goddess at that year's recently completed temple festival. In the early 1990s, there had been a mere handful.

The rumoured attendance of police and army at the temple was nothing new. In the 1990s, Saktirani was occasionally asked to help young Sinhalese men from the armed forces with their troubles. Another oracle was summoned by senior army commanders and government ministers to offer her vision of the future of the region (Lawrence 1997: 106). In the many cases that Lawrence documents in the closing chapters of her thesis, Muslims as well as Tamils bring their troubles to her. (During her regular sessions, Saktirani tries to deal with Muslim supplicants first, so they can leave before anyone needs to unburden themselves on issues to do with the LTTE.) Empowered by the goddess, Saktirani herself is free to transgress the normal disciplines of dress, gender and comportment. The space she creates around her is one in which other people can cross boundaries of their own: between communities and between speech and silence. In one extraordinary moment, another oracle turned on the army in a moment of high drama:

At the Kallady Kali temple in 1992, several thousand local people had gathered to witness firewalking on the seventh evening of the annual propitiation. It was dark, and the crowds were kept clear of the wide sacred area around the firepit by constant patrolling of the temple *vannakar* (trustees). The firepit was prepared for hundreds of devotees to walk over the fire in a few minutes. The oracle who would lead the firewalk was wearing a red sari with white plumes of *kamukampu* (areca palm flower) at his waist. At this heightened moment of ritual, three tall Army officers from the nearby Sri Lankan Army camp strode boldly into the cleared circular space surrounding the hot bed of coals as if to position themselves there for the event. There were rumours that arrests were imminent. Suddenly, the oracle rushed from the shrine, tore furiously across the space and, growling angrily at them in the unbearable rage of Kali, chased them out. And the officers did quickly move out. (Lawrence 1997: 258–9)

There is a particular configuration of space at work here: one that allows people at times to step outside the deadly constraints of everyday life. In this particular case, it is a space of demotic religion, where ordinary people bring their problems, ignoring, however briefly, the political forces that otherwise divide them. At points in her text, Lawrence tries to locate this new space in terms of the familiar division between the public and the domestic. In Batticaloa in the early 1990s, she says, circumstances 'were so repressive that temple rituals were one of the very few active and viable social spaces outside the household' (Lawrence 1997: 88). Later she elaborates:

Public roads and streets are dangerous spaces inside Sri Lanka's war zone. [Saktirani] counters the landscape of danger by reconstituting her domestic space at home as a public space for treating survivors of torture and a wide range of desperate problems in the local population, most of which are related to broken family connections and the disruption caused by war. (Lawrence 1997: 106)

Temples can become safe – like domestic spaces, but unlike other public spaces – under the protection of the goddess. But a domestic space can itself become like a temple – and therefore a safe but public place – in the hands of a skilled oracle. What Lawrence is describing is a form of life lived 'under the radar' (as other observers in the east have described it: Gaasbeek 2013, Walker 2013); somewhere where people can forget the skein of fear and surveillance that otherwise dominates the everyday.

There are two types of Hindu temple in the east: small, village temples, many of them dedicated to the Amman goddess, and much bigger, more hierarchical temples, which bind together villages and castes across a territory. These are known as *tecam kovils*, temples that serve (and constitute) a 'minor polity' or 'principality' (Theyvanayagam 2006: 300). Lawrence's work concentrates on developments within the smaller Amman temples. Mandur, a village on the land side of the Batticaloa lagoon, where the anthropologist Mark Whitaker lived in the early 1980s, is home to an altogether grander *tecam kovil*, the Sri Kantasvami Kovil. When Whitaker returned on a brief visit in 1993, he too was struck by the contrast between the ravaged landscape of war and the many signs of prosperity and rebuilding around the region's temples. If the landscape is the product of what he calls a certain kind of 'modernist' politics, the politics of Sinhala nationalism and Tamil counter-nationalism with all the violence and suffering that this confrontation has brought about, then what is happening at the temple, where old arguments about status and position are still being fought out in the register of honour, represents an 'alternative' or 'non-modern' politics (Whitaker 1999). Reporting on his first return to the region after a gap of 15 years in 1993, in a piece parallel to Whitaker's, Dennis McGilvray comments on the contrast between the war-ravaged landscape and the shining paintwork of renovated and rebuilt mosques and *kovils*. He describes a Pillaiyar (Ganesa) temple in Akkaraipattu in dire straits in the 1970s but now the subject of expensive rebuilding. Alongside it is a new orphanage for Tamil boys, built by the Ramakrishna Mission under the aegis of the temple trustees, which 'exemplifies an obvious connection between the unspeakable trauma of the war and the reinvigoration of Hindu religious institutions' (McGilvray 1999: 218). Just as the temples were able at times to stand outside the logic of colonial rule, so too they provided a place outside the logic of friend-and-enemy that fuelled the war. This seems to have been a view shared, at least most of the time, by the LTTE. Although the LTTE sought to establish as total a control as possible over Tamil society, when it came to the temples of the east, it held back: 'Religion is not part of the consciousness of the struggle' as one LTTE figure told Lawrence (1997: 40). In London, and elsewhere in the Tamil diaspora, the LTTE controlled the temples and used them as vehicles for fundraising and political work; back in eastern Sri Lanka, the LTTE kept these central institutions of Tamil life as far as possible at arm's length (Maunaguru and Spencer 2012).

This earlier work by Lawrence, Whitaker and McGilvray, was an important inspiration for our own project. In particular, it illuminates a number of different modes of religious response to the war. At the level of demotic religion, the war creates suffering and new forms of popular religiosity address that suffering. They do that, moreover, in ways that to some extent ignore the boundaries that divide different religious and ethnic communities. The bigger, more established *kovils*, like the Mandur temple, share one aspect of this – the apparent capacity to isolate themselves from the toxic politics of the war itself. Old-style temple politics, jostling for positions and 'honour' within the temple structure, carry on through the years of war, but these stand in what Whitaker (1999: 188) describes as an 'orthogonal' relation to the divisions of the war itself. Perhaps not surprisingly, the people most engaged in the intense scrabble of temple politics did not appear in our own ethnographic encounters with public religious leaders and organisations such as Batticaloa's Inter-Religious Organization for Peace (IROP: discussed in Chapter 6). The big question of the 'religious response' to the war splinters into smaller questions to do with modes of religiosity, organisational structures, and the making and crossing of boundaries – between religion and politics, and between the public or visible, which is always inherently a space of danger, and that which is relatively hidden and therefore relatively safe.

Religion as Identity

In December 2006, at the start of our fieldwork, we spent a few days in the small town of Sammanthurai, a predominantly Muslim settlement positioned halfway between the Tamil-Muslim-dominated coast and the town of Ampara, centre of the Sinhala-dominated Gal Oya scheme and, not uncoincidentally, home to several large bases for different wings of the state security forces. We stayed in Sammanthurai because it is home to the official guest house of Southeastern University, a small, almost entirely Muslim, institution with its main campus about 10 miles away on the coast, where two of the team were helping revise the sociology curriculum.

The first sign that something was amiss came on the second day of our stay when we noticed that our dinner was being served later than usual, and what we eventually received was modest to say the least. The guest housekeeper explained that it was hard to get fresh ingredients because the shops were closed. Why? Because a *hartal* had been declared in the town. This was in response to an incident that had occurred while we were on campus on our first day. A truck driven by a Sinhala man from

Ampara had hit and killed a pedestrian in the town. The driver, realising his predicament, tried to drive off to escape the angry crowd that had swiftly assembled. Two young men on a motorcycle chased him. When they overtook the truck, the bike was knocked over, killing one of the riders but also jamming itself under the truck. The driver climbed out of the now immobile vehicle and ran for it, but his companion, also Sinhala, was less lucky as he was trapped in the cab as the crowd torched the vehicle. Or this is the version of events we eventually pieced together, having entirely missed the original drama. By the time we learned of the *hartal* the air was thick with rumours. Busloads of Sinhala thugs were on their way from Ampara we were told; a major escalation of the violence seemed both inevitable and imminent.

At this point, the first set of rumours started to play off another, rather more reassuring story. The members of the local mosque federation, we heard, were trying to contain the situation. They had assembled in town, and were attempting to broker a meeting with their counterparts – Buddhist monks, Christian priests, as well as senior police officers – from Ampara. And over the days that followed, that was what happened: meetings were indeed held, the situation was contained, peace of a sort returned to Sammanthurai.

Two days later, we learned some more about the mosque federations and their capacities. One of our colleagues at Southeastern tells us the story of an incident that had happened a year earlier in a nearby town. On the day after the presidential elections, someone had thrown a grenade into the Grand Mosque at Akkaraipattu, killing four and injuring many more during Friday prayers. Although it was unclear whether this was the work of the LTTE, or of their rivals the Tamil Makkal Viduthalai Pulikal (TMVP; or Karuna group as they were still known at this time), no one doubted that it was the work of Tamil paramilitaries of one sort or another, their presumed motive the desire to provoke retaliation which in turn would enable them to present themselves as defenders of their own community. Our colleague explained how he and other senior members of the Akkaraipattu Mosque Federation had acted swiftly to forestall escalation: groups of men were posted on roads leading to Tamil parts of town to block any attempt to administer immediate revenge, while appeals for calm and restraint were broadcast from the loudspeakers at the mosque. There was no retaliation. The situation gradually calmed.

In his recent ethnography of Muslims and Tamils in Sri Lanka's east, Dennis McGilvray discusses the demise in authority of mosque trustees at the time of his original fieldwork in the late 1960s and early 1970s.

At the time, mosques were usually administered by hereditary matriclans of trustees, known as *maraikkars*. In the past, he was told, these trustees had wielded considerable influence in local community affairs, but their authority had been eroded from two principal directions: alternative sources of knowledge and authority in Islamic matters had appeared from one direction, while party politics had intruded in its own divisive way from another (McGilvray 2008: 275–9). A decade on from McGilvray's earlier fieldwork, as the Muslims began to see themselves squeezed between a state in the hands of Sinhala Buddhist nationalists, and emerging militant groups of young Tamils eager to break away, so new forms of Muslim organisation began to take shape.

Before the 1980s, Muslim political leadership in Sri Lanka tended to be based in Colombo, even though it tried at times to speak on behalf of the big concentrations of Muslim population in the east of the country. As 'the conflict' in general put most pressure on Muslims living in the east (and north), so the east became the source of new leaders and new parties. The most important figure in this transition was M.H.M. Ashraff, a charismatic lawyer and politician from the east, who founded the Sri Lanka Muslim Congress (SLMC) in the early 1980s, and entered Parliament later in that decade. Ashraff served as a minister in the coalition led by Chandrika Kumaratunga in the 1990s before dying in mysterious circumstances in a helicopter crash in 2000. After his death, his party split into various factions, each led by different political 'big men' (at least one of whom was a woman – Ashraff's widow).

The story, which we return to in the next chapter, is complex and highly contested so this is not intended to be at all definitive. In its early stages, Ashraff himself appears as a kind of chameleon, making a name for himself as a student in the Islamist Jamaat-i-Islami, then appearing as a delegate at the 1976 Vaddukoddai conference which brought together a number of Tamil opposition parties under the call to establish a separate state of Tamil Eelam, then working for the fledgling Muslim Congress. Here are parts of a version of it we were told by a long-time activist from Akkaraipattu, who had been involved with the Muslim Congress from the very start. He tells the tale of Ashraff's SLMC and the rise of the mosque federations as a single narrative. The key dates in the narrative are 1983, 1985, 1990 and 2002. The SLMC in its earliest days was primarily a youth organisation, organised as he put it, for both security and social reasons. In 1983, after the government-backed attacks on Tamils in Colombo and elsewhere in the south, Tamil separatist groups, notably Eelam People's Revolutionary Liberation Front (EPRLF), started to mobilise youth in this part of the east, and at first a number of young Muslim men joined them. Muslims had no separate representation *as Muslims* in the all-party conference summoned by the government after the 1983 violence, and as the SLMC took up the political challenge in the name of eastern Muslims, so the new mosque federations started to organise at village level. One of the concerns for the federation's founders was the need to keep 'their' youth out of the hands of the militants. A series of clashes between Tamil militants and Muslims in 1985, which set in motion the polarisation of the two groups for the next two decades, took care of that problem. The forced eviction of the entire Muslim population from Sri Lanka's Northern Province by the LTTE, and a sequence of attacks on eastern mosques along with other brutalities in 1990, firmly entrenched the Muslim–Tamil divide, despite a long history of intertwinement, close cultural and linguistic ties and continued economic interdependence. In the political developments that followed the moment of definitive separation, something of a division of labour emerged in which Muslim politicians aligned with the SLMC looked after Muslim interests in the realm of national politics, while the mosque organisations dealt with religious and 'social' issues. With each twist and turn of the conflict, the mosque federations grew in strength. In 2002, with a bilateral ceasefire between the government and the LTTE (and no place at the table for the Muslims), the LTTE took on increasingly visible policing functions in the areas under their control. The mosque federations responded by urging 'their' people to bring issues to them, not to the LTTE, and by uniting different town-based federations at district level.

What is important about this version of local history is the way in which the activist at once stresses the coevality of the Muslim Congress and the mosque federations, both born of the troubles of the 1980s, *and* their striking divergence over subsequent decades. In the political realm, Ashraff's attendance at Vaddukoddai suggests some degree of imitation of the Tamil United Liberation Front, the pan-Tamil party, which was born there and which was briefly the main opposition party in the late 1970s and early 1980s. But the mosque federations present themselves as operating 'outside' politics and in the interests of the community as a whole; the politicians are seen as inescapably individualistic and divisive in their activity, the moment of unity represented by the founding of SLMC now little more than a fading memory.

While the worsening ethnic conflict impelled east coast Muslims to create strong modes of collective organisation and representation, other forces, many emanating far from Sri Lanka, swept through the Muslim towns and villages of the east, dividing that same community in often fierce arguments about reform and tradition. Much of that story is explored in Chapter 5, but there is another contrast to note here. When we spoke to representatives of the Kattankudy Mosque Federation in 2008, they explained their roles in these terms: if there is an incident or a problem here with another community people will be selected from the mosque federation to go to their area and talk to their leaders and intellectuals. But this activity has a structural problem, because in Tamil areas there *are* no equivalent organisations, and leaders of the same sort were harder to find. We could put this another way, the space in which the mosque federations tried to operate was to some extent precisely the space that Tamil people tried to avoid in taking their troubles to the oracles in the temples. Religious institutions provided strong and enduring organisational structures in the conflict, but while Muslim groups could use this as a platform for public interventions, the situation was altogether more problematic for Hindus, for whom significant public roles attracted equally significant risks of attack from one or other of the warring parties in the area.

The Social Life of the Priesthood

'Before I can answer your question, I think we have first to discuss the change in the social mission of the priesthood after Vatican II.' The conversation was not going entirely as planned. We were trying to discuss our ideas for some collaborative research with the Catholic NGO Eastern Human Economic Development (EHED) in and around Batticaloa. Our interlocutor, a senior priest from the east, had a different agenda for the conversation: before we even started to talk about ideas for research and collaboration, we needed first to get a proper understanding of the changing role of the Catholic priesthood, and for this we had to start with events and circumstances seemingly far away from the civil war in Sri Lanka and its causes. We were a little baffled by what seemed to be a surprising digression. In retrospect though, it is clear that our friend the priest was right to insist on his agenda for the conversation. To some extent, Catholic priests provided the leadership for the Tamil community that failed to materialise from Hindu institutions and Hindu organisations. Their links to arguments and ideas from Rome in the 1960s may have been an embarrassment in Sinhala majority areas in a time of rising nationalism; in Tamil areas, it would seem to have been an important source of strength.

Our consideration of the position of Catholics in the area of our study is then founded on a striking contrast with earlier writing on Catholicism in Sri Lanka. Stirrat's publications on Sinhala Catholics constitute one of the subtlest and most incisive analyses of religious change in postcolonial Sri Lanka. His 1992 monograph, *Power and religiosity in a post-colonial setting* tells a rather downbeat tale of gradual decline, in Catholic influence and confidence, in post-independence Sri Lanka. Changes in the liturgy, including increasing use of the vernacular, and changes in the official role of the priesthood, have left both clergy and laity disconsolate and more than somewhat disoriented, especially in the context of a resurgent and increasingly vocal Sinhala Buddhist nationalism. New kinds of popular religiosity address the uncertainties of life in a postcolonial setting, but in doing so they seem to draw on modes of popular Buddhist religiosity, raising the prospect of a slow 'entropic' dissolution of Catholic boundaries (Stirrat 1992: 149). Stirrat's analysis is impressive in several different ways. It is grounded in an unusually careful account of the longer history of the Catholic church in Sri Lanka; it provides a nuanced sense not merely of changing modes of religiosity but also of systematic differences in dominant styles of religiosity in different settings; and it is probably the best ethnography we have of the everyday entanglements of religion and politics in Sinhala Sri Lanka.

As that final point indicates, Stirrat's study and Stirrat's conclusions are explicitly limited to Sinhala Catholics. At various points, he makes it clear that things may be quite different for Tamil Catholics, but this is not a topic on which he claims any authority. Just how different things are is clear in a more recent article by Deborah Johnson (2012) on the Church in the context of Sri Lanka's war-to-peace transition. Johnson focuses on Catholic priests' capacity to act as 'brokers' within a highly contested space – crossing checkpoints, mediating between armed factions and the local populace, sometimes able to gain access to spaces (like the controversial detention camps established at the end of the war in 2009) which were closed to other outsiders:

Different priests brokering different situations drew on various kinds of capital, including institutional, aesthetic and moral. The institutional basis of the church (its network, international links and financial resources) facilitates much brokerage. The Church has been able to 'deliver' and, through CARITAS [the international Catholic NGO] served needy Sri Lankans of all faiths and ethnicities. Aesthetically, the garments of priests make them immediately visible, and interviewees spoke of the sacred authority this dress conveys, and the protection it affords. Morally, the commitments of priests and the vows they take in a community of support and brotherhood, the sacred and ritualistic element of their existence, are the powerful capital for self-motivation and wider recognition and respect. (Johnson 2012: 84)

In a neat inversion of the situation described by Stirrat, it is precisely the aspects of Catholicism that make it an object of suspicion for Sinhala nationalists – especially its foreign origins and enduring transnational structure – that make it a source of potential strength for those living in the shadow of LTTE-dominated Tamil nationalism. The new emphasis on the social engagement of the priesthood could produce as much puzzlement for the laity in the east as in the Sinhala areas described by Stirrat – indeed similar issues were reported by socially engaged Methodist ministers during our fieldwork – but more importantly it provided priests with a space and a role to inhabit in the conflict. Indeed, in the absence of other visible alternatives, in many cases Christian priests were able to speak for a much wider Tamil community than the relatively small congregation of Tamil Christians in the east. Our interlocutor was indeed right: we needed to understand internal processes of change in the global Catholic Church if we were to understand the place that the Church occupied in the war in eastern Sri Lanka.

Buddhism Entangled

November 2008, two years on from the Sammanthurai incident, and two of us are experiencing the predictable downside of any collaborative enterprise. We had been dropped several hours earlier at a Buddhist temple in a border village, originally established as part of the Gal Oya scheme near Ampara town. Rain falls in sheets as we wait in the monk's lodging. Our vehicle left hours ago to collect another member of the research team from Oluvil and has not returned. Somewhere close by, the US Ambassador is opening a new USAID project: maybe the delay has been caused by the security consequences of having foreign VIPs in the area. Whatever the reason, all that has happened since is the rain, which has been sheeting down for hours, turning the temple compound into a temporary pond. But the delay is not entirely bad, for it turns a useful interview into a much longer, more free-ranging discussion with the temple's incumbent monk.

He is an incomer to this area, born in Galle in the south of the country and ordained at Kegalla, but has worked in and around this village for many years. He is extremely open about his political connections – he was very close to former President Premadasa and also to J.R. Jayewardene (in whose honour he once edited a book in Sinhala), but he was also an admirer and associate of the charismatic Muslim politician M.H.M. Ashraff. He describes the village and its difficulties, including the years of intermittent attack from the LTTE who controlled the Tamil areas on the other side of the village paddy fields. The village is poor and in dire need of development initiatives, with most households depending on employment of some sort with the government security services – the civil guard, the police and the army – to keep them afloat. The monk sees himself as a central figure in village development efforts, especially brokering access to resources from the state and from external donors too.

The conversation ranges widely and sometimes loops back to go over topics for a second or third time. The rain continues to fall. He tells us about the work the temple organised after the tsunami, which devastated the Tamil and Muslim settlements along the coastline a few miles to the east. About a thousand Tamil villagers came and stayed in the village immediately after the tsunami. He got very friendly with them and is now often invited back to their villages for weddings and other big events. He does not speak Tamil but enough Tamil people can manage a bit of Sinhala for basic communication. He then decries the activities of hardline Sinhala nationalist parties like the JVP and Jathika Hela Urumaya (JHU). Buddhism, he says, does not discriminate between races and ethnic groups. The Buddha ridiculed caste so you simply cannot discriminate. We are all human beings. That is the true principle. The problem comes from people in Colombo who never interact with Tamil people. If you interact with them, you realise some are good people, even if some are extremists. But these people who do not meet them are the ones deciding how to treat them. It should be us living in the border villages who live with them who should be consulted.

There is a lot of contextualisation and unpacking to do here, but we should first make clear that this monk, whose liberalism on the ethnic question seems strikingly at odds with our received idea of Sri Lankan *bhikkhu*s as staunch nationalists, is by no means atypical. In an interview near Vavuniya in 2006, a monk in the northern border area complained to Iselin Frydenlund:

The JHU and the JVP are in Colombo. They call for war to end this problem. They don't know the situation at the border. Here, the people don't want the war ... The rich monks in Kandy are not interested in helping out in the border areas. (Frydenlund 2011: 68)

Or as a Buddhist lay activist in Ampara put it: 'It is the outsiders who make the problems. Local people here are very close' (Frydenlund 2011: 215).

There are also strong historical antecedents. In *The work of kings*, H.L. Seneviratne draws on a vivid description of this very area, provided by an activist monk who had visited it to preach at the villagers' request in the late 1940s. The village in question, which is extremely close to the one where we held our conversation 60 years later, is described even then as a border village. Tamil–Sinhala intermarriage is common and people mix vocabulary from the two languages in their speech. In his preaching, the monk is at pains to reassure the villagers that, despite appearances to the contrary: 'This country is Sinhalese, and is ruled by them'; but to soften the apparent chauvinism of this statement, Seneviratne then points to the monk's long and open engagement with Tamil language and culture (Seneviratne 1999: 105–8). The monk himself petitions the Batticaloa Government Agent for support and is able to help the villagers establish a cooperative that removes them from the snares of outside merchants. Although six decades separate the two, his role is not so different from that of the development-oriented monk we interviewed.

In *The work of kings*, Seneviratne presents a broad picture of the changing position of Buddhist monks over a period of roughly 100 years. He roots his account in the figure of Anagarika Dharmapala, the turn-of-the-century lay activist often cited – accurately or not – as the founder of so-called Protestant Buddhism. Seneviratne discerns two distinct agendas for the *sangha* within Dharmapala's project: one is the narrowly nationalistic and intolerant political engagement that has shaped so much of the post-Independence history of the island; the other is a more socially engaged, cosmopolitan and development-oriented vision of the role of the *bhikkhu*. The two are instantiated in two rival Buddhist training institutions: Vidyodya and Vidyalankara. The monk preaching to the border villagers in 1948 is an example of the Vidyodaya option. Someone like Walpola Rahula, historian of early Sri Lankan Buddhism, and in his last years advocate of a military solution to the Tamil problem, is an example of the Vidyalankara option. The tragedy, for Seneviratne, is the long-term eclipse of the Vidyodaya position by the Vidyalankara one.

The history of the Buddhist *sangha* in the east does not easily fit into these neat categories. Rather it is a story of initial expansion and consequent entanglement, in which social service, community development, politics and nationalism, are all mixed together in different configurations and to different degrees. The main division is not between two competing visions of the monkhood, but between centre and periphery, Colombo (or Kandy) and the east. The expansion of the *sangha* in the east has come in three distinct but overlapping modes. Most obviously, temples have been founded in areas of new Sinhala settlement as part of official government colonisation projects. Second, particular branches of the *sangha* have at different times established themselves in areas with few Sinhala settlers, often around sites of archaeological significance, and claimed links to the sacred geography of the Buddhist chronicles: Seruwila near Trincomalee, Dighavapi (which we discuss in Chapter 4), Buddhangala near Ampara, Somawathie. But as well as these, since the 1930s there have been concerted efforts by some sections of the *sangha* to bring temples (and schools) to isolated areas of the country. Often, it is difficult to separate one of these modes from another: the same branch of Amarapura Nikaya that re-established a temple at Seruwila, also founded a string of temples in Tamil–Muslim areas on the coast – in Batticaloa, Kalmunai and Akkaraipattu – and then went on to establish a major monastery in Ampara, a town built as the heart of a new government settlement project. But in all these cases, the same thing seems to have happened: in Leach's terms, those who moved into the area and those who already lived there were forced, as much by necessity as initial choice, to 'have relations with each other' and, out of these entanglements with other communities, a grudging tolerance was born.

Meanwhile, Buddhist monks of all persuasions have had closer links to the state and to government politicians, and, despite frequent complaints about the perils of mixing politics and religion, have taken on various kinds of activist, development-focused roles in the areas they settled. From the very start of modern mass politics in Sri Lanka in the 1930s, the issue of the propriety of monks engaging in public politics has been a source of debate and anxiety (Abeysekara 2002: 67–108). Quite apart from the problem of the war against the LTTE, the exuberant but often unseemly mode of party politics in Sri Lanka renders too much visible engagement by monks somehow inappropriate from the point of view of both lay Buddhists and other monks. But the close identification of the *sangha* with the project of Sinhala nationalism means that monks have often intervened politically while claiming to speak from a position that transcends the agonism of everyday politics. The opposition to S.W.R.D. Bandaranaike's attempt to resolve the Tamil question in the late 1950s – in which protesting monks camped outside his private residence (Manor 1989: 286) – is a good example, as is the build-up to the emergence of the JHU in late 2003 and early 2004. In the early 2000s, the charismatic monk the Reverend Gangadovila Soma built up a huge following, especially among the new middle classes of the Colombo area, preaching a radical reform of religious practice, and highlighting what he saw as the corruptions visited upon the nation by foreign influences of all sorts. In the period before his sudden death in late 2003, he turned his attention on the moral failings of politicians and started to talk about entering politics himself (Berkwitz 2008: 96). His baton was immediately picked up by the *bhikkhu* activists of the JHU, who managed to gain nine seats in the 2004 parliamentary elections (Deegalle 2004). The subsequent involvement of these monks in a fight in the parliamentary chamber itself reinforced many Buddhists' suspicions of the dangers of mixing Buddhism and politics too closely.

The East as a Field of Possibilities

What then have we learned from this brief and incomplete survey of public religion in eastern Sri Lanka? First and most obviously, we were right to be wary of essentialism. There is no singular 'Muslim' or 'Christian' or 'Catholic' or 'Buddhist' pattern in recent religious changes. In Chapter 5, we look more closely at two apparently different cases of religious change in Muslim towns 57 km apart from each other, in an effort to tease out the intersection of local political economy, transnational reform movements, and the peculiar dynamics of minority identity in a time of war. However, as that case also illustrates, there is no uniform logic to 'the conflict' either: there are other conflicts at play as well as the conflict between the government and the rebels. This is not a story that can be told in terms of the determining influence of single factors, whether these be religious, political, or even institutional. Instead, the religious traditions of the east, in conjunction with the wider histories of which they are a part, provide a field of possibilities, within which some options have opened up and flourished – the mosque federations, the social mission of the Catholic clergy – while others have been more muted or undeveloped.

One predicament that cuts across all the cases so far is the fraught relationship between religion and politics. In Whitaker's account of Mandur temple politics, religious institutions offer a different mode of politics, one that can serve as a 'kind of refuge' from the politics of the war and its consequences (Whitaker 1999: 191). In the case of the Muslims, religious forms of self-organisation, such as the mosque federations, exist in parallel with the more agonistic claims of local party politics. Buddhist monks may engage in a great deal of political activity, but this does not prevent many of them complaining about those monks who have entered the realm of party politics *tout court*. These different responses are not stable and settled, either in time or across space: the monks around Ampara complain about the activities of Colombo-based activists, what may have been a singular project for Muslim activists in the 1980s has split into different modes by the 2000s. In that respect, it does not make sense to talk about a singular Muslim or Buddhist relationship between religion and politics. But nor does it make sense to say, as Stirrat does, that the very categories 'religion' and 'politics' are 'unsuitable' for use in a setting like Sri Lanka, and any distinction between them is 'little more than formalistic' (Stirrat 1992: 174). The categories are as recognisable to our informants as they are to outside analysts, and the rather unstable boundary between them is, as we shall show, at once a source of constraint and a source of potential strength. The point is to recognise their rhetorical, or tactical, importance in local life, without any accompanying analytical assumption about their reality, or not, as social 'things'.

What we have presented so far is necessarily selective, intended to introduce a set of issues that will be explored more fully in the chapters that follow. These issues can be organised in terms of a few, rather approximate, typological distinctions – between the demotic and what we might call the official, between the unbounded and the bounded, and between the public, or visible, and the domestic, or invisible. As well as these distinctions, the shaky and shifting boundary between religion and politics is an issue that occupies the minds of all the people we met and talked to in our research.

So, for example, Lawrence's work on popular Hinduism during the worst days of the war is located very firmly at the demotic end of the continuum. People seek out oracles for help in dealing with disappearances and loss. The oracles are themselves classically marginal figures; the temples at which they work are small, often low caste. Their followers come from all religious and ethnic communities. But this zone of popular religiosity does not produce public leaders, capable of mediation and able to stand up in the face of external threats, in the way that the mosque federations or the Catholic churches have produced public leaders. As these examples suggest, what seems to have been most effective at moments of crisis is a kind of leadership which, in other circumstances, is more often focused on the reproduction and policing of the boundaries between religious traditions. The kind of religiosity that most obviously addresses the travails of the conflict is often the least bounded, but also the least effective as a ground for public action.

That point is reinforced by one further example: the new Pentecostal Christian churches that have grown across Sri Lanka in recent years. Their modes of operation have been the source of huge public controversy at national level, especially from Buddhist nationalists who accuse them of practising 'unethical' conversion. In the east, they seem to have recruited most strongly, not from Buddhists or Muslims, but from low-caste Hindus and the more established Christian denominations. The classic Pentecostal conversion story hinges on healing, either of physical ailments or of the more inchoate sufferings of war and poverty. The afflicted take refuge in their new community of fellow believers, but that community does not seem (as yet?) to provide a platform for any form of sustained public engagement. The new churches are notable for their absence from the citizens' committees and peace committees that have done so much work during the war. Even more than the oracles studied by Lawrence, they represent that promised space 'outside' the conflict. And, as we shall see in Chapter 7, they may prove to be the biggest religious beneficiaries of the end of the war in 2009.

The capacity for publicly engaged leadership is clearly a product of particular institutional arrangements. Members of the Society of Jesus, for example, can draw on certain institutional capacities that are simply not available to people with other religious affiliations. But even institutional structures are mutable at times of crisis. The mosque federations and the SLMC did not exist before the war, and it is an open question how long they will endure now the threat posed to the Muslim community by the LTTE is no more. The same question is posed for Catholic priests: can they retain their prominence in local affairs – and do they want to – as the tensions of war recede? Early in the fieldwork, when we started to notice the limited role of Hindu leaders in public engagements, we wondered how much this was a product of the organisational structure of the big *kovils*, where the trustees wield power and priests are merely their servants, and the community is explicitly divided on caste or village lines. But there is some evidence that new *kovils* in the Tamil diaspora have created platforms for community leadership comparable to those found in the other religious traditions in the east. So, the question remains why they did not perform those political functions in the east.

Two threads run through the story so far. One concerns the political mobilisation of religious communities. In the 1950s, Buddhism provided much of the symbolic language in the rise of Sinhala nationalist political forces. Other religious communities did not, on the whole, mobilise on religious grounds in response. Tamil opposition to the Sinhala nationalist project was based in language and territory, rather than in the claims of particular religious groups. Catholic opposition to specific outcomes of the rise of Sinhala nationalism – the nationalisation of church schools for example (Stirrat 1984) – was short-lived and fizzled out in the face of a demographic reality, in which Catholics were massively out-numbered by Buddhists. Muslims participated in electoral politics mostly through one or other of the Sinhala-dominated national parties, the United National Party (UNP) and the Sri Lanka Freedom Party (SLFP). But the coming of the war, and the threat posed by the LTTE in particular, gave impetus to the rise of the SLMC, a party founded above all on the claims to a common Muslim identity. The new Christian churches, possibly mindful of the same demographic constraints as the Catholics, have shown no sign at all of any national-level political ambitions. Their only role so far has been as the target of attacks by Buddhist activists. Yet uniting this apparent diversity, we would argue, there is a degree of convergence on a shared understanding of the relationship between politics and religion, a relationship that is unstable and potentially dangerous. Normatively, there should be a clear boundary between politics and religion. Practically, that boundary often dissolves, but the consequences for religious actors are rarely good. Religious fields are never simple. Neither are political fields, as we shall see in the next chapter.

3

Land and Water, War and Not War

When the war restarted in July 2006, it started in the east and the issue was land and water. Or that is how it was presented at the time. At a place called Mavil Aru, south of Trincomalee, the LTTE closed a sluice gate feeding lands worked by Sinhala farmers in an ethnically mixed area of irrigated rice land. The ostensible motive for the LTTE action was the exclusion of certain Tamil villages from a proposed new drinking water project, and the closing of the sluice gate seems to have been intended as a relatively trivial way to put pressure on the government to resolve the issue (Gaasbeek 2010a: 178 n.153). But the gesture misfired horribly. The government used the closing of the sluice gate as the pretext for a carefully planned, and remarkably successful, offensive against the LTTE presence in the entire Eastern Province.

From the start, the offensive was presented as a 'humanitarian' intervention, initially on behalf of the farmers deprived of water, and subsequently on behalf of the civilians ('hostages' in the official rhetoric) trapped with the retreating LTTE forces. At first the LTTE responded by taking over the predominantly Muslim town of Mutur on the edge of

Figure 3.1   Paddy fields near Akkaraipattu, 2008 (photo by Jonathan Spencer).

Trincomalee Harbour, but the army responded quickly, pushing them out of Mutur, and also their stronghold in the neighbouring town of Sampur soon afterwards. After the army had retaken Mutur, the executed bodies of 17 local workers for the French NGO Action Contre la Faim were found in the organisation's compound. Official ceasefire monitors blamed government forces for the murders. Government forces using heavy artillery forced the LTTE to retreat down the coast towards the town of Vakarai. By January 2007 Batticaloa town was beginning to fill with internally displaced persons (IDPs) fleeing the fighting to the north. By July 2007, the LTTE had retreated from its former territory inland of the coastline, and the government was able to declare victory in the east. In less than a year, the LTTE had entirely withdrawn from the region, falling back behind their defence lines in the northern Vanni. Although far from obvious at the time, the incident at Mavil Aru was the beginning of the end: less than three years later, in May 2009, the LTTE would be finally and comprehensively defeated in their chaotic last stand on a narrow strip of beach north of Mullaitivu.

The main plan for our research in the east was framed in a period of official ceasefire, but then had to be carried out through a time of rapid transition. In the final decade of the old millennium, the government of Sri Lanka and the LTTE seemed to have fought themselves into a weary stalemate. This was the context in which the government started to actively seek the help of a third-party mediator, eventually settling on Norway in 1999. Norwegian diplomats facilitated the signing of a Ceasefire Agreement in early 2002. Although this was followed by several rounds of talks between the government and the LTTE, negotiations made little progress and would have been quickly abandoned if not for pressure from major aid donors, but they started to unravel when core political issues came in sight. When we wrote our original research proposal, in early 2006, the signs were not good: a new President had been elected, seemingly committed to a much more belligerent approach to the problem, while the LTTE was openly preparing for what it promised would be the 'final war' (Human Rights Watch 2006).

By the time we started the field research in late 2006, war had broken out in the region, but by the time we completed it, the war itself was a receding memory, and an uneasy victor's peace prevailed. If the immediate circumstances of the 2006 events at Mavil Aru were not predictable, the broader pattern was. In the second half of 2005, both the government and the LTTE exchanged increasingly belligerent gestures. In November 2005, Mahinda Rajapakse was elected President, with the support of smaller hardline parties like the JVP and the JHU, while the LTTE, which had organised a boycott of the vote in Tamil areas, started a major fundraising drive from their supporters in the diaspora, promising the imminent start of the 'final war': a war, they claimed, which would drive government forces out of the north and east within two months of its start (Human Rights Watch 2006). Norwegian diplomats, supposedly still mediating an official peace process, stood by and watched in dismay (Goodhand, Klem and Sørbo 2011). By early 2006, it was already clear that the northern part of Eastern Province, especially Trincomalee District, was too volatile to be included in our planned research. We watched anxiously later in 2006, as Batticaloa town filled with displaced villagers fleeing the fighting to the north, then relaxed a little as the LTTE systematically withdrew and the government declared victory. The rest of our fieldwork coincided with the launch of the government's programme for reconstruction in the region (Nagenahira Navodaya – the 'awakening of the east'), and the transition to 'normal' local politics, albeit a local politics dominated by the former paramilitaries of the TMVP.

Land and Water

The Eastern Province of Sri Lanka is a long strip of land that hugs the island's eastern seaboard, from the boundaries of Yala National Park in the south-east, to the beaches and lagoons north of Trincomalee some 250 km to the north. It is divided into three administrative units – from north to south, Trincomalee, Batticaloa and Ampara districts. This book is primarily based on research in two of these, Batticaloa and Ampara.

Although the Mavil Aru stand-off was probably chosen as the moment for the launching of the military campaign for propaganda reasons (it allowed the government to claim the humanitarian high ground), it does remind us of the importance of natural resources, and access to natural resources, as a component in wider patterns of conflict. In particular, it directs our attention to land and water – but land and water not only in its material sense. Land and water have also been important symbolic markers of spiritual and political significance – with the irrigation tank and paddy field as the cradle of Sinhala Buddhist civilisation, battles over the sacredness of space as 'archaeological sites' of Buddhist significance or the claim of a specific territory as 'Tamil Eelam'. But while these symbolic significations are powerful, the physical geography of the east also shapes and channels the landscape within which the military contestation was fought out.

The landscape of Eastern Province is for the most part flat and, in its uncultivated condition, relatively arid, with the central mountains of the island on its western border, and the Indian Ocean to the east. The population is densest along the seaboard, especially between Batticaloa and Thirukkovil to the south, where towns sprawl into each other in a near-continuous belt of human habitation. West of the urban belt is a string of shallow lagoons, and then a broad swathe of quite intensive paddy cultivation. Beyond the paddy, in the foothills of the mountains, is an area of wilder country known as the *Bintenna*. The whole area lies within what is known as the Dry Zone, that part of the island solely dependent on the north-east monsoon for its rainfall. This is a landscape defined by the presence or absence of water, and it is a landscape shaped by recurrent human efforts to channel the water.

Sometimes water defies all human attempts at control. In 1978, before the war, more than 700 people were killed in a fierce cyclone that hit the east coast. In 2004, the Indian Ocean tsunami caused more than 10,000 deaths in Ampara District and almost 3,000 in Batticaloa District. Altogether 20,000 homes were destroyed along this stretch of the coast. But away from the global headlines, floods (and droughts) are recurring features of the landscape. This is a place of too little water and too much water.

Batticaloa is an anglicisation of the local *mattakalapuwa*, meaning 'muddy lagoon'. A Portuguese observer in the sixteenth century came up with a different – almost certainly spurious – etymology, in which Batticaloa was said to mean 'kingdom of rice'. An early twentieth-century Government Agent elaborates:

> Most people in Ceylon have heard of the great irrigation works of the Batticaloa District, and of the vast extent of paddy land irrigated by these works, but it required a personal visit to the District to enable me to realise what figures fail to convey to the mind. A drive along the South Coast road from Kalmunai to Karunkoddittivu is Akkarari pattu [Akkaraipattu], a distance of fourteen miles, and thence along the road to Sakaman tank, comes to one as 'revelation'. On the east side of the road are densely populated villages situated in coconut gardens, with here and there a large estate. On the west side of the road, almost as far as the eye can reach, is a vast stretch of paddy land extending without a break, not merely for the fourteen miles mentioned, but north and south of that distance. (1907 *Administration Report*, quoted in Denham 1912: 91)

The scene that so impressed the Government Agent was in part the fruit of early colonial attempts at 'improvement' based on the restoration and revival of irrigation works. From the 1850s onward, irrigation tanks were restored and land opened up for relatively intensive paddy cultivation, making Batticaloa District a substantial net exporter of rice by the start of the twentieth century. This was especially remarkable given the poor quality of transport links: rice was either shipped up the coast for sale in Jaffna to the north, or else transported by bullock caravan to the tea estates in the mountains around Badulla. By the 1950s, Batticaloa District was the site of a quite distinct agricultural economy, dominated by large landowners (so-called *podiyars* or 'big men'), large operational units and wage labour (rather than the share-cropping found elsewhere in the island). The towns along the coast provided a labour force for the paddy fields, as well as facilities like rice mills to process the grain. In some areas, Muslim owners employed Tamil labourers; elsewhere Tamil owners sometimes employed Muslim labourers.

Away from the sites of improvement, the story seems to have been rather different. In 1921, the Government Agent described the District as 'probably the least progressive … in Ceylon', with 'little to attract the capitalist or settler' (Festing, in Canagaratnam 1921: vi). Two decades earlier, a colonial official had characterised the inland area to the east of the paddy fields as a 'tangled trinity' of 'chenas [swidden], lepers, and relief works for the unemployed', with a population 'miserable in appearance' and 'nearly all' sick (Freeman, in Denham 1912: 90). The melancholy tone of this official is a stark contrast to the can-do optimism of an American geographer reporting on the same area immediately after independence:

> The seemingly fanciful dreams of a mere half-dozen years ago of bringing rehabilitation and abundant life to Ceylon's Gal Oya Valley jungles are today beginning to materialize in amazing and heartening fashion. Here, in a small segment of Ceylon's vast Dry Zone, thousands of acres of long-idled lands are now being methodically cleared and watered, to bring them once again into agricultural production to help feed a sadly food-deficient population. (McFadden 1954: 271)

The Gal Oya scheme, which transformed the region in the early 1950s, represents a combination of three somewhat different sources of inspiration. It was in part a continuation of earlier colonial work to restore and improve Dry Zone irrigation works, work which had already transformed agriculture in the region. For the Prime Minister of newly independent Ceylon, D.S. Senanayake, it also represented a self-conscious attempt to emulate the supposed glories of the pre-colonial kings. And, at the same time, it was conceived as a flagship project for the new developmental state, organisationally and ideologically modelled on the Tennessee Valley Authority (TVA) and the New Deal in the USA, and paralleling efforts elsewhere in Asia like the Damodar Dam in India (Klingensmith 2003).

The Gal Oya project changed the demography and politics of the region irreversibly. Although the first allocations of new irrigated land were pretty evenly divided between Sinhala and Tamil cultivators, the Sinhala cultivators were almost all immigrants from Wet Zone areas far to the west and south, whereas the Tamil cultivators were mostly from villages closer to the coast at the further end of the irrigation canals (Farmer 1957: 208). The incoming settlers moreover brought others with them – as many as nine in a single family (McFadden 1954: 281). The Sinhala population in the area trebled between 1946 and 1953, and trebled again between 1953 and 1971 (Table 1). The image of the Gal Oya project as a politically 'clean' technocratic solution to the island's dependence on food imports took a blow in 1956, when shortly after the election of S.W.R.D. Bandaranaike's government, with its commitment to 'Sinhala-only' language policies, the Gal Oya valley burst into flames with the first Sinhala–Tamil riots in the modern era: 'Sinhalese toughs – inspired as always by fantastic rumours – seized government cars, bulldozers and high explosives and for a few days terrorised the Tamil minority in the colony' (Manor 1989: 262). Over 100 people were killed.

Table 3.1   Batticaloa and Ampara population by ethnicity 1946–2007

	1946	%	1953	%	1971	%	1981	%	2012	%	increase 1946–2012 (%)
Tamil	102,264	51	130,377	48	243,817	46	317,941	44	495,225	42	384
Sinhala	11,850	6	31,107	12	93,828	18	157,017	22	257,145	22	2,070
Muslim	83,375	41	106,033	39	187,254	35	240,798	33	416,328	35	399
Others	3,697	2	2,975	1	4,427	1	3,929	1	4,511	>1	22
Total	201,186		270,492		529,326		719,685		1,173,199		483

Source: Department of Census and Statistics, 1946, 1953, 1971, 1981 and 2012 Census.

Economically, the Gal Oya project was a disappointment in the long term. A 1975 FAO report describes a dismal scene:

Many canals have scoured out and many others have silted in; others, some in the primary system, are in almost immediate danger of washing out completely ... Drainage facilities earlier installed have become so clogged and closed, some purposefully by cultivators and encroachers, that they have largely ceased to function ... [N]early all gates leak 24 h[ours] a day. Padlocks have disappeared, gates have been damaged and destroyed, extra pipes and siphons have been installed, and canal banks have been cut by the cultivators; there is very little discipline or enforcement. (FAO in Uphoff 1996: 29, n. 3)

Although the scheme benefited both Sinhala and Tamil farmers, at least in theory, it did little to bring them together. Tamil farmers at the lowest ends of the water distribution often complained they received less water than they needed. More seriously perhaps, the Sinhala settlements that grew up as a result of the scheme oriented themselves to the new town of Ampara, 15 miles inland, and from there on to other Sinhala-dominated areas further inland. Tamil villagers at the other end of the scheme looked to Batticaloa and the densely populated Tamil–Muslim towns along the coast. Politically, Gal Oya's failings were ignored, and the governments of the 1970s and 1980s threw themselves behind even bigger, and more grandiose, irrigation projects, notably the Accelerated Mahaveli Scheme further to the north (Dunham 1982). Muslims and Tamils observing the consequences of the earlier project took all this as a direct attack on their interests (Peebles 1990).

The demographic consequences of the Gal Oya project were considerable. In the quarter century following independence, the Sinhala population in the area grew from 6 per cent to nearly 20 per cent of the total (Table 3.1). In the late 1950s, local administrative structures were reorganised to reflect this change. Batticaloa District was split into two administrative units, with the creation of Ampara District. With some notorious gerrymandering, the new district covered the area of both the Gal Oya project, and the southern stretch of the Muslim–Tamil coastal strip. Demographically, the new district was split between Tamils (21 per cent in 1981), Muslims (42 per cent), and Sinhala (37 per cent).

The east coast society of the early 1980s, which was about to enter a quarter century of civil war, was characterised by striking inequalities. Post-independence development projects had brought a substantial bloc of Sinhala migrants to the inland areas, with the new town of Ampara emerging as a hub for trade and administration. While the Gal Oya scheme failed to generate the prosperity its planners had anticipated, earlier colonial land policies had created a distinctive political economy, with much greater concentration of ownership, and much higher levels of landlessness, than in any other part of the island (Herring 1972). The big landowners formed a thin elite stratum, their agrarian income often supplemented by government or professional employment. Their children attended the sprinkling of top schools, such as St Michael's in Batticaloa. The landless, in contrast, were usually wage labourers rather than sharecroppers (the most common pattern elsewhere), often travelling out of the district altogether for seasonal employment (Farmer 1957: 62). Away from the elite schools, educational levels were poor: in 1981, Batticaloa District had the lowest literacy levels in the island. It also had the lowest average cash income per household (O'Hare and Barrett 1996: 118).

War

For many years, the 1956 riots in the Gal Oya valley seemed little more than an aberration, a one-off disturbance in the longer history of grudging accommodations and everyday coexistence in the east. When young people in Jaffna started to lose patience with the futility of mainstream political representation in the 1970s, eastern youth did not at first follow them. Up to 1983, the year of the fateful attacks on Tamil homes across Colombo and the island's south, there were few signs of overt militancy in the east. But within a year of the July 1983 violence, the army and police had started to impose themselves on the Tamil population, while young men, little by little, started to slip away to join one or the other of the different Tamil militant groups (Whitaker 1990). And, from 1984, the east became the site of some of the most bitter events of the war.

The early history of the war – from the early 1980s to the mid 1990s – in the east of Sri Lanka remains so far unwritten, and most of the published accounts of the war concentrate far more on the island's north where the war began, and eventually ended (Weiss 2011). We do however have some remarkable accounts of particular episodes from the war in the east. A Dutch NGO missionary cum aid worker, Ben Bavinck, drove around the east on a regular basis in the late 1980s and early 1990s, delivering supplies to Christian development projects and listening to stories of round-ups and killings. His diaries of those years give a strong sense of the confusion of the early years of full war (Bavinck 2011). Anthropologists like Dennis McGilvray (1999) and Mark Whitaker (1999) have contributed snapshots of the effect of the war on the places they knew best from their previous research. Patricia Lawrence's unpublished PhD thesis provides us with a vivid account of events in the Batticaloa area in the early 1990s. And throughout the war, the University Teachers for Human Rights (Jaffna), who were quick to acknowledge the political importance of the multi-ethnic east for the struggle that was unfolding, published regular reports on particular events and developments there. A somewhat clearer picture emerges for the subsequent years, when in the latter part of the 1990s, a degree of equilibrium emerged between the LTTE and the Sri Lankan military with a low-intensity type of war. The political economy of war in this period has been studied in depth by a number of authors (Goodhand and Lewer 1999; Goodhand et al. 2000; Korf 2004, 2005; Korf and Fünfgeld 2006). Similarly, the time after the 2002 Ceasefire Agreement when, paradoxically, violence in many parts of the east increased rather than decreased, is also relatively well documented (Bohle 2007; Bohle and Fünfgeld 2007; Gaasbeek 2010a; Walker 2013).

We can, for convenience sake, identify three phases in the history of the war in the east. In the first, between 1983 and 1990, a complex scene with multiple actors resolved into the more familiar bipolar logic of the war between the government and the LTTE. Immediately after the 1983 violence, different militant groups emerged in the east (Thangarajah 2003), especially more conventionally leftist ones like the Eelam People's Revolutionary Liberation Front (EPRLF) and the People's Liberation Organisation of Tamil Eelam (PLOTE). Initially, the militants were eager to recruit Muslim as well as Tamil youth, while the government was equally eager to foment divisions between the two communities. In 1985, violence broke out between Muslims and Tamils in a number of towns up and down the east coast. In 1987, the Indian Peace-Keeping Force (IPKF) arrived to police the implementation of the Indo-Lankan Accord, signed between India and Sri Lanka, and intended to pacify the LTTE. Having imposed itself on both parties, the Indian forces soon became embroiled in the war when the LTTE refused to disarm and the incumbent Premadasa government sought to sabotage the agreement. The IPKF quickly became embroiled in their own fight with the LTTE, while the government was distracted and faced a brief but highly violent insurrection by southern youth under the banner of the JVP. In the second half of the 1980s, the LTTE set about the elimination of all rival Tamil political formations, killing as many leaders as they could. The remnants of groups like the EPRLF were co-opted as proxies to work on behalf of the Indian forces.

When the IPKF finally withdrew in the course of 1990, the LTTE took over the villages on the inland side of the Batticaloa lagoon, initiating the second phase of the war. From 1990 to 2004, those villages remained under more or less unbroken LTTE control. In the first years of this phase, government forces transposed to the Tamil villages of the east the same scorched-earth counter-insurgency policies that had eventually broken the JVP in the late 1980s. At the same time, the LTTE launched a series of attacks on Muslims, many of which provoked counter-attacks against Tamil civilians by armed Muslim groups, some of them operating in the shadow of the government forces. The government strategy against the LTTE was less successful than it had been against the JVP, and little by little the patchwork sovereignty established in 1990 came to seem like a 'normal' state of affairs. Within that state of affairs, the poor villages of the east became the prime recruiting ground for the LTTE, whose main battles were being fought elsewhere in the north and the Vanni. Recruitment started as a predominantly voluntary process, but little by little the degree of coercion increased. The seeming 'normality' of war also comprised a hardening of faultlines. The east became a region fragmented by frontlines, checkpoints, curfews and entrenched ethno-political boundaries. Security regimes, patronage politics and restrictions on livelihoods had distinct impacts on the Sinhala, Muslim and Tamil communities, and this drove deep wedges between them (Goodhand et al. 2000; Korf and Fünfgeld 2006; Bohle 2007; Bohle and Fünfgeld 2007). The 2002 Ceasefire Agreement with the government enabled the insurgents to consolidate their rule in the areas they controlled, while also expanding their political work in government-controlled territory. That in turn became a growing source of resentment, and this second phase ended when the eastern leader of the LTTE, Karuna, announced his split with the leadership in April 2004. What started as the 'Karuna faction', morphed into a paramilitary group-turned-political party called the TMVP, again acting in the shadow of the government forces. With their support, the government was able to recapture LTTE territory and declare victory in the east in 2007. The final phase, which continues as we write, involved the elimination of the LTTE as an alternative source of power and authority in the region, and the reversion to a pattern of 'normal politics' which is not always so very different from the politics of wartime.

Two vignettes from the long years of war capture some of the shifting contours of warscape in the east. The first is from July 1990, when the first phase was at the maximum point of flux and confusion. The second is from 1998, when the government and the LTTE had settled into some kind of long-term accommodation in the area around Batticaloa itself. In 1990, a temporary and unlikely alliance between President Premadasa and the LTTE forced the Indians to start the process of withdrawal from the island. As the IPKF left, the LTTE detained a large number of policemen in the Batticaloa area; hundreds, Sinhala and Muslim, were murdered. The LTTE also started their own attacks on Muslims, for which there were further reprisals, while the government forces conducted round-ups and atrocities of their own on Tamil villages. In his diary, Ben Bavinck records his impressions of a trip to the east at the height of the killing and confusion:

> *8th July 1990, Batticaloa.* Early this morning, I set out for Chenkaladi. Alas! In the dim light of dawn I passed six bodies lying on the streets, burning on car tyres. Here, in Batticaloa too!
>
> In Urani, I briefly visited the CSI [Church of South India] pastor, Earl Solomon, and his wife and, after passing a strict checkpoint at the Airport Road junction, I was back in Tiger-land. South of Kiran, several big buildings had been blown up by the Tigers, allegedly to prevent the army from ever using them. This is common practice with these 'boys'! ... In a conversation with Rev. Alfred, he vented his feelings of despair about the Tigers. He felt that they did not have any realisation that a people slowly build up their material resources. If one destroys all these, they have to start again from scratch. 'We have been set back a 100 years,' he said.
>
> I went on to Valaichchenai, where I heard that the army had killed 150 people, many with knives.
>
> In Chenkaladi, all the shops have been ransacked by the 'boys'. (Bavinck 2011: 113)

Bavinck then goes on to describe the worsening violence between Muslims and Tamils that had been sparked by the killings of the policemen ('from one Muslim village alone, Addalaichchenai, 105 police constables have been killed' [2011: 115]). He also describes attempts by local worthies in some places to mediate between the Tigers and the other forces, and minimise the violence – 'the Assistant Government Agent, the bank manager, the Roman Catholic priest' (2011: 114).

The entry from Bavinck's diary represents one of the most volatile moments in this history of the war. A few years later, the arrangements set in place in the early 1990s had begun to acquire an air of permanence. In 1998 an Indian journalist reported on the LTTE's attempts at state-building from its stronghold of Kokkadichcholai, a village a few miles across the lagoon from Batticaloa town (the latter remaining in government hands):

> At the heart of the 'state structures' in Kokkadicholai [sic] is the LTTE's political office, which is kept ticking by its intelligence wing. Here, a political representative of the LTTE briefs this correspondent on the intricacies of 'Eelam ethos' and gives matter-of-fact replies to some questions and parries others. Keeping vigil all the while is Tulasi, evidently an intelligence official. Tulasi saw action in the battle for Jaffna, just before the Sri Lankan military forces overran the LTTE stronghold in the northern peninsula in January 1995. He is particular that no photographs be taken of LTTE fighters, as distinct from guards or sentinels, in Kokkadicholai [sic].
>
> On the streets of Kokkadicholai [sic] one sees LTTE fighters, including women. A 'court of justice' and a 'police station' run by the LTTE constitute the centrepiece of the power structure. There is, however, no chamber of representatives of the people. This is in line with the LTTE's theory of state; the organisation favours a system of centralised power in the hands of a 'supreme leader'. The absence of a chamber of people's representatives also points to the fact that although for all practical purposes this terrain is in the administrative control of the LTTE, it has not broken free of the sovereign Sri Lankan state. The relative free movement of people and goods across the dividing line between Kokkadicholai [sic] and the Batticaloa segment is a sure sign of a continuing, perhaps sustainable, interaction between the two sides. (Suryanarayana 1998)

A village like Kokkadichcholai played a two-fold role in the LTTE strategy: at once an exemplar of the new world of Tamil Eelam to be shown off to foreign journalists (and the occasional gullible anthropologist [Trawick 2007]), and a source of fresh recruits to be sent to the north where the 'real' war was being pursued remorselessly. In a few short years, the violent chaos of the early 1990s had settled into a state of grudging mutual accommodation, war-as-usual rather than the unpredictable and unruly violence of a few years earlier.

The stalemate of the second half of the 1990s did little to help the enfeebled economy of the area. Much of the richest paddy land was now either in the zone controlled by the LTTE (and therefore subject to their efforts at taxation) or on the contested borders between Sinhala, Tamil and Muslim areas. Some fields had to be abandoned, others suffered from labour shortages as no one wanted to work in such potentially deadly locations. Lagoon fishing was also hit by curfews and government (and LTTE) harassment (Goodhand et al. 2000; Bohle and Fünfgeld 2007). Transport links to the rest of the island were disrupted by checkpoints and a general deterioration of the roads, limiting the opportunities to access markets for local produce. The impact of this regime was unequal in ethnic terms: while Muslims were largely denied access to their paddy fields in LTTE-controlled areas, many Tamil farmers could still cultivate paddy, but faced difficulties to bring it into cleared areas to the markets.

Politically, a significant development of the 1990s was the rise to importance of the Sri Lanka Muslim Congress (SLMC) under the charismatic leadership of M.H.M. Ashraff. Until the late 1980s, Muslim politicians across the island had tended to align themselves, more or less opportunistically, with one or other of the two Sinhala-dominated national parties, the UNP and the SLFP. There was also a long-term trend in which Muslim politicians from the richer areas of the south-west attempted to speak in the name of the poorer Muslim communities of the north and east (McGilvray and Raheem 2007). In its formation, Ashraff's SLMC reversed both these trends. It was a party that attempted to mobilise Muslims as a single bloc across the island, led by a man born and raised in the east. Ashraff himself was clearly influenced by the rise of Tamil identity politics. As a participant at the Vaddukoddai meeting in 1976, where the Tamil United Liberation Front (TULF) leadership set down the terms for their goal of a separate Tamil nation, Ashraff is said to have presented himself as the 'younger brother' of TULF leader Amirthalingam, promising to deliver Eelam should Amirthalingam fall short (Ismail et al. 2004: 195). Leaving Tamil dreams of Eelam behind, Ashraff's SLMC played down any specifically Islamist strand within its political project, concentrating instead on protecting the interests of the Muslims conceived as a single political entity. Founded in 1981, the party rose swiftly as the eastern Muslims found themselves increasingly squeezed by the rise of the Tamil militant movements. The SLMC won enough seats to become the biggest opposition party in the short-lived North-East Provincial Council in 1989, and gained four MPs in that year's parliamentary election. In 1994, it won seven seats in parliament, and was brought into Chandrika Kumaratunga's ruling coalition, with Ashraff using his position as Minister of Ports and Shipping to promote the development of harbour facilities in the east. But the so-called 'Ashraff factor' went far beyond the confines of the harbour sector and was manifest in new public buildings in Muslim settlements across the east.

When Ashraff died in a helicopter crash in 2000, the prospects for Muslim political unity seem to have died with him. Two figures from the Kandy area, Rauf Hakeem and Ashraff's widow Ferial Ashraff, claimed the succession, and when Hakeem emerged as leader, Ferial founded an alternative party. Since then, although the SLMC are still frequently treated as if they are the pre-eminent representatives of Muslims in general, Muslim political power has fragmented, with more or less autonomous Muslim leaders holding sway in particular areas. What endures, more than anything, is the importance of patronage, the ability to be seen to deliver state resources to your supporters. The need to tap into state power severely impedes the scope of these political entrepreneurs to advocate 'the Muslim cause' – the collective rights of the Muslim community as a self-defined ethnic group – as that would place them in opposition to the government from which they demand resources and in which their politicians hold ministerial portfolios. In this respect, both Sinhala and Muslims in the east in the 1990s could see the state as a potentially benevolent source of benefits. Eastern Tamils, with little or no political leverage in Colombo, were left out of patronage networks, with only the repressive machinery of the security apparatus to remind them of the central government's claims on them. This imbalance between the two minorities – the Muslims and the Tamils – in their relative political leverage and patronage power led many Tamils to label Muslims as 'war winners' in the east – another source of resentment between the two ethnic communities.

The security apparatus itself grew as the war proceeded, providing an increasingly important source of income for people in the poorer areas of the country. Recruitment to the growing military sector was not simply skewed to poor parts of the country like Eastern Province; it was also heavily skewed to young Sinhala Buddhist men. A World Bank survey in 1999–2000 revealed that in Eastern Province, a quarter of Sinhala men in the 18–30 age group were directly employed in the military (Venugopal 2009: 114; see also Korf 2006). As well as joining the police and the army, both Sinhala and Muslims were drafted as part-time fighters in the Home Guard units that were set up in the late 1980s. This brought a significant proportion of young men and their (extended) families in these settlements to depend on this source of income, creating an inflated cash economy in these frontier villages.

Not War

When exactly should we say the war ended in the east? The question is much less straightforward than it may appear at first. Three possible dates suggest themselves. In 2002, the government and the LTTE signed a Ceasefire Agreement brokered by Norway acting as a third-party mediator. That agreement was only formally abrogated by the government in 2008, but by then the same government had already declared 'victory' in the east. It is clear that the LTTE was comprehensively defeated in the final battle in May 2009, but many would argue that even this did not represent a clear 'end' to the conflict. Indeed, in 2008 and 2009 we were often explicitly told by activists in the area not to take away the impression that anything had really changed or improved with the departure of the LTTE from the local political scene. Violence continued; political claims had not been resolved.

The story of war in Sri Lanka's most diverse region is a uniquely eastern narrative with many localised elements, rather than simply a derivative of the national sequence of events. However, given that both the government and the LTTE centres lie outside the region, we do need to place the east coast's experience of war in the context of Sri Lanka's wider political and military developments. The defeat of the LTTE ended a long and turbulent period of ceasefires, peace talks, military re-escalations and new stalemates.

The story of how and why the war ended in Sri Lanka remains bitterly contested. By the late 1990s, there was a strong sense that the war had become unwinnable by either side. Chandrika Kumaratunga's government had been elected in 1994 with high hopes for peace, but optimistic early signs of dialogue with the LTTE withered almost immediately. War restarted, and after retaking control of Jaffna from the LTTE, government forces became bogged down in an attritional struggle for territory in the LTTE stronghold of the Vanni. The government persevered with an attempt to combine a political strategy to build consensus around a set of constitutional proposals that would address Tamil grievances once and for all, while pushing back the LTTE on the military front. It also actively pursued international support for its efforts to find an end to the conflict. For the LTTE, with its dense networks of support in the growing Tamil diaspora in Europe, Australia and North America, the struggle had also long since become an international one. This was the situation in which Norway came forward as a potential third-party mediator. The formal process commenced in 1999 with President Kumaratunga's request for Norway to start a dialogue with the LTTE, and reached its high point with both sides agreeing the Ceasefire Agreement in February 2002.

The CFA was followed by six rounds of formal negotiations in the months that followed, but by the middle of 2003 the talks had reached an impasse. The tangled story of the Norwegian intervention is immensely complicated, involving as it does not merely the LTTE, the government and the Norwegians but also other important international players such as India, the USA and the major aid donors (mainly the World Bank, the Asian Development Bank, the UK, USA, Japan and the EU in particular), who had collectively positioned their sizeable aid budgets and promised huge amounts of aid as inducements to keep the peace process alive (Goodhand et al. 2011). On the ground in the east, the CFA had a number of immediate implications. Travel became easier all over the island, and the LTTE were able to set up offices and hold rallies in government-controlled areas like Batticaloa town. The Norwegian effort was heavily concentrated on the problem of bringing the LTTE to the table and keeping them there: this meant there was no formal role for other affected groups like the Muslims, let alone dissident Tamils who did not support the LTTE project. For the excluded, the process itself carried the veiled threat of future LTTE dominance in the north and east.

Despite the lack of progress at the talks, the immediate consequence of the process itself was destabilising for both opposed parties. By the time the CFA was signed, Kumaratunga had lost control of Parliament to the opposition UNP and was forced to work with a bitter political enemy, the new Prime Minister Ranil Wickremesinghe. The agonistic dynamic of Sri Lankan party politics worked its malign magic, encouraging Kumaratunga's supporters to target the Norwegians and Wickremesinghe as stooges working in the interests of the LTTE. On the LTTE side, the destabilisation was less predictable in the direction it took but, as it turned out, completely fatal in its consequences: the aforementioned Karuna split drove a major nail in the LTTE's coffin. On 3 March 2004, Karuna – then the LTTE commander in the east – announced that his forces would no longer take orders from the LTTE hierarchy in the north. A month later, it looked as if the breakaway group had been comprehensively defeated by forces loyal to Prabhakaran, the LTTE leader. Karuna himself escaped, and with the support of the army, was able to regroup and, little by little, strike back against the LTTE in the east. Meanwhile Wickremesinghe's government was defeated in a snap parliamentary election, in which hardline nationalist parties opposed to the Norwegian efforts prospered. A little over two years on from the ceasefire, both signatories found their position undermined by divisions on their 'side' of the war.

Our book's subtitle ('A Collaborative Ethnography of War and Peace') does not, then, indicate a simple transition between two known states (from 'war' *to* 'peace') but an exploration of an unresolved state (both 'war' *and* 'peace'). In the years leading up to the 2002 CFA, the 'hot' war had shifted to the north, and it was in the Vanni that the government and the LTTE were fighting themselves to a standstill. In the east, the lines of demarcation between so-called 'cleared' and 'uncleared' areas were known and, most of the time at least, relatively uncontested. The situation was not exactly what any of the parties wanted, but people at least knew where they stood. As a Catholic priest told us in 2008:

> It used to be quite simple. If somebody wanted to communicate with the LTTE, I could take my motorbike on the ferry and cross the lagoon and take the message. There were two sides and everyone knew who they were. But now ...

His voice trailed off, leaving us to complete his thought. This feeling of complete confusion about who was standing on whose side framed the common saying, 'You only open your mouth to eat.'

The former 'Karuna Faction', the TMVP, had filled some of the political space occupied by the LTTE until their withdrawal the previous year. Following Karuna's absence from the east, the TMVP had split again. A contentious election had seen the leader of one TMVP faction (Pillayan) installed as Chief Minister of the Eastern Province in 2008, while another (Karuna) served in senior government positions in Colombo. But this veneer of respectability did little to cloak the less respectable situation on the ground. The TMVP were a rag-tag force of ill-trained and very young armed men – some of them forcibly recruited from the same villages the LTTE had used for their forcible recruitment in the recent past (Sánchez Meertens 2013). Their local pre-eminence owed everything to the protective shadow of the Sri Lankan Army. Moreover, their election victory brought to a head the internal divisions between those around Pillayan and those more attached to Karuna, who was by now a minister in the Colombo government. The two TMVP factions started to target each other. A week before the conversation with the priest, a group of Pillayan supporters had been murdered in the TMVP office in Chenkaladi north of Batticaloa. Disappearances were common. Bodies sometimes washed up on the banks of the lagoon. Officially, this may have been 'peace', but it certainly did not feel at all secure. Not for the last time, we had to suppress our surprise when people looked back nearly nostalgically to the clarity and certainties of the war between the LTTE and the government.

The period of 'not war, not peace' was also the high point of 'not government' in the east, not in the sense of a decline in state activity, but rather in the sense of a proliferation of action in the name of the 'non-governmental'. A small number of international non-governmental organisations (INGOs) had been active in Eastern Province since the early 1980s, and almost from the start their presence and their commitments opened them up to political attack, especially from Sinhala nationalists for whom the very idea of the 'non-governmental' was a political anathema. As the war proceeded, both national and international non-governmental agencies became increasingly embedded in everyday life in the east (and the north), not least because they offered a politically convenient way for international donors to support populations in the war-affected areas. In so far as the worst affected populations were likely to be Tamil, it was not surprising that INGO work was usually concentrated in Tamil areas, nor was it surprising that this in itself, in the eyes of their nationalist critics, could be taken as proof of covert support for the LTTE and its political project. The signing of the CFA raised the profile of non-governmental activity in the shadow of the war. The Norwegians, in particular, poured aid into a range of NGOs promising peace-related interventions, generating a short-lived 'peace industry', in which 'peace entrepreneurs' skilfully pitched their organisations to international donors eager to be seen to be associated with what promised to be the decisive intervention that finally ended the long, bitter war. And, when war broke out again in 2006, and especially as it reached its eventual denouement in a wave of official patriotic fervour in 2009, the same organisations and entrepreneurs found themselves forced to distance themselves as far as possible from the very concept of 'peace' (Walton 2012).

On top of the peace boom, the Boxing Day tsunami that hit the coastline of the east on the morning of 26 December 2004 brought in its wake what was often referred to as a 'second tsunami' of aid (Korf 2005; McGilvray and Gamburd 2010). The first tsunami killed just over 10,000 people in Ampara District, which had the highest death-toll in the island, and a further 3,000 in Batticaloa District. Altogether 20,000 homes were destroyed in the two districts. But the damage and immediate suffering were confined to a narrow strip along the coast, while infrastructure, housing and services a mile or more inland were unaffected. This narrow strip, though, was among the most densely settled areas in the country. Prompted by a huge flow of donations, agencies of all sorts scrambled to find some kind of activity they could attach themselves to, especially in the weeks after the initial disaster when communications had been restored and transitional housing provided for the displaced, in a spirit aptly captured in Stirrat's term 'competitive humanitarianism' (Stirrat 2006;

Gaasbeek 2010b; see also McGilvray and Gamburd 2010). In the months that followed the disaster, the roads along the coast were choked with INGO vehicles, with their agency flags and waving satellite phone aerials. Towns like Batticaloa experienced a brief property boom as INGOs sought space for their new offices. Local organisations with the personnel and experience to make a contribution found themselves inundated with funding and offers of cooperation. By late 2006, though, when the fieldwork for this book began, the humanitarian tide had already started to abate. Agencies were packing up and pulling out, housing projects were being completed, new emergencies elsewhere beckoned.

Politically, the tsunami was another blow for the Norwegian-backed peace process. This outcome was not immediately self-evident, however. In the first hours and days after the disaster, the LTTE and government forces forgot about their antagonism and joined together in the search for survivors. But as the scale of external aid became apparent, old grievances about ownership and control of resources swiftly resurfaced. The major international donors saw the emergency as an opportunity to force both sides to build more cooperative structures for rehabilitation and reconstruction work. Under donor pressure, a mechanism for the distribution and management of aid through local community-based structures which couldn't simply operate as informal wings of either the government or the LTTE – called P-TOMS (Post-Tsunami Operational Management Structure) – was put together. Anti-NGO sentiment and anti-Norwegian sentiment coalesced around the P-TOMS proposal, and after a short but intense campaign in which the JVP left the government coalition, the proposal was ruled unconstitutional by the Supreme Court in July 2005. Something that had started as an attempt to bring the two sides back into dialogue, ended with the LTTE nursing an even stronger sense they were being systematically excluded from access to external aid. And, while the P-TOMS proposals were gradually grinding to a constitutional halt, both sides were quietly stepping up the pressure. In February 2005, the LTTE political leader in the east was ambushed and killed in government-controlled territory. In April, the well-known Tamil journalist Dharmaratnam Sivaram was murdered in Colombo. In August 2005 the Foreign Minister Laksman Kadirgamar was killed by a sniper in Colombo. In October the Principal of Central College in Jaffna, a known opponent of LTTE child recruitment, was killed at his school.

In the year that followed the tsunami, and the huge level of international attention that accompanied it, the country slid slowly back into war. In November 2005, Mahinda Rajapaksa was elected President, promising a much more belligerent approach to the LTTE and the crumbling peace process. His opponent Ranil Wickremesinghe's chances were widely believed to have been scuppered by an LTTE call for Tamils to boycott the vote. Events then moved swiftly, if not always especially clearly. The LTTE–Karuna killings continued in the east, while in the north paramilitaries aligned with the government attacked a range of 'soft' LTTE targets, like the families of LTTE 'martyrs'. The LTTE tried to respond by marshalling a citizens' uprising – an Eelam Intifada – against the government. Rajapaksa's brother, a former army officer, was installed as Secretary to the Ministry of Defence. A clear change of strategy followed. Tensions rose around Trincomalee after a series of incidents, including the widely publicised killing of a group of Tamil students in January 2006 (UTHR(J) 2006). Although the period of official ceasefire did not end violent contestation, it transformed and fragmented the patterns of violence: although the overall condition was more peaceful than the overt war that had preceded it, a degree of violence had persisted (as evinced by the ceasefire violations routinely reported to international monitors). But after the split in the east, there was a slow process of escalation, culminating with the Mavil Aru incident with which we started this chapter.

The East as a Political Field?

Our fieldwork was carried out, then, towards the end of the long years of war. When we started, Karuna's supporters, the TMVP as they started to call themselves, were beginning to make themselves a visible presence in the landscape. Offices bearing their name appeared in towns, almost always adjoining, or even within, army or police bases, thus making clear the logic of protection that enabled them to function. The army and the LTTE engaged in what can now be seen as a rehearsal for the final events of 2009: government forces softened up LTTE positions with heavy shelling and the LTTE would slowly cede territory rather than engage in prolonged open combat. Often the shelling would be directed into villages and other areas of concentrated population, followed by accusations and counter-accusations about civilian casualties and which side was to blame for those that occurred. One immediate consequence of the Mavil Aru events was a cutting of the LTTE supply routes between the east and their stronghold in the northern Vanni. Within a year, they had entirely withdrawn from the east (thus cutting them off from what had been their most consistent recruiting ground).

The Mavil Aru incident coincided with a Supreme Court ruling that broke up the unitary North-Eastern Province, an administrative unit which linked the main Tamil areas of the east and north in a single structure, and which had been established originally in the wake of the Indian involvement in 1987. Soon after the announcement of victory in the east, the government started planning elections to the Provincial Council for the revived Eastern Province. These were held in May 2008 and, amid some confusion and accompanied by sporadic acts of violence, the TMVP leader Sivanesathurai Chandrakanthan, known as Pillayan, became Chief Minister, much to the concern of the Muslim electorate who now outnumbered the Tamil vote. Even then, disappearances and killings continued, albeit at a lower level than in previous years, as factions loyal to Pillayan and Karuna clashed within the TMVP.

This was the immediate political context for our field research. In comparison with the events of the 1980s and 1990s, the return to war was brief in the east, but when the confrontation between the government and the LTTE ended, it was not replaced by a straightforward peace. Instead one group of paramilitaries (the LTTE) had been superseded by another group of paramilitaries (the TMVP), a group whose leadership had themselves been members of the LTTE only a few years earlier. In terms of the three phases of the war, our work was carried out in the third phase, that is the period after the LTTE split of 2004. This is a period which can be characterised by two slightly contradictory trends – on the one hand a continued move away from the high levels of violence of the late 1980s and early 1990s, and, on the other, a fragmentation and multiplication of possible sources of violence, more reminiscent of the earliest years of the war. The atmosphere in which our fieldwork was carried out was objectively safer than it had been for many years, and yet subjectively for many people we spoke to it was felt to be more uncertain.

The incidence of violence is never the only story, and there is always a danger that a fascination with overt conflict may distract the observer from noticing other less dramatic stories (Lubkemann 2007). Certain themes shape the longer history of the east as we have told it here. The history of the last two centuries is dominated by land and water, by the economic potential they possess, and by the visions of improvement that captivated first colonial officials and then postcolonial politicians. The state is of course integral to that story of improvement, and therefore central to the shape of the emerging political economy of the east. The state provided the impetus for the expansion of paddy agriculture, and that in turn was the foundation for a new class structure of big landowners and landless workers, serviced by the shopkeepers and rice-mill owners of the coastal towns. In contrast to India, the colonial state in Sri Lanka did not acknowledge and structure its activities around the divisions of caste, but it did see the world through an ideology of 'race'. Colonial officials lamented the absence of Sinhala farmers in the east, and their political successors saw it as self-evident that a scheme like the Gal Oya project should in part attempt to build a new Sinhala society on the borders of the more established Tamil and Muslim communities.

In some sense then, the landscape of the east, with its shoreline, lagoons, paddy land, rivers, tanks and canals, provides a potential source of coherence, binding together different communities and religious groups – a point of convergence in Baumann's (1996) terminology. The ubiquitous presence of the state, in everything from the construction of irrigation works to the everyday working of schools and post offices, further reinforces these processes of convergence. At this point, we might see political economy as representing a centripetal force working against the centrifugal impulse that might send religious and linguistic groups on divergent courses. But this is to ignore the extent to which people's engagement with state institutions and state resources is assumed to be framed by ethnicity, language or community: in the next chapter we examine at greater length the story of a controversy, ostensibly over land and religious space, but in fact predicated on the 'ethnicisation' of entitlements to state resources. The very shape of the state's administrative structures tells its own tale in that respect. The division of Batticaloa District to form the new Ampara District in the late 1950s created a space that could be administered by Sinhala officials (the Government Agents for this district have never been Tamil or Muslim). During the years of war, lower-level administrative boundaries were drawn and redrawn in some areas to create parallel bureaucracies, to match other parallel institutions (schools, and in bi-ethnic places like Kalmunai, even hospitals) for Tamils and Muslims. In the 1980s, the new North-Eastern Province was created in response to Tamil demands for an autonomous homeland; the 2007 de-merger signified the end – for now – of that particular political possibility.

Competitive party politics has also worked in contradictory ways, sometimes uniting communities as communities, but then dividing them again, as shown most clearly in the history of Muslim politics in the east and, paradoxically, in Tamil politics after the Karuna split, which triggered a further fragmentation into a multitude of former militant groups now acting as political parties. In the immediate post-independence period, local politicians established themselves by hooking up with national political parties and promising patronage to their followers. The rise of Ashraff's SLMC seemed to break that pattern by mobilising Muslims as a unitary political bloc – but only temporarily. When the SLMC joined Chandrika Kumaratunga's coalition in the 1990s, the flows of patronage restarted; after Ashraff's death, there was a slow reversion to the pattern of local leaders opportunistically cultivating links with government. Immediately before the war, and the hiatus in 'normal' Tamil politics occasioned by LTTE dominance, the eastern Tamil population aligned themselves electorally with the TULF, a move that more or less automatically removed them from the regular flow of party-based patronage. Pillayan's victory in 2008 might have represented a decisive reversal of this pattern, but the new Provincial Council was starved of resources, and its autonomy curtailed by the actions of the Governor, who was Sinhala and a former military commander appointed directly by the centre. In the most recent elections in 2012, the TMVP has been decisively defeated on the Provincial Council, with another Tamil party, the Tamil National Alliance (TNA), assuming the TULF's place in permanent opposition.

Through all this the state endures, both as a material reality (children go to school, babies are born in hospitals) and as a focus for the political imagination (the promised land of Tamil Eelam, the vision of a new Sinhala Buddhist order in the Gal Oya and Mahaveli projects). Sometimes state-like agencies have appeared, apparently taking on the work we might expect the state to do – NGOs, paramilitaries. But apart from the mosque federations in Muslim areas, these have come and gone, temporary interventions leaving the state as important as ever in the lives of most people in the east. But at the same time, the state sporadically left important political spaces to be ordered, policed and secured. This is where we often find religious actors taking responsibility for the maintenance of local order.

4

Making Sacred Space

November 2008: The monastery we are visiting is built around a much older Buddhist site on a rocky hill with glorious views over deserted scrub jungle. Driving up the track to the monastery we notice tell-tale heaps of elephant dung by the road, emphasising the remote, jungly quality of the location. When we finally arrive, the monastery turns out to be bigger and more elaborate than we had expected. There is a police post with two resident police officers, as well as several buildings, and a row of rooms built into the overhang of a large rock. A pond has been artfully created in a dip of the rock, with a new bridge crossing it, leading to a site of ongoing construction: a replica of the famous statue of the reclining Buddha from Gal Vihara at Polonnaruwa is being built here. There is an impressive *dagäba* (stupa) and, fenced off and protected, a sapling planted from a branch of the original bo-tree under which the Buddha gained enlightenment. Power lines follow the road up the hill and there seems to be a radio mast of some sort above the police post. We have arranged a meeting with a very well-known monk, a former army commander who has changed course and ordained in late middle age. We are early so find ourselves wandering round the place, talking to other monks about its history, and looking at concrete manifestations of that history – an inscription high on the rock in Brahmi script, more recent stones recording openings, constructions and donations, and photographs of visits by more or less every Sinhala politician of note from the last four decades.

Eventually we are told that our host is free to see us. As we enter his room, he is closing down his laptop. He has just been emailing some Thai followers who were in a long-term conversation with him about meditation. He explains that he has access to a satellite link that allows him a good quality connection, even here in the back of beyond. His fame is quite unusual. He has only been formally ordained for a year, but already he is the centre of a great deal of attention from the media and from lay Buddhists eager to hear his teaching. Some – but not all – of this is almost certainly due to the peculiarities of his biography. For most of his life – he is now in his early 60s – he was a career soldier, actively involved in the war against the LTTE and the insurgency by southern youth in the late 1980s.

The interview proceeds. The monk is a captivating and charismatic speaker, and we are soon content to let him decide what he is going to tell us. It is late afternoon and we decide to move out of his quarters and finish the interview in the open air, with vast views of the arid landscape spread out behind us. Eventually we move on to the topic of the conflict and the role of religion in the conflict. There are those, he tells us, who argue that Buddhism is the property of a particular people. (In this context it would be the Sinhala people.) But this is clearly wrong. The Buddha did not give his teaching for any particular category of people. The Buddha gave his teaching for everyone. Similarly – and apparently in allusion to the nationalist monks of the JHU who were now Members of Parliament – he did not ask the *sangha* to get involved in politics. This was not their duty. It was hard to disagree with what he told us and we were impressed by his lucid and unambiguous commitment to a non-chauvinist version of Buddhism. This argument, we said, is so clearly both true and important, and you command a great deal of authority and respect among ordinary Buddhists. Why don't you go out and challenge those Buddhist monks you believe are preaching a distorted version of the Buddha's teaching? Ah, he said, that would be to fall into their trap. It is not the *dhamma* of a monk to engage in politics like this, and even to argue against such engagement is itself to commit the same mistake.

This was a memorable conversation, not least for the paradoxes that framed it. Here was the monk who had himself been a soldier. Here was a forest hermitage, but with its own police post and a satellite internet connection. Here was a refusal to enter the world of politics, yet here were so many photographs on display of prominent politicians visiting the monastery and providing visible support for it. And as we left, we were given a copy of a small pamphlet on this history of the monastery, written by the Reverend Ellawala Medhananda, at that time the leader of the JHU in Parliament.

In this and the following chapter, we shift our attention from '*the conflict*' – the war between the government and the LTTE – to look more closely at religion itself as a potential source of conflict. In Chapter 5, we compare the fate of Muslim reform movements in two towns, one of which has seen violent confrontation between religious factions and one which has not. In this chapter, we focus on what, from a certain angle, looks pre-eminently like a 'religious' conflict – the stand-off between Muslims and Buddhists over the Buddhist site of Dighavapi. But as the chapter unfolds, we also look at two different ways to contextualise the Dighavapi dispute. First, we trace a history of the idea of a 'sacred space' as it is worked through in Anuradhapura and Kataragama, and specifically at the way in which the sacred becomes by definition a space which excludes the political, yet at the same time is a space which depends entirely on the political for the ratification of its claims to sacredness. This paradox should become clearer as our argument moves forward. The second context loops back to the previous chapter, placing the Dighavapi dispute back into the history of people, land, and water by reading it alongside the many other disputes over access to resources in the immediate area. From this perspective, the 'religious' is just one of many registers that might be employed to pursue access to resources in a world where the ethnicisation of entitlements has become more or less axiomatic. That rather crowded statement will be also unpacked and explained as we proceed.

The Dighavapi Story

In June 2009, the Sri Lankan Supreme Court, chaired by Chief Justice Sarath Silva, pronounced on a case that had been discussed before it the previous year. The case was brought forward under the name of the Reverend Ellawala Medhananda, the JHU leader, and five others, including the chief monk of the Dighavapi temple. Dighavapi temple is located about 8 km east of Ampara, and a similar distance from the coastal villages of Oluvil and Palamunai. The case was filed against the District Secretary for Ampara District and 64 others, and it was just one in a series of legal declarations and challenges concerning the Dighavapi temple and the area in its vicinity.

The Supreme Court judgment makes for fascinating reading, not least for the way it moves seamlessly from claims about the ancient past, to fundamental principles of religious freedom, to the apparently more prosaic issues of political patronage and proper bureaucratic procedure in disbursing state land. As such, it illustrates an important point about the place of 'religion' in the making of local disputes: what appears to one party as pre-eminently a problem about religion, appears to another as a straightforward fight over access to resources. It also exemplifies processes well documented elsewhere in South Asia by which potentially containable local disputes become amplified beyond recognition through the intervention of agents working within a much wider political arena (Tambiah 1996; Brass 1997). It is not, however, a classic case of a

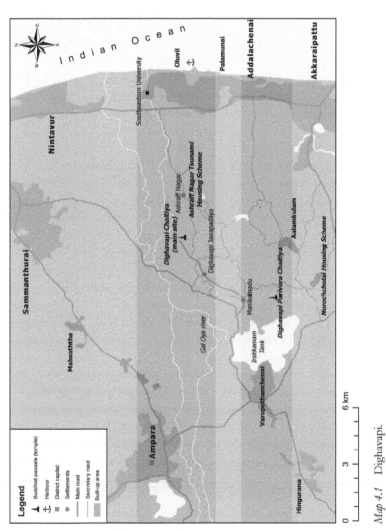

Map 4.1 Dighavapi.

Note: Religious buildings are not displayed exhaustively; a selection was made of those most relevant to this book.

contested religious site – such as Babri Masjid in Ayodhya, to take an obvious example – in two respects. First of all, so far the dispute has not reached the level of overt violence, however much it may have contributed to tensions between religious communities in the immediate area. Second, only one side to the dispute sees it as a religious dispute at all; there are, as yet, no claims of Muslim or Hindu *religious* rights to the place. In other words, there is an asymmetry to the dispute, and this is what the Supreme Court judgment illustrates so clearly. We shall return to the judgment itself later in this chapter.

The Dighavapi case brings together two threads from earlier chapters. Until the 1980s, the story of Dighavapi was an exemplary case of the process of Buddhist expansion and entanglement described in Chapter 2. A Buddhist presence was established in an area beyond existing Sinhala settlement and went on to attract a small number of new settlers around it. But with the passage of time, the Buddhist leaders at Dighavapi gradually established good relations with local Muslim politicians. Muslims here, as elsewhere along the crowded coastal belt, were keenly aware of the pressures on their land and of the constraints on expansion into new land. The response to the 2004 tsunami, which affected coastal communities but left inland areas untouched, destabilised an already tense situation. The war, which further complicated local issues of landholding and cultivation, was never the prime source of the conflict at Dighavapi, although it is significant that the dispute reignited just as the LTTE ceased to be a threat in the area. But the dispute illustrates the tension between centre and periphery, Colombo and the east, in Buddhist perceptions and Buddhist politics.

Dighavapi (literally 'long tank') refers to an ancient stupa or *caitya* reportedly built by King Saddhatissa, brother of the celebrated Sinhala king Dutugämunu, and according to some popular accounts containing the sacred nail relic of the Buddha, and also to a Buddhist temple and land and settlements surrounding the *caitya*. The place now identified as Dighavapi is a large, partially renovated, ancient stupa with an accompanying Buddhist temple situated in between the heavily congested Muslim and Tamil settlements along the eastern coastline and the inland Sinhala settlements mostly established under the Gal Oya Valley project dating back to 1949. Situated in the Addalachenai Divisional Secretary (DS) area of Ampara District, it marks the border area between mainstream Sinhala populations in the western part of the district and a predominantly Muslim belt spreading from Kalmunai to Akkaraipattu in the east. The temple currently controls 585 acres of a total of 20,758 acres in the Addalachenai DS Division (about 3 per cent of all land). There are a number of partially ruined ancient irrigation tanks as well as numerous other ruins, collectively referred to as Dighavapi Janapadaya (colony) in the popular Sinhala nationalist literature (Medhananda 2000). Muslim and Tamil concentrations spread along the narrow coastline but they hold cultivable paddy and highland in interior areas with a lower density of settled population. The main economic activities in the area are rice cultivation, livestock husbandry, limited *chena* (swidden) cultivation, the extraction of gravel for building purposes, and sugar-cane cultivation that was started by a private company in 1973 under the auspices of the ruling government at the time. Even though the area came under the Gal Oya project, irrigation, colonisation and related services were not extended to this eastern bank of the Gal Oya river, leaving it more or less untouched by the 1950s settlement project.

The first reference to a place called Dighavapi occurs in the first chapter of Sri Lanka's Buddhist chronicle, the Mahavamsa. The chapter records the Buddha's three legendary visits to the island of Lanka. After his third visit, to Kelaniya (just outside modern Colombo), he is said to have continued on to Dighavapi: 'And the Master seated himself with the brotherhood at the place where the cetiya (thereafter) stood, and gave himself up to meditation, to consecrate the spot' (Mahavamsa I, 79). This record of the Buddha's visit places Dighavapi in the list of 'sixteen great places' (*solos-mahasthana*) for Buddhist pilgrimage. Later in the chronicle, Dighavapi appears as the seat of Saddhatissa, the pious brother of Dutugämunu, who is defeated by his warrior brother before the climactic war against the Tamil king Elara, a war which dominates the first volume of the chronicle and continues to provide a symbolic template for Sinhala Buddhist self-understandings across the island.

Despite this, Dighavapi seems to have been lost to the official record for many centuries: in Geiger's 1912 translation of the Mahavamsa into English, a footnote says Dighavapi is 'probably' a tank about 30 miles south-south-west of Batticaloa (Geiger 1912: 8 n.1). Canagaratnam, in his 1921 *Monograph of Batticaloa District*, says that Dighavapi has 'never been satisfactorily identified', but agrees with Geiger that 'there is every probability that it is the tank now known as the Kandiyakattu or Maha Kandiya' (Canagaratnam 1921: 53). And in his 1935 *Ancient Irrigation Works in Ceylon*, R.L. Brohier also records that Dighavapi has never been convincingly identified: he also thinks it most likely is Maha Kandiya (Brohier 1935). The site in question is just west of Ampara town, about 6 miles from the place now identified as Dighavapi.

In local accounts, the Dighavapi ruins were first discovered by the British surveyors who surveyed all potential Crown Land in the wake of the Crown Lands Encroachment Ordinance of 1840 and the 1897 Waste Lands Ordinance. Although temple lands were normally not declared as Crown Land, in keeping with the Kandyan Convention of 1815, Dighavapi land was not treated as temple land, presumably because there was no functioning Buddhist temple on the site at the time of the survey. In 1916, a highly committed monk named Godakumbure Revatha, reportedly sent by the Bibile Rajamaha Vihara in Uva Province, built a temple near the ruins and claimed that the sacred site had been identified as that of the Mahavamsa's Dighavapi, and the accompanying land belonged to the Bibile Rajamaha Vihara, to which the land along with all its assets, including villages, cattle and buffaloes, had been donated through a *sannasa* (deed inscribed in rock) by the Kandyan King Kirthi Sri in 1756.[1] One unconfirmed story widely circulated among local Sinhala people is that when the Reverend Rewatha first visited in 1916, Muslim villagers were removing bricks from the *caitya* site to build their own houses, which in turn prompted him to stay on site in order to safeguard what remained of the stupa. In 1916 the Reverend Rewatha petitioned the then Governor, requesting that land to the extent of 1000 *amuna*s (roughly 3,000 acres) be restored to the Bibile temple. As there was no immediate response, the monk sent a reminder in 1924 and, reportedly, a team headed by the Commissioner of Archaeology, A.M. Hocart, was sent to the site. The team did not grant the monk's request, however, and instead proposed to find him an alternative site where his temple could be built with government permission. But the monk clung to his original request and continued to live in the Dighavapi temple, asserting what he considered as his legitimate right to safeguard the sacred site. Thus, initially there was only a conflict between the temple and the colonial state over the control of the site, and there was no conflict along ethnic lines whatsoever between the temple and nearby Muslim communities.[2] This only happened as a result of nationalist campaigns that unfolded in the post-Independence era.

The chief monk at the Dighavapi temple, the Reverend Rewatha, was killed by an unknown party in the 1950s. This potentially explosive event suggests some local friction, but it did not lead to any rise in ethnic tension as such at the time. Meanwhile his successor, the Reverend Nannapurawe Buddharakkita, continued to live in the temple and looked after what he claimed as temple land. He brought some peasants from Bibile and settled them in the vicinity of the temple in order to facilitate its upkeep. Some of the temple land, however, was leased out to Muslim tenants from nearby villages, indicating that some degree of trust had been established over time. In addition, cattle from neighbouring villages were allowed to graze freely on temple land, irrespective of the ethnic identity of the owners. Following representations from Ampara-based Sinhala politicians, Mrs Sirimavo Bandaranaike, the then Prime Minister, arranged to transfer the title of 585 acres of land to the Dighavapi temple through a Gazette notification issued in 1973. The boundaries of the allocated land were not marked, however, and this gave rise to inevitable confusion in time to come. This confusion was amplified by the fact that the amount of land reportedly donated by the kings to the temple varied according to different sources. According to the Reverend Medhananda (2000), all land within the hearing distance of a *lokada tamatama* (a deep-sounding drum typically used for announcing royal decrees) was originally granted to the temple by King Saddhatissa. He estimated that this amounted to some 12,000 acres. This elastic and expandable notion of land allowed militant Sinhala nationalists to claim that all the surrounding villages were actually encroachments on Dighavapi temple land.

In 1973, a leading Sinhala politician in the area established a Sinhala Buddhist settlement of 100 families, selected from second-generation colonists in the Gal Oya project, on nearby vacant Crown Land. The reported aim of this settlement was to facilitate the upkeep of the Dighavapi temple. These settlers were initially provided with highland allotments only. Subsequently some 130 to 140 acres of paddy land in Ponnanwelli, previously cultivated by Muslim farmers from nearby villages under annual permits, were transferred to the new Sinhala settlers by government officials (under the influence of the same Sinhala politician), creating understandable hostility from long-established Muslim residents in the area. In the 1970s a sugar factory was established by a private company at Hingurana, about 16 km from Dighavapi, under the auspices of the government; Crown Land was allocated to Muslim and Tamil villagers, and to Sinhala settlers, for sugar-cane cultivation. It appears that local Sinhala politicians used this opportunity to expand Sinhala settlements around Dighavapi temple, in an attempt to establish a substantial Sinhala Buddhist presence in the vicinity of the site. The Sinhala population in the area increased substantially, which of course was seen as reducing the possibilities for the densely packed Muslim villages along the coast to expand inland.

In 1980, the Cabinet approved a scheme to renovate Dighavapi, identifying it as an important Buddhist site. Only the base of the stupa was renovated, however, and the larger project seems to have been abandoned due to shortage of funds. From 1987 onwards, many villages in the area became depopulated due to LTTE threats and attacks targeting Sinhala settlements and some Muslim villages. In an LTTE attack in 1987, some 13 Muslims and 12 Sinhalese in border villagers were killed, and many of the remaining people in these villages moved out to safer areas with a larger concentration of people belonging to their community. People only started returning to the abandoned villages after the inception of the Norwegian-backed peace process in 2002.

Dighavapi next came to national prominence in 1997, when M.H.M. Ashraff, leader of the Sri Lanka Muslim Congress and at the time an influential member of the Cabinet, was accused of 'bulldozing' certain Dighavapi ruins in an attempt to provide alternative land to Muslim people who had lost land in Ponnanwelli. Subsequent archaeological investigations revealed that the damaged ruins were those of an old *dagäba*, claimed by some nationalist scholars as a *parivara caitya* (satellite *dagäba*) of the main Dighavapi *caitya*. This received great publicity in the Sinhala nationalist press and Ashraff was accused of deliberately demolishing sacred Buddhist ruins and thereby erasing ancient Sinhala Buddhist presence in the area. This in turn led to a hostile reaction from the Buddhist public. The bulldozing took place at a place called Pallekadu, just outside the Dighavapi temple premises. An area of Crown Land under thick forest cover had been identified for distribution among Muslim peasants by Ashraff, who was apparently under considerable pressure from his Muslim voters to secure alternative land in compensation for the lands they had lost in Ponnanwelli. According to Muslim accounts, the damage to the ruins was accidental rather than deliberate, in what appears to have been a haphazardly planned and executed, and politically motivated, project to provide land to Ashraff's Muslim constituency. A combination of public pressure and bad publicity immediately stopped the project, and plans for distribution of land among Muslim peasants were abandoned. Ashraff was a major provider of state patronage to the Dighavapi temple, providing electricity, telephone connections as well as many other services.[3] As a result, he had established a good rapport with the chief monk by this time. He admitted responsibility and apologised for the accidental digging up of the ruins and tried to correct his error by having the Dighavapi site surveyed once again, this time clearly demarcating temple lands and erecting boundary markers. He also commissioned an archaeological survey in the surrounding area, identifying and marking over 30 new archaeological sites nearby, some of which overlapped with

Muslim and Tamil villages. The aim of this exercise was to prevent any further accidental damage of such sites by actual or potential users of the land and to facilitate any future restoration work in the relevant sites.

At this point a new figure appeared on the scene. The Reverend Gangodavila Soma, popularly known as Soma *hamuduruvo*, was a charismatic Buddhist monk who had returned from a period of Buddhist missionary work in Australia to his home temple in a Colombo suburb. In the late 1990s, he attracted a very large following, mainly through his popular preaching style on television (Berkwitz 2008). He was instrumental in drawing public attention to the Dighavapi issue, openly charging Ashraff with a deliberate attack on Buddhist heritage. He challenged Ashraff to a television debate on the issue, a challenge that Ashraff readily accepted. The debate was conducted in Sinhala and is still widely remembered. In the debate Ashraff, who was a lawyer by profession and who came armed with maps and other information about the area, emphasised the peaceful relations that had existed between Buddhists and Muslims in the east, the services he had personally rendered to Buddhist establishments, including Dighavapi, and denied any conscious or deliberate effort to alienate or damage Buddhist sites. The Reverend Soma, who made several unsubstantiated or poorly supported claims about Muslim encroachment on Buddhist sites, was less impressive. As an urban monk, whose prominence had come through the Colombo-based mass media, he demonstrated a certain lack of understanding of the ground realities in the east during the debate.

The Reverend Soma's engagement with Dighavapi was part of a wider concern with the need to protect and restore the relics of the Budddhist past in the Tamil-speaking areas of the north and the east. Seruvila, south of Trincomalee, became the focus of Buddhist settlement and served as a symbolic focus for hardline Sinhala nationalists like the UNP politician Cyril Mathew in the 1970s. It was declared a sacred area in 1979 (Kemper 1991: 155; see Chapter 7). Mathew's role as a champion of Sinhala expansion through popular archaeology passed after his death to figures like Soma, and especially Ellawala Medhananda. The Reverend Medhananda's book *The Sinhala Buddhist heritage in the east and north of Shri Lanka* (2005) is a compilation and translation of dozens of articles about particular archaeological sites, published over the years in popular Sinhala newspapers. The ideological mission of the collection is straightforward enough – to demonstrate that the island has been a unitary state for millennia, that this state was Sinhala and Buddhist, and that the archaeological record demonstrates the presence of Buddhists in all parts of the island (this in contrast to claims for traditional Tamil homelands). The heritage, it goes without saying, is in danger from 'Muslim fundamentalists' (Medhananda 2005: 30), 'terrorists' and the 'so-called cultivators belonging to minority races' (Medhananda 2005: 10). For Medhananda and his generation of hardline Buddhist activists, to some extent Dighavapi occupies the place that Seruvila did for Mathew and his allies in earlier decades: a privileged symbol of Sinhala Buddhist claims on the whole island.

Just as the dust was settling from the debate between Soma and Ashraff, the December 2004 tsunami hit the coastline of Sri Lanka. At first, it led to some easing of ethnic tension, as many displaced Muslims and Hindus were helped by Buddhist temples and organisations in Ampara. Apart from providing temporary shelter for tsunami victims from the coast, many Buddhist organisations provided relief items collected from donors, in an outpouring of ethnic-blind sympathy towards the disaster victims. The situation changed, however, with the influx of NGOs and INGOs, all seeking to channel a flood of external assistance to those affected by the disaster. Both state agencies and international donors, charged with resettling victims away from the affected coastline, looked towards the interior hinterland, which up to this point had been an expanding Sinhala frontier. The state policy of resettling tsunami victims in alternative sites led to considerable tension along ethnic, caste and social class lines. In the east, the majority of tsunami victims were Muslims, followed by Tamils, and then Sinhalese. Finding alternative sites to resettle Muslim IDPs posed a serious problem; the Muslim bazaar towns along the coast were already seriously congested and Muslim IDPs were reluctant to move to areas outside Muslim concentrations due to security concerns and possible reaction from host communities belonging to other ethnic groups (McGilvray 2008).

The Norochcholai Housing Scheme was established by the National Housing Development Authority under Mrs Ferial Ashraff, the widow of M.H.M. Ashraff, as the minister in charge, with Saudi support for housing Muslim tsunami victims from the east coast. The 500-unit project was built on Crown Land, selected for the purpose in 2005, in Norochcholai, which is 13 km away from the Dighavapi temple. The project is actually located not in Addalachenai DS Division, but in the adjoining Division of Akkaraipattu. Similar tsunami housing projects for Muslim tsunami victims (for example, the Ashraff Nagar housing project, which is 1 km from the sacred site) had already been established closer to Dighavapi itself, in Addalachenai Division – but they mostly went unnoticed by Sinhala

Figure 4.1   Norachcholai housing scheme, 2008 (photo by Tudor Silva).

nationalists. An increasingly public argument between Ferial Ashraff and rival Muslim politicians first drew attention to the Norochcholai scheme. Once it had become a public issue, the project triggered an immediate reaction from activist Buddhist monks in Colombo and Ampara. Newspaper articles in the Sinhala nationalist press accused Muslim politicians of using the tsunami as an excuse for encroaching on sacred Buddhist land. The housing scheme was interpreted as an unacceptable expansion of the Muslim frontier in close proximity to the Dighavapi sacred site. The Digamadulla Sangha Sabha, a 'non-political' organisation open to Buddhist monks from all three Nikayas and all political parties, was formed in 2007.[4] To some extent, the structure of the organisation mimicked the structure of the mosque federations which had become regionally organised under external threat in the years of war (see Chapter 5), but the Sabha was also in part a Colombo initiative to which local monks signed up. Their activities included a protest march to Dighavapi temple, where a *dharma salava* (preaching hall) had been built by Mrs Ashraff in memory of her dead husband, and named after him. The signboard was forcibly removed by the protesters in spite of opposition by the incumbent chief monk. The Digamadulla Sangha Sabha also made representations to leading politicians including the President himself. They called on the President to immediately stop the allocation of newly built houses to

Muslim IDPs. They further requested him to declare the Dighavapi area as a sacred site. In 2008, the Dighavapi temple premises were duly declared as a sacred site under the Urban Development Authority through a Gazette notification. This created restrictions on the use of Dighavapi land for anything other than approved religious and archaeological purposes. This move did not satisfy the nationalist monks, however, as it did not address the allocation of housing in the Norochcholai Housing Scheme, which lay outside the demarcated sacred area.

In 2008, the fundamental rights suit was filed in the Supreme Court by a group of Buddhist monks led by the Reverend Medhananda. The suit argued against the allocation of housing exclusively to Muslim IDPs, claiming that 'the settlement of such a large number of Muslims within close proximity to the Raja Maha Viharaya would bar further expansion of Sinhala residents who are now living close to the Viharaya', and this would 'infringe the freedom of religion'.[5] Although the chief incumbent of the Dighavapi temple was one of the petitioners in this case, he appears to have been co-opted by militant monks from outside. An interim order preventing the allocation of housing to any beneficiaries was obtained and, in June 2009, the Supreme Court found in favour of the petitioners, not so much on grounds of religious freedom (the central right they claimed had been infringed) but simply because the land allocation had completely ignored the correct legal process. This, of course, is far from unusual in the world of Sri Lankan political patronage.

This case shows how a certain historical perception about Dighavapi, and its conceptualisation as 'a sacred site' exclusively belonging to the Sinhala Buddhists, has emerged as a serious threat to the land rights of another religious community in eastern Sri Lanka. While the Buddhist monks from Ampara we interviewed did not necessarily agree with the external nationalist representation of what was happening, the more militant among them strongly held the view that the Norochcholai housing should be distributed only among Sinhala peasants from the area, ignoring the reasons for funding and constructing the scheme in the first place. Some held the opinion that the housing should be distributed among tsunami victims following national ethnic proportions. Many Buddhist monks complained that the Muslim politicians from the east were using their disproportionate political power in the government to divert resources, including land and development funds, to support their Muslim constituencies, while Sinhala politicians merely looked after their own personal interests without helping their constituencies as such. In this, these monks made the majority the vulnerable victim of the failure of its own politicians in a kind of cultural criticism of corrupt politics: they had failed to deliver their task to protect the Sinhala Buddhist nation.

The Supreme Court Judgment

The Supreme Court issued its judgment on the Dighavapi case on 1 June 2009, just a few days before the then Chief Justice Sarath Silva retired from the court. This was one of a number of high-profile cases presided over by Silva during the time of his controversial tenure as Chief Justice; others include the striking down of the Post-Tsunami Operational Management Structure (P-TOMs) in 2005, and the ruling that the merged Northern and Eastern Provinces (a measure introduced during the late 1980s Indian intervention) should be immediately de-merged in 2006. Silva had originally been Chandrika Kumaratuna's Attorney-General, moving to his role in the Supreme Court in 1999. Rather unusually for a senior judge, by 2009 Silva was also the presenter of a weekly TV programme, which he used as a vehicle to deliver sermons on Buddhist issues.

The case was brought as an infringement of three fundamental rights guaranteed under the Constitution: freedom of thought, conscience and religion (Article 10); equality before the law (Article 12 (1)); and no discrimination on grounds of race, religion, language, or caste (Article 12(2)). The case was brought by the Reverend Ellawala Medhananda as first Petitioner, together with representatives of the Dighavapi temple and various associated Buddhist groups. The Ampara District Secretary and 64 others were named as Respondents.

The judgment starts with a summary of the complaint:

The alleged infringement is the executive and/or administrative action taken to alienate the land in question which is about 60 Acres in extent to 500 families being entirely for the Muslim community. The land is located 13 kilometers to the south of the Deeghavapi Raja Maha Viharaya. The case of the Petitioners and the Respondents referred to above who support the Petition is that the settlement of such a large number of Muslims within close proximity to the Raja Maha Viharaya would bar further expansion of Sinhala Buddhist residents who are now living close to the Viharaya. They allege that the infringement results from a total failure on the part of the Respondents, to act in terms of the applicable law, being the 13th Amendment to the Constitution and the Land Development Ordinance and to follow a fair and equitable process in effecting the impugned alienation of lands. It is alleged that the alienation is arbitrary and discriminates against Sinhala and Tamil persons who are without land and have requested that they be alienated State land and, is biased in favour of Muslims. It is further alleged that the settlement of 500 families of Muslims in an area proximate to the Viharaya would infringe the freedom of religion. The infringement of the fundamental rights guaranteed under Articles 12(1), 12(2) and 10 are alleged on the aforestated basis.

The main substance of the judgment concerns the circumstances in which the allocation of the contested housing was made, and the process of allocation itself. According to the judgment, there has been 'no compliance' with the legislative and constitutional requirements for land allocation, and no attempt to suggest otherwise on the course of the action. Rather, there is evidence – in the form of a 1998 letter from M.H.M. Ashraff to the then Minister of Land, requesting the allocation of Norochcholai land to landless Muslim farmers from Akkaraipattu – that the plan for this particular allocation pre-dated the tsunami by some years.

The issue of freedom of religion is, however, dealt with rather differently in the body of the judgment, where it receives a single, quite striking paragraph:

> The Petitioners and the Respondents who support the petition submitted that the Deeghavapi Rajamaha Viharay is one of the 16 most venerated sites of Buddhists in this country. According to the Mahavamsa the Buddha in his third visit to Sri Lanka attended the site of the Viharaya. These matters urged by the Petitioners are supported by the comprehensive report of the Director General of Archaeology, which has been produced by the 1st Respondent himself marked 1R9. According to this report the name Deeghavapi has been used from the 2nd Century B.C. and the Viharaya was constructed by King Saddhatissa in the 1st century B.C. Further, the sacred Viharaya had been reconstructed by King Kirthisri Rajasinghe of the Kandyan Kingdom in 1746 A.D. In the circumstances nothing further need to be stated as regards the sensitivity which has been affected by the impugned action from the perspective of the Buddhist, not only in that area but in the entire country.

This is the only paragraph that specifically addresses the religious basis of the court action. Dighavapi, it is argued, is important because of its place in the Mahavamsa and because it is said to have been reconstructed by King Kirthi Sri Rajasinghe (whose reign actually started in 1747). Sensitivity is, then, self-evident: as the judgment puts it, 'nothing further need to be stated'. In other words, the religious case is not argued through at all: religious issues do not *drive* the argument of the judgment, rather they *frame* it.

The judgment concludes:

> State land is held by the executive in trust for the People and may be alienated only as permitted by law. For the reasons stated above I hold that the impugned alienation is bereft of any legal authority and has been effected in a process which is not bona fide ... On the preceding analysis of evidence, the Petitioners have established an infringement of the fundamental rights guaranteed by Article 12(1), 12(2) and 10 of the Constitution.

There are, then, three strands in the judgment, corresponding to the three fundamental rights invoked in the original petition. The first concerns the distribution of state land to the landless. The second concerns the identification of beneficiaries on the grounds of ethnicity, in this case the decision to benefit Muslims exclusively. The third concerns religious 'sensitivity'. The background to the first of these issues lies in the mid-nineteenth century when the colonial government declared all land without obvious title to be Crown Land. Over the following century, large blocks of Crown Land were sold off for plantation development in the central mountains and the south-west Wet Zone. Here in the east, the main development was the opening up of new irrigated rice land. With the advent of mass politics in the 1930s, the process of allocating state land has been administratively erratic, or highly politicised, or both (Moore 1985: 43). Therefore, the procedural shortcomings in the Norochcholai case are by no means unique, but it took the other two issues to bring them to the attention of the Supreme Court.

This leaves us with the religious basis of the judgment. While the process of allocation, and to a lesser extent the ethnicised rationale for the allocation, are subject to some degree of legal reasoning in the judgment, the challenge of religious freedom is presented rather differently. The judgment here merely reiterates the self-evident importance of the site for Buddhists across the island. Yet for a housing scheme 13 km away to affect Dighavapi itself, it is necessary to introduce another argument – that the existence of Norichcholai has the potential to limit the expansion of the Buddhist population. And this in turn contains an implicit assumption –

that Dighavapi *requires* an expanding and exclusively Buddhist population in the surrounding area – which works within the same logic of ethnicised distribution of resources which in other respects the judgment challenges.

Making a Sacred Space

The Supreme Court judgment was only one of a series of important rulings on Dighavapi. In February 2008, at a *poya* day ceremony at his official residence, the President handed over a document promising to develop Dighavapi as a sacred area. As the government newspaper, the *Daily News*, put it in its editorial: 'The move by the President to declare Deegavapi as a sacred area which would naturally encompass the vast surrounding lands said to contain ... artifacts would be a matter of great solace to all Buddhists.' And followers of other religions should also, it claimed, be pleased as the President's decision, 'would also significantly contribute to religious concord and amity and remove suspicion and misgivings among those professing other faiths' (*Daily News* Editorial, 22 February 2008).

What does this mean in practice, and where does the idea of the sacred area come from? The answer lies in the confluence of Buddhist historiography, modernist planning and colonial divisions of the world. The modern history of the Buddhist centre of Anuradhapura in the North-Central Province provides something of a template for subsequent claims to sacred space. The pilgrimage centre of Kataragama to the south provides a more recent variant. Between them, though, we find a peculiar combination, in which that deemed to be sacred is clearly divided from the non-sacred in spatial terms, yet the precise meaning of the sacred is much less clear. For Buddhist leaders campaigning against colonial developments at Anuradhapura, the sacred is explicitly opposed to the political. But later in the Anuradhapura story, the sacred is implicitly identified with a particular community, Sinhala Buddhists, and the non-sacred refers to non-Sinhala non-Buddhists. At Kataragama, despite a process of general 'Buddhicisation' at the shrine, the sacred area includes Muslim, Hindu and Buddhist elements, and the sacred then becomes identified with some sense of religion in general, and is opposed to all kinds of worldly activity.

The Buddhist chronicle, the Mahavamsa, which occupies the ideological heart of Sinhala Buddhist nationalism, tells the island's story from the perspective of one of the two great monasteries at Anuradhapura, the Maha Vihara. Anuradhapura itself served as the centre for both Buddhism and kingship from roughly the fourth century BCE until the tenth century, when power shifted to Polonnaruwa, some 50 km to the east. By the time the British established their rule across the island in the early nineteenth century, Anuradhapura itself was mostly a collection of half-forgotten ruins in a thinly populated and isolated part of the country. Among those ruins, though, was the temple that housed the sacred bo-tree, said to be grown from a cutting from the tree under which the Buddha himself attained enlightenment. Even in the earliest days of British rule, when a certain understanding of Anuradhapura as forgotten and engulfed by jungle was built up, pilgrims continued to visit the bo-tree and battles for control of the temple occupied the minds of British administrations and local elites alike. In the course of the nineteenth century, Anuradhapura grew into a significant centre for local administration, aided by the coming of the railway to the town, while the remains of the old city were investigated by archaeologists and, little by little, restored by Buddhist activists.

The fractious history of colonial Anuradhapura has been meticulously documented and analysed by Elizabeth Nissan (1985, 1989) and we draw heavily on her account here. Reading Nissan's account, it is striking how much of the Dighavapi story is foreshadowed at Anuradhapura. So, for example, some of the most important early efforts at restoration were the work of a low-country Buddhist monk, who settled at the ruined Ruvanvelisaya – a stupa celebrated in the Mahavamsa – and attracted support from Buddhists in other parts of the island. Another monk settled at Isseramuni and set about attracting support for its restoration. In arguments about control and restoration of the ruined sites, a certain reading of the Mahavamsa – stripped of its mythical and symbolic dimension in keeping with the historiographic expectations of the times – was used to buttress Buddhist claims. In 1894, the Chief Monk at the Bo-tree Temple claimed that a Muslim shopkeeper was using materials from the ruined Abhayagiri site for building works (Nissan 1985: 261–3). What complicates the story, when compared to Dighavapi, is the presence of British colonial archaeologists, who were just as likely as the Buddhist activists to read the landscape through the prism of the Mahavamsa, but whose activities were the source of considerable anxiety and occasional overt protest. The other complication is the growth of the town itself, with its mosque and church and butcher's shops, not to mention courts and government offices – all anathema to the increasingly vocal Buddhist protesters.

As in the Dighavapi case, Buddhist protests about what was happening in Anuradhapura were orchestrated and supported by Buddhist leaders from outside the area. An especially important figure in this history is

Walasingha Harischandra, an associate of Anagarika Dharmapala, who more than anyone initiated the campaign for re-establishing the 'sacred city' of Anuradhapura in the early years of the twentieth century. Harischandra published a small guide to the area called *The Sacred City of Anuradhapura*. Although primarily descriptive, it contained an important argument about the relation of the sacred city to temporal power. Harischandra starts his account of Anuradhapura with the gift of what came to be known as the Mahamegha garden by King Mutasiva in the fourth century BCE. The gift is significant for Harischandra because, he claims, it signifies a physical distinction betweeen the royal capital, somewhere to the west of the main Buddhist sites, and the sacred city itself, which was contained within the Mahamegha garden and which belonged entirely to the *sangha*. The British administration had mixed up government offices with sacred sites, 'either by ill will towards our national religion or by ignorance of the true history of the Sacred City' (in Nissan 1985: 265).

So, at the heart of Harischandra's campaign to restore Anuradhapura as a sacred city, there was a strong division between the sacred (that which has been gifted to the *sangha*) and the rest (including the mundane work of government). The division is based on one of the deep structural principles of Sri Lankan Buddhism – the boundary that separates the *sangha* from the distractions of worldly life – which in this case has been adjusted to fit a colonial reality in which government increasingly tried to distance itself from engagement in the world of public religion. But Harischandra's 'sacred city' was not just about the presence or absence of government offices. He was equally concerned with the presence of the wrong kind of people and the wrong kinds of activity in proximity to sacred areas: 'It is most regrettable to state that certain Officials of the Ceylon Government have ignored this fact, and have endeavoured to convert this ground of most hallowed shrines, into an ordinary bazaar with taverns, liquor shops, meat stalls, and such other things' (Harischandra 1908: 4). In his view, 'all land in Anuradhapura and within a circuit of 48 miles was for Buddhists only, and … no other religions, nor other practices contrary to Buddhism, could be tolerated in this area' (Nissan 1985: 267). Here the 'sacred' became the property of a particular religious community and could be invoked to exclude other religious communities from the town and its surroundings.

Harischandra's project for Anuradhapura to be remade as a sacred city had to wait another 30 years before it started to take real shape after the political reforms of the early 1930s, which handed over most of the work of government to elected local politicians. The cause was taken up by the young S.W.R.D. Bandaranaike who, as Minister for Local Administration, piloted the Anuradhapura Preservation Ordinance into law in 1942. This grafted Harischandra's concerns on to a modernist planning framework for a New Town at some remove from the key Buddhist sites. Clifford Holliday, a British architect and planner who had been heavily involved in urban planning in Jerusalem, was brought in to help (Nissan 1985: 298). The New Town was inaugurated in 1949 and, little by little, offices, shops, churches and mosques in the old town were demolished and rebuilt on the new site. What is left is the sacred city as visitors find it today – an area disembedded from the flow of everyday life, and organised for the benefit of two overlapping groups: tourists and Buddhist pilgrims.

The case of Kataragama can be dealt with more quickly, if only because we lack the kind of documentation provided by Nissan's research. Kataragama is a classic example of a South Asian multi-religious centre. Located in what was until recently a very remote, jungly spot in the far south-west of the island, the main ritual attraction is the annual festival celebrating the visit of the god Kataragama (Murugan to Tamil worshippers) to the island, and his dalliance with a beautiful jungle girl he meets there, a dalliance that arouses the fury of his powerful but barren South Indian wife Theyvanniamman. The shrine itself dates back to Kandyan times if not earlier, but its popularity increased with the arrival of migrant plantation workers from South India in the second half of the nineteenth century, working on tea and coffee estates in the high mountains of the interior. They brought with them new devotional practices and, in the twentieth century, their intensely emotional style of religiosity attracted increasing numbers of Sinhala Buddhist pilgrims. Kataragama and its devotees have been the focus of some of the most important analyses of religious change in Sri Lanka, most notably Gananath Obeyesekere's *Medusa's hair* (1981). In *Buddhism transformed* Obeyesekere and his co-author Richard Gombrich document a process they call the 'Buddhist appropriation of Kataragama', a process in which control of the key shrines has passed to Sinhala Buddhists, and Tamil devotees have found themselves edged to the margins, while new myths circulate linking the shrine to key figures from Sinhala history like King Dutugämunu (Gombrich and Obeyesekere 1988: 411–44).

Obeyesekere opens *Medusa's hair* with a description of the route taken by a visitor to Kataragama (Obeysekere 1981: 2–5). To reach the shrine, pilgrims first have to cross the river, the Menik Ganga, which runs past the temple complex. The complex itself consists of the main shrine to the god, with smaller shrines to his legitimate wife Theyvanniamman and to his brother Ganesh. About 200 metres away from this cluster of buildings is the shrine to the god's mistress Valli Amma. Between the two is a mosque containing the tomb of a Muslim saint, where Sufi devotees gather for their own rituals at the time of the main temple festival to Kataragama himself. Behind the main shrine to the god is a large bo-tree, and beyond that is a gleaming white Buddhist stupa, the Kiri Vihara. Obeyesekere's account emphasises the different affective quality of the spaces that the pilgrim passes through, first from the everyday world across the river to the area around the temple itself, then the route of the god's procession to his mistress, which, with its displays of passionate devotion, constitutes a zone of sensory excess, of colour, eroticism and sensuality, a zone in stark contrast to the tone of Buddhist restraint and calm around the Kiri Vihara.

But the landscape that Obeyesekere evokes so memorably from the early 1970s has now, like that of contemporary Anuradhapura, been replaced by a relatively recent construct. Until the 1950s, the route of the god's procession was lined with shops, stalls, restaurants and pilgrims' rests (Wirz 1966: 31). Kataragama was declared a sacred area in 1961 and, little by little in the decades that followed, the area around the shrines was cleared of all reminders of mundane needs and their fulfilment. If pilgrims needed a place to eat or sleep, they would have to seek it in the New Town that was constructed on the other side of the river from the sacred area (Frydenlund 2003: 58–62). The 'sacred' in this re-arrangement of sacred space was not exclusively Buddhist (as it had been in Anuradhapura), not least because the whole *raison d'être* of Kataragama is of course the shrines to the god himself. 'Sacred' here necessarily denotes a space devoted to religion in general, which includes Hindu, Buddhist and Muslim shrines within it: what makes the space 'sacred' is the deliberate exclusion of mundane activity. This of course echoes Harischandra's argument against the mixing of government offices with the Buddhist ruins of Anuradhapura, but there is a further irony to the working through of this logic at Kataragama. Buddhist monasticism does indeed have a deep structure based on the need for the renouncer to remove himself from the distractions of worldly life (as well as a long history of interdependence between monastic order and kingly power). But the religiosity celebrated at Kataragama is intensely engaged with worldly concerns: pilgrims come to seek the god's help with exams and employment, marriages and political campaigns. Seen in this light, the material 'disembedding' of 'religion' from the rest of life, concretised in the division between the New Town and the sacred area, seems to rather miss the point of the place itself.

The Kataragama example of space that has been officially designated as 'sacred' differs from Dighavapi in two ways then, one rather more obvious than the other. The obvious difference is between a multi-religious site being declared sacred, where members of particular religious communities cannot be evicted or excluded on simple religious grounds. The less obvious difference is this question of disembedding. In the original complaints about the allocation of land to Muslim families in Norochcholai, it was argued that the presence of Muslim families would prevent the settlement of Buddhist families, which in turn would deprive the Dighavapi temple of the lay supporters it might need for its own day-to-day existence. Religious space is in this case not separated from mundane space; rather religious space needs to include both the *sangha* and the laity. And 'religion' is not disembedded from everyday existence, but rather is expanded to include an entire religious community, both monks and laity.

Meanwhile, the idea of the sacred area continues to cause problems in post-war Sri Lanka. In September 2011, the BBC reported that a small Muslim shrine in Anuradhapura had been destroyed by a group led by a Buddhist monk: 'The monk who led the group told the BBC he did it because the shrine was on land that was given to Sinhalese Buddhists 2,000 years ago.'[6] A year later, a more spectacular protest in Dambulla, site of an old and famous cave temple, attracted global attention. A prominent local monk led a demonstration demanding the removal of a small mosque from what he claimed was sacred Buddhist land. The demonstration was unruly, and video footage of a Buddhist monk apparently exposing himself at the site of the mosque circulated widely on the internet (Heslop 2014). In the political and legal confusion that followed, the Colombo NGO, the Centre for Policy Alternatives, put out a short document entitled 'Legal Framework Governing Places of Religious Worship in Sri Lanka.' The authors examined the various relevant pieces of legislation before reaching a surprising conclusion: despite the frequent declarations by politicians, the concept of the 'sacred area' has no legislative foundation whatsoever in Sri Lanka (Centre for Policy Alternatives 2012: 7). Declaring something sacred is, to invoke J.L. Austin, a performative, one of those speech acts – like 'I do' in a wedding ceremony – that can shift the boundaries of the social world. And the people most likely to make these declarations and try to separate off a protected place for religion are, of course, politicians.

5

Conflict in the Plural

In late 2006, two of the authors travelled together from Peradeniya to Sammanthurai, and then on to Eastern University, just north of Batticaloa. It was very early in the project and we were still slowly acquiring a general sense of what we might be dealing with in addressing the question of religion and conflict in the east. A few days further down the road, one of the travellers asked the other if there were significant conflicts *within* the Muslim community in Sri Lanka. 'You remember our journey the other day from Sammanthurai to Batticaloa?', he replied. 'Yes.' 'You remember

Figure 5.1　Kattankudy Mosque Federation, 2008 (photo by Jonathan Spencer).

passing through Kattankudy?' 'Yes.' 'Have you heard what happened there later that day?' 'No.'

This is what happened in Kattankudy in December 2006. A Sufi leader from Kattankudy called Payilvan had died in Colombo. He had been exiled from Kattankudy as part of a long-running dispute about the supposedly un-Islamic content of some of his teaching and practice. When Payilvan died, his followers brought his body back to Kattankudy by helicopter for burial there. In the violence that followed, houses were torched and a number of people were killed and injured. Some days later, Payilvan's large and impressive meditation centre by the beach was attacked and a tower torn down by a crowd armed with cables and other equipment. With incidents like this, it was naïve to assume that there was only one 'conflict' at work in this part of Sri Lanka. Our problem was not one in which 'religion', a relatively inert cluster of institutions and practices, responded to problems generated by '*the* conflict', that is the war between the government and the LTTE. The multiple religious traditions of eastern Sri Lanka were themselves the site of many kinds and layers of conflict, and our eventual analysis would need to come to terms with the existence of conflict in the plural. This chapter uses this example of conflict among Muslims in Kattankudy as a point of departure. The story of religious change and religious dispute in Kattankudy revisits those issues of community, purity and spatiality raised in the previous chapter's analysis of the Dighavapi dispute. But a comparison of Kattankudy with another Muslim centre, the town of Akkaraipattu some 60 km to the south, brings out the complexity of relations within just one of the religious traditions we are dealing with. The comparison, however, also returns to the issues in the previous chapter about what might be thought to make a conflict 'religious'. The divisions within the Muslim community are in some sense irreducibly religious: they are conflicts within, and therefore about, a shared Muslim tradition, and therefore not obviously interpretable as, say, conflicts about resources that the protagonists have misapprehended in religious terms. Nevertheless, the shape these religious arguments have taken in different places is clearly conditioned by local demographic, political, and politico-economic, circumstances.

The Broken Minaret

The Muslim meditation centre of Payilvan, a Sufi sheikh, has a history that is both short and dramatic. It was built in 2002 on the southern edge of Kattankudy, a Muslim enclave on Sri Lanka's east coast, yet it already represents a scar on the face of Muslim harmony and unity. Until recently, visitors reaching the beach site would have found the minaret lying flat on its back. The rubble and metal bars awkwardly sticking out of the foundation bore silent testimony to the events of 16 December 2006, when a crowd of people came to attack the shrine and tear down its tower. They brought heavy-duty equipment and a video camera. (This was not an entirely spontaneous attack.) The footage shot that day (and sold in Kattankudy on DVDs afterwards) does not show, as one might expect in this place where war had formally restarted months earlier, Tamil rebels or Sinhala army soldiers attacking their Muslim neighbours. This is not an obviously 'ethnic' flashpoint: the events of December 2006 feature a Muslim crowd attacking a mosque in a small, densely populated, Muslim enclave surrounded by army checkpoints and Tamil-dominated settlements. A few years on, the minaret has been rebuilt, but its destruction has not been forgotten.

The incident was no exception. It was the culmination of a much longer sequence of hostilities directed against the followers of Payilvan. On the same December day, Payilvan's body – which had been buried just over a week earlier (he had died ten days before) – had been taken out of his saintly tomb and burnt, a deeply desecrating act for Muslims. And in the years before, Kattankudy's other prominent Sufi leader – Rauf Maulavi – was formally excommunicated by the *ulama* for transgressing the boundary of Islamic thought. The followers of both Sufis suffered intimidation, grenade attacks and forced displacement from their Muslim townsmen, spearheaded by a relatively new arrival in the town: the Islamic reform movements known locally under the umbrella term Tawhid Jamaat.

While the events following Payilvan's death are quite exceptional in the Sri Lankan context, the underlying processes at work are familiar developments among the country's Muslim community. In recent decades, we have seen a coming together of a number of important historical shifts. The liberalisation of Sri Lanka's economy, global changes in the Muslim world after the Iranian revolution, the increased international connectedness of Islamic revival movements, and the escalation of the war in Sri Lanka: all started in the late 1970s and early 1980s. Each of these developments strongly affected Sri Lanka's Muslim community, through a gradual process of increasingly visible 'Islamisation', with increased importance attached to Muslim identity, and a concomitant contestation of ethnic and religious boundaries (McGilvray and Raheem 2007; Klem 2011; McGilvray 2011). The events in Kattankudy thus need to be read as part of a larger narrative about a Muslim enclave in which anxieties and external pressure have generated an acute preoccupation with the preservation of 'Muslimness' and Islamic purity, which in turn provokes argument about how those categories are defined.

But for all the force of these common processes, in some ways Kattankudy is quite different from other Muslim settlements in the east. Akkaraipattu, some 60 km south, is a superficially similar place. It is also a somewhat urbanised Muslim pocket in a region characterised by an 'ethnic checkerboard' geography. It has undergone the bitter history of war and is far from a haven of peace. Yet Muslim reformists, in this case mainly Tablighi Jamaat, but also Tawhid and Sufi followers, live there in relative harmony. Islamic interpretations are a source of difference and debate, but not of outright antagonism and violence.

It is this striking contrast between two apparently similar localities that we explore in the final part of this chapter. How can we make sense of violent struggle between Muslim groups in Kattankudy and relative peace among Akkaraipattu's Muslims? The existing literature on contemporary developments within Sri Lanka's Muslim community is relatively thin and gives us little help in answering this question. The answer we put forward is provisional and involves the interaction of different factors operating at different scales. Somewhat schematically, these can be summarised under three headings: arguments about community and tradition elsewhere in the region; the political geography of armed conflict; and the socio-economic antecedents of religious revival.

Our argument runs as follows. First, at the core of the problem we find divergent interpretations of Islam and resulting rifts and contestation between streams of Sufism and Islamic reformers. This contestation has its own dynamic, discourses and origin, and in that sense resembles tensions that have been observed elsewhere in South Asia, and elsewhere across the Indian Ocean (Van der Veer 1992; Eickelman and Piscatori 1996; Bayat 2007; Robinson 2008; Osella and Osella 2008a, 2008b). Second, three decades of war have shaped and reinforced arguments around Islamic reform in Sri Lanka. The recent history of violence between Tamil separatists, the government, and other armed groups breeds an acute awareness of group identity, group boundaries and concomitant concerns with internal purity (Knoezer 1998; McGilvray and Raheem 2007; Nuhman 2007; Goodhand et al. 2009; Klem 2011). Religious contestation thus builds on gradual changes in the political geography. This is particularly clear in the case of Kattankudy, because of its location as an ethnic enclave, but we see similar dynamics around ethnically infused borders in Akkaraipattu. Third, there are important connections between religious change and processes of socio-economic transformation, in particular questions of employment, labour migration and education. The main difference between Akkaraipattu and Kattankudy is probably to be found in the rather different economic histories, histories that condition differences in other registers: kinship relations, education, occupation and religious orientation. Partly as a paradoxical consequence of its enclave nature, in Kattankudy people move around more, and we find a *madrasa*-educated, geographically mobile, urbanised lower class that has embraced Tawhid, while the agro-town of Akkaraipattu has a large number of state-educated professionals, sons and daughters of the region's big paddy landowners, many of whom have joined Tabligh.

While each of these issues – religious contestation, the political geography of armed conflict and socio-economic change – has its distinct causes and dynamics, they are also closely related. They reinforce and contradict each other, but they do this in locally distinctive ways. Kattankudy and Akkaraipattu share the same ingredients: arguments about proper Islam link in to socio-economic changes and produces rifts that are dramatised by the anxieties of the separatist insurgency. The story that ties these ingredients together, however, is different in the two places and as a result we find violent clashes in Kattankudy and relative peace in Akkaraipattu. The encounter between contemporary Islam, socio-economic change, and armed conflict is thus a highly localised phenomenon.

Kattankudy: Divergent Interpretations and Authority

At its heart, the controversy in Kattankudy concerns issues of Islamic interpretation. Both Payilvan and Rauf Maulavi represent the Sufi tradition that is found across South Asia and other parts of the world. Following its dispersal across the Indian Ocean (McGilvray 1998), Sufism has long been part of the Islamic mainstream in colonial and postcolonial Sri Lanka. While conceiving of themselves as devout Muslims, and embracing the five pillars of Islam, Sufis have a long track-record of accommodating themselves to divergent local customs. (The five pillars are: faith in Allah and the Prophet, daily prayer, annual fast, alms-giving, and pilgrimage. They will return as an issue later in the story.) Meditation, saint worship and associated festivals often echo popular Hindu and Buddhist practices, and are common among Payilvan's and Rauf's followers. Both Payilvan and Rauf combine the mysticism and the charismatic leadership that often characterise Sufism.

Sufism has also on occasion been a source of controversy. It was in part in response to the 'folkloristic' practices of Sufism that a wave of reform movements emerged in South Asia (North India in particular) during the late colonial era, in an attempt to purify Islam and 'Islamise' Muslims, though there have been important differences between various movements in the extent to which they emphasise more personalised, everyday piety, or more collective and worldly political Islam (Metcalf 1982; Ahmad 1991; Sikand 2007). It was only after Sri Lanka's Independence, however, that these movements – mainly Tablighi Jamaat and Tawhid Jamaat – really established themselves, and they only became significant in the east in the late 1970s and early 1980s.

Both revival movements propagate Muslim purity, but there are important differences between them. Tabligh was founded by the Indian Islamic scholar Muhammad Ilyas in the 1920s to call on Muslims to bring their everyday life in line with Islam. The credo of the movement can be summarised in his aphorism, 'Oh Muslims, become Muslims.' Tablighis aim to purify Islam from 'undesirable' customs that have blended with Islam during the centuries of its expansion. Sufi practices like mysticism, meditation and saint worship are tolerated as an advanced form of Islam, but they are not encouraged. Tablighis see themselves as a *da'wa* movement, that is, they educate the rural masses and disentangle them from 'un-Islamic' habits (Sikand 2007; Robinson 2008). Tawhid on the other hand is an older movement originating from Saudi Arabia, which has gained new momentum in recent decades. Also known as Wahhabism, it is known for its strict observance and purging of what are perceived to be recent Islamic innovations. The Arabic word *tawhid* stands for the uniqueness and unity of God and this principle stands at the core of their doctrine. Unlike Tablighis, who emphasise everyday practice and eschew theological debate, Tawhid has a more thoroughgoing agenda. Where Tablighis position themselves as explicitly apolitical, Tawhid's doctrinal positions, while not necessarily synonymous with political Islam, certainly leave less space for dividing politics off from religion. Sri Lankan Tawhid first emerged in the Kurunegala area in the centre of the country, and a brief period of enthusiasm in Kalmunai on the east coast caused intense theological debate in the 1960s. Kattankudy was not in the forefront in Tawhid's spread across the country. It started to become prominent there in the 1980s and its support base rose sharply in the following decade; dedicated mosques and *madrasas* – in turn divided between different Tawhid splinter groups – abound. Using television, radio, books, pamphlets, discussion groups and demonstrations, alongside religious practice, adherents propagate a return to the fundaments of Islam and call on others to distance themselves from 'infidel' practices like saint worship and mysticism.

Controversies around Sufism in Kattankudy preceded the arrival of Tawhid, however. Rauf Maulavi, a native from this town, first became the subject of debate in 1976 following a public speech. The main source of trouble was his argument that God is in everything, which in turn gave rise to the interpretation that everything is God. Subsequent speeches and pamphlets fed the tension and he was eventually charged with heresy and excommunicated by the All Ceylon Jammiyathul Ulama in 1979. The date matters, because it makes clear that antagonism over Islamic interpretation predates the civil war and many of the socio-economic developments we will discuss below. Rauf's case reminds us that the intra-Muslim conflict to some extent has its own dynamics and origin. Payilvan was a part of those dynamics as well, but he is a much more recent arrival to Kattankudy itself. He suffered a similar experience to Rauf in Maruthamunai, his hometown 40 km to the south, where the local *ulama* excommunicated him in 1989. His name is Tamil for 'wrestler' (he was for a time a professional wrestler as his physical appearance shows). Payilvan's alleged sin was to argue that spiritual growth could be achieved through meditation – without complying with the basic duties, that is, the five pillars of Islam. Despite the ruling against him, his presence and following in Kattankudy increased and an impressive new Islamic meditation centre was constructed.

Sufis, Tabligh and Tawhid thus flourished more or less in parallel in Kattankudy. Supporters of Tablighi Jamaat had long been sceptical about both Rauf and Payilvan, but with the arrival of Tawhid Jamaat in the late 1980s, resistance entered a new, more militant phase. A movement was organised against Rauf and the subsequent disturbance resulted in the displacement of some 2000 of his followers to the neighbouring Tamil settlement of Arayampathy (a place we will return to in the next chapter) in November 2004. In the same month, a grenade was thrown into his mosque, while a few days earlier Payilvan's newly built mosque was attacked.

In subsequent years, the controversy around Rauf de-escalated, in part due to the intervention of the local MP Hizbullah. The *ulama* withdrew his excommunication, but the underlying issues and tension continued to simmer. Meanwhile, Payilvan died (of natural causes) in Colombo on 6 December 2006. That same day, his followers wanted to bury 'the wrestler' in his Kattankudy mosque and create a tomb, as is common among saint-worshipping Sufis. Tawhid followers protested and resisted. Payilvan was

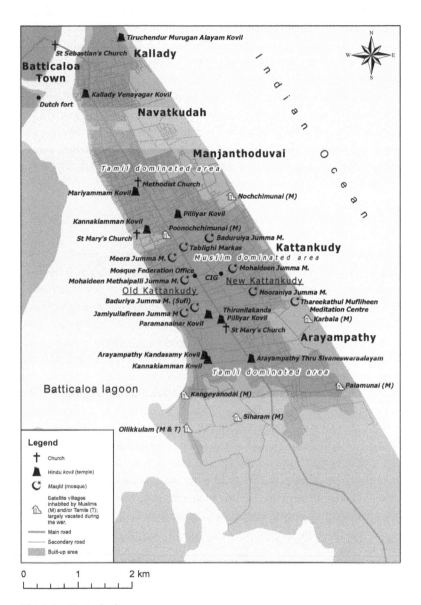

Map 5.1   Kattankudy.

Note: Religious buildings are not displayed exhaustively; a selection was made of those most relevant to this book. .

buried as planned, but tension continued until the District Court ruled against the placement of the body on the 14 December. Violence increased, and shops owned by 'Payilvanists', as well as government property, were damaged (protesters felt the police were biased against them) and this was the prelude to the scene with which we opened this chapter: Payilvan's body was dug up and set on fire and a small crowd marched to the mosque to tear down the minaret. About 300 families fled the town, fearing for their safety. Tensions among Sufis and Tawhid remain in Kattankudy. No violent incidents have been recorded recently, but each side continues to stand its ground. The Payilvanists have rebuilt their meditation centre, though they did not put a new minaret in place, and each of the groups continues to claim to represent true Islam.

Political Geography: Boundaries, Identity and Purity

The developments discussed so far resonate with tensions between Sufis and Islamic reformers elsewhere in Asia, for example sectarian strife in Indonesia (e.g. between Jemaah Islamiya and Javanese mystics: Hefner 2000; Sidel 2007) or in India (Metcalf 1993; Jasini 2007; Osella and Osella 2008a, 2008b). In both these settings, however, scholars have pointed out that Islamic contestation does not take place in a political vacuum. This is no different in Sri Lanka, and it brings us to the second point in our analysis. Although religious dispute in Kattankudy has its own origin and dynamics, the context of the war makes a difference. It is significant that intra-Islamic violence escalated in Kattankudy, which is not an entirely typical Muslim settlement. Kattankudy is famous for a combination of things: a very high number of mosques and *madrasas* which attract people from all over the country; a high population density; as a Muslim enclave in the heart of Tamil territory; and a place where Tamil rebels perpetrated one of the most traumatic acts of violence against the Muslims. We are thus directed to Kattankudy's political geography.

The Kattankudy enclave is located on the coast, which is marked by a jigsaw of Tamil and Muslim settlements. The political violence and warfare that ravaged Sri Lanka since 1983 created a warscape, marked by heightened military presence, military checkpoints, guerrilla attacks by Tamil militants, counter-insurgency measures, killings, and 'white van' abductions. The Muslim community tried to stay outside the battle between Tamil militants and Sri Lankan military forces. Influential Muslim politicians from the east became ministers in different governments, siding with one or other of the major Sinhala political parties. This allowed

Muslim politicians to generate patronage resources for their community in the form of infrastructure investments and public jobs. But the more Muslims attempted to keep outside of the military battle and to cater for their community politically, the greater the antagonism between Tamils and Muslims (Ismail 1995; Hasbullah 2001; McGilvray and Raheem 2007; Nuhman 2007; Goodhand et al. 2009; Klem 2011; Lewer and Ismail 2011; McGilvray 2011).

Kattankudy has been a famous place in Sri Lanka's east and a stronghold of Muslim politicians. It is considered a stronghold of Islam and brings together manifold religious institutions, traditions and a clergy famous for giving influential religious verdicts (*fatwas*). Contrast this image of a stronghold with its territorial vulnerability as a small enclave surrounded by Tamil settlements. Kattankudy is the most important of three Muslim enclaves within the largely Tamil-dominated Batticaloa District (the other two being Eravur and Oddamavadi). Tamils and Muslims have long had social and economic ties (Ruwanpura 2006; McGilvray 2008), but the escalation of the armed struggle of the LTTE since the early 1980s turned Tamil–Muslim relations increasingly sour and contested. By early 1990, the LTTE had established itself as a controlling force in Tamil-majority areas, particularly on the land side of the lagoon, while the coastal belt became ruled by a shadow regime of Sri Lankan security forces and proxy groups of Tamil and Muslim paramilitaries (Goodhand et al. 2000; Hyndman and de Alwis 2004; Korf 2005; Korf and Fünfgeld 2006; Bohle and Fünfgeld 2007; Gaasbeek 2010a; Korf et al. 2010). Kattankudy became territorially confined to an enclave located on a thin coastal strip surrounded by sea (east), lagoon (west) and Tamil settlements (north and south). It was surrounded by non-Muslim spaces, making it highly vulnerable to attacks from the LTTE, evidenced by arguably the worst atrocity against Muslims since the war started in 1983: the LTTE massacre in Kattankudy on 3 August 1990, which killed more than 100 worshippers (UTHR(J) 1990).

In the jigsaw of Tamil and Muslim settlements along the east coast, Muslims tend to live in cramped, densely populated settlements. In Batticaloa District, for example, Muslims make up approximately 25 per cent of the district's population, but their settlements are confined to 2 per cent of the territory. Kattankudy is one of the most densely populated areas in Sri Lanka. This population pressure is a direct result of what we call its territorial confinement. Since its establishment as a separate administrative entity, the territorial demarcation of its boundaries has not changed. Territorial expansion was not possible to the east (sea) and west (lagoon) for reasons of terrain, an expansion into the north or south was not possible for ethno-political reasons, because the neighbouring villages were Tamil. Increasing ethnicisation of politics in Sri Lanka made it impossible for Muslims to settle on 'Tamil soil', that is, to buy land in adjacent Tamil settlements. The deterioration of Muslim–Tamil relations in the 1980s, and especially the 1990 mosque massacre, made territorial boundaries between Tamil and Muslim settlements especially significant, thereby hardening Kattankudy's boundaries with its Tamil neighbours in the north (Manjanthoduvai, on the outskirts of Batticaloa) and south (Arayampathy).

In addition, the enclave experienced extraordinary population pressures, first from a high internal birth rate, and second through in-migration of Muslims from adjacent Muslim satellite settlements as a result of ethnic polarisation and violence. Seven satellite villages were located in relative proximity to Kattankudy: Kangeyanodai, Palamunai, Siharam, Ollikkulam, Nochchimunai, Poonochchimunai and Karbala (see Map 5.1). All are within 2–3 km from Kattankudy, but are in Tamil-majority areas and come under the jurisdiction of other, Tamil-dominated, administrative units. All these satellite settlements had strong family, economic and political ties to Kattankudy, which was considered as the 'mother' settlement. During times of heightening military confrontation in the 1980s and 1990s, many Muslim inhabitants of these satellite villages chose to move to Kattankudy because they did not feel safe surrounded by Tamils and governed by Tamil administrators.

This in-migration from the satellites increased population density, but was also beneficial to some segments in Kattankudy: many in-migrants were available as cheap wage labour (to replace Tamils from neighbouring settlements who had been hired before). Former satellite inhabitants moved into less attractive locations, where local landowners sold land to them: those places closer to the sea in the less densely populated western part of Kattankudy. Often, migrants were also settled into the frontier spaces of the boundary areas between Muslim and Tamil settlements. Kattankudy has now been separated into 'Old Kattankudy' (presently GN Division Nos 1–10) and 'New Kattankudy' (GN Division Nos 11–18), which is mainly comprised of those newer settlements closer to the coastline. The inflow of Muslims from the satellite villages changed the inner structures and politics of Kattankudy. For example, the satellite Muslims provided a potential block vote for politicians who provided patronage to them (e.g. land on which to settle).

Three decades of war thus transformed Kattankudy into a densely populated Muslim enclave 'under siege'. This perception is firmly entrenched in local discourse, and a preoccupation with the town's uniquely Muslim identity, its boundaries, and the persistent threat from its Tamil surroundings, pervaded all our interviews and discussions in the town. Clearly, being Muslim matters more than it did before the war, which accounts for the salience of Muslim identity and the strong urge to mark out the land: this is Kattankudy, a Muslim place, with its Islamic entry gates and its numerous mosques as the most obvious markers. The preoccupation with Muslimness, however, embodies a number of paradoxes, such as the visibility of militancy in internal disputes versus the self-image of a peaceful people who live in harmony with their neighbours, but also the near obsession with Muslim unity and purity that is at odds with the continuous rifts and internal struggles that form the heart of this chapter.

Ironically, the anxiety to stand united only seems to deepen the divisions. As we have suggested elsewhere (Klem 2011), the strong desire to demarcate the boundaries of 'Muslimness', and to preserve the purity of the stuff enclosed by them, adds charge to the question of how Muslimness is defined. Sufis resort to the history of local belonging. Mirroring the reasoning that underpins much Tamil and Sinhala nationalism, the long historic presence of Sufi shrines and traditions bolsters Muslim claims on the land and a concurrent political agenda of minority rights. Sufi thought in eastern Sri Lanka – and we see this both in Akkaraipattu and in Kattankudy – thus emphasises its many linkages with local places and cultural practices. Old saints' tombs throughout the region attract worshippers from far away, Muslims as well as Hindus and Christians, and thus reinforce the Muslim claim to belong to this place.

Reformist movements like Tabligh and Tawhid, on the other hand, propagate Islamisation by shedding this genealogical attachment to place, which they see as 'folkloristic' pollution. Both groups see their primary mission as purifying Islamic practice. 'Non-Islamic' cultural influences like saint worship or Hindu-style meditation are transgressive for them. Followers of Tawhid, however, are much more aggressive in this respect than Tablighis, who treat Sufism as a special form of Islam that might be suitable for spiritually gifted people. For the masses, however, Tablighis encourage the simple pursuits of praying, eating, sleeping and so on, in an Islamic way.

Both Sufism and the two reform movements thus address the idea of Muslim identity, but while Sufis emphasise local grounding and local tradition, Tabligh and Tawhid de-emphasise them. Instead, they foreground connections to the global *umma* and the non-Sri Lankan history of Islam. Kattankudy's political geography adds meaning and significance to these pre-existing tensions around Sufi theology. Issues of Islamic interpretation have assumed paramount importance in defining us and them, friend and foe. The intricacies of 'proper' Muslim thought are no longer simply a form of Freud's 'narcissism of minor difference'. The urgent, existential need to preserve Kattankudy as a Muslim enclave adds charge and significance. The project of religious 'purification' propagated by Tawhid, the dominant movement in Kattankudy, is boosted by a political sense of urgency to root out what is 'un-Islamic'. The hostility towards the followers of Payilvan and Rauf is thus steeped in a need to reinforce ethnic boundaries and purify the Muslim enclave they surround.

Making a Muslim Community

The anxiety instilled by Kattankudy's political geography is aggravated by what is perceived to be the weakness of formal political leadership. While to some extent stoking the fire of ethnic claims and rights, by and large Muslim politicians in Sri Lanka have been pragmatists, who needed to retain flexible loyalties and ideologies in order to secure patronage for their constituencies. Keeping together their block votes is at the core of their strategy. Uncompromising religious standpoints, and strife within their constituency, thus pose a threat. Vote banks tend to hinge on alliances with the old elites of their rural towns, which often have Sufi allegiances. Muslim politicians thus have difficulties grappling with strong or inflexible demands from their electoral base, be it ethno-nationalism (which impedes their ability to join government) or exclusivist Islamism (because it divides the voters).

The politicians' pragmatism in turn feeds a sense of frustration among parts of the electorate, the younger generation in particular. The turmoil in Kattankudy is in part a result of that frustration. M.L.A.M. Hizbullah, the dominant politician from Kattankudy, is a representative of the old Sufi elite and has made remarkable turns and crossovers in pursuit of key portfolios within successive administrations, which he has in turn used to deliver returns to his constituency. The violence against Sufis is also an expression of anger towards his political leadership, which is seen to be unresponsive, biased towards the old bourgeoisie, and contaminated by materialism and the dirty games of politics. While the bulk of the violence that we witness in eastern Sri Lanka is instigated and controlled by political leaders or their proxies, the attacks against Payilvan and Rauf Maulavi seem to comprise a form of 'violence from below', a response to a sense of weak or unprincipled political leadership, rather than the result of shadowy political games.

Hizbullah was first elected as MP in 1989. He was appointed a minister in 1994 and was very successful in directing government funding to the town, as manifest in numerous public buildings erected during his term as minister. Hizbullah's power and influence ended termporarily when he was not re-elected in the 2000 elections. He regained a seat in 2001, lost it again in 2004, and won it back in 2010. During the war years, Hizbullah had already been an 'absentee' MP, living in Colombo, because he could not return to Kattankudy for security reasons. Hizbullah had the reputation of being an outspoken advocate of Muslim interests and a critic of the LTTE, which made him a potential LTTE target. The enclave geography of Kattankudy made his presence and his travel back and forth from Colombo to Kattankudy highly insecure. When the attack on the Kattankudy mosques happened in 1990, Hizbullah even had to be flown in by helicopter to attend the funeral of the victims of the massacre. As a result of this situation, Hizbullah was able to direct funding to Kattankudy, but he was unable to be present in his fiefdom himself. Local political matters could therefore not be resolved through the influence and patronage of the local MP. This created a vacuum in Kattankudy as a political space.

This vacuum was – at least partly – filled by the local Federation of Mosques and Islamic Institutions (or 'mosque federation'). The federation was registered in 1987, when Tamil–Muslim relations deteriorated and when the activities of Tamil militants undermined public order and security. The mosque federation was founded and first hosted at the Methaipalli mosque, which was recognised as the congregation place for Friday prayers (before the numbers of Friday congregations proliferated) and as an especially 'sacred place'. The Methaipalli mosque had traditionally been a place where community issues were discussed. The increasing deterioration of public order in the mid 1980s created the feeling that these meetings should be formalised. The federation's organisational strength increased over the years of war and conflict. The federation was able to negotiate with LTTE and talked to military personnel at times of crisis. Step by step, its role had further extended to dealing with broader issues, such as land and the political rights of Muslims.

After visiting the mosque federation in 2008, we suggested that there seemed to have evolved a division of labour between Muslim politicians (MPs, ministers, etc.) and the federation (Spencer 2012). The politicians had to look after Muslim interests in the realm of national politics (and the distribution of patronage resources) – albeit with shrinking leverage after the demise of Hizbullah as MP. Meanwhile, the federation ruled over local religious matters, coordinated social welfare and negotiated local agreements with the Tamil militants and the Sri Lankan security forces to safeguard their security, to regain access to their occupied lands, and to ensure the unity of the community in matters that dealt with its security and strength as an enclave amid Tamil militant rule in a highly militarised landscape. This seems to comply with the self-representation of the federation's leading figures who suggested that the mosque federation fulfilled two functions: to unify the community and to provide a forum for collective decisions. Both functions emphasise the unity, the commonalities of Muslims in Kattankudy.

To be able to accomplish its role as a voice of the whole community, the mundane practices of politics-as-usual – the mostly divisive politics of political parties – had to be kept outside of the federation. So the federation not only filled a political vacuum, it also provided an innovative political mechanism based on the staging of what Hansen calls 'antipolitics' – a moral critique of political leaders and the field of patronage politics within which they operate (Hansen 2001: 35, 38; cf. Spencer 2007: 142). This anti-political register was based on a tradition of community service through which the federation gradually expanded to include almost any civil society organisation, from sports clubs to cultural groups. During the time of our main fieldwork from 2007 onwards, the mosque federation represented over 48 mosques from Kattankudy and satellite settlements, and more than 110 other organisations. The federation held weekly meetings on Saturdays to which all associated organisations could send representatives; decisions were mostly taken unanimously, based on consensus.

The performance of widely acknowledged welfare services, and mediation in security issues, gave the federation its role as a 'community voice', allowing it to act as a political mechanism for collective decision-making in the register of anti-politics. It is in this sense that the federation constituted an innovative political mechanism which emphasised unity, tolerance and inclusion, and distanced itself from the exclusionary and divisive mechanisms of electoral politics, which function on the basis of block votes, party affiliations and patronage networks. The federation became the prime source of social welfare and appointed a number of sub-committees to deal with distribution of welfare benefits to the poor and needy, to organise pilgrimage to Mecca, and to resolve marriage disputes and other conflicts. The federation developed its own funding system and subsequently became a wealthy organisation by taking on the responsibility of collecting and distributing *zakat*, or alms-giving. The federation also established regulations to govern the community and intervened in social, religious and cultural matters, such as dress codes and codes of proper conduct. Although those regulations were not necessarily welcomed by all, the decisions were generally accepted because the federation had gained legitimacy through its role as a spokesperson for the community, in particular vis-à-vis the LTTE and the security forces.

The paradoxical achievement of the federation was to provide a political forum by keeping politicians out, by purifying its political space from the damaging influence of party politics. But this does not mean that this political space was devoid of politicians: they were present in the forum, but not *as* politicians. In other words, the politicians were kept out, but only as politicians, not as individuals, for example, as representatives of a civil society organisation (Spencer 2012). And so, the mosque federation and political figures have always been connected in everyday practice. Already a key founding figure of the federation, the then town council chairman and chief trustee of the mosque, Mr A. Ahamed Lebbe, was also one of the initiators of the SLMC, the Muslim political party (although M.H.M. Ashraff from Kalmunai became the party leader later on). Similarly, federation leaders, though they kept party politics out of the federation's forum, have not necessarily abstained from taking sides publicly in election politics. For example, the then President of the federation, Mr U.L.M. Subair, was listed on the supporters' platform for Hizbullah's candidacy for the 2010 parliamentary election. However, this was not seen as an involvement by the federation in party politics, as the President signed up in his capacity as a respected individual, not as federation chairman. Again, this can be seen as a mechanism to keep the Federation's space purified from the disturbing elements of party competition – as a move in the register of anti-politics.

The federation therefore not only filled the political vacuum that bureaucratic failure and the demise of electoral politics brought about, but it created a register of anti-politics that sought to purify politics from its divisive elements. In fact, the work of purification worked in two registers: an anti-political one to separate the federation's business from that of the politicians, and a register of inclusion and tolerance to provide a space of community, through which antinomies of community (that the divisive practices of electoral politics nurtures) were overcome. But, in fact, the paradox of this purification was that tolerance and inclusion were not complete – there was a boundary that could not be transgressed: the limits of proper Islam. This limit to toleration was marked by the violent attack against a Sufi sect whose supporters were not considered as Muslims and were thus not welcome, not included in the community.

Kattankudy and Akkaraipattu: Class, Education and Labour Migration

To sum up our observations so far: intra-Muslim contestation in Kattankudy has its own religious origins and dynamics, but these were transformed and reinforced by ethnic politics and war. When the political leadership proved unable or unwilling to act, Islamic reformists acted themselves on the perceived need to preserve boundaries and purify Muslim practice. This resulted in violence against Sufis, who were seen to accommodate 'impure' Hindu or Tamil influences. At the same time as the community confronted what could be seen as a threat from within, it also organised itself through the mosque federation in an idiom of unity and harmony. It did this by systematically keeping a space between the federation and the work of politics.

When we travel the short distance from Kattankudy to Akkaraipattu, although some of what we see is very much the same, for example, a well-organised mosque federation at work there, other parts are quite different. Although Akkaraipattu lacks the 'enclavic intensity' of Kattankudy, in terms of surface area (it is larger), population density (lower), and lacks a single event as iconic as the 1990 mosque massacre, the difference is merely one of degree. Akkaraipattu is also part of a slightly more dispersed Muslim enclave that encompasses a few other villages (Addalachenai, Palamunai, Ninthavur). The border between Muslim and Tamil settlements runs through the heart of the town. The northern half and neighbouring villages are Muslim, the southern half and neighbouring villages Tamil (see Map 5.2). Akkaraipattu is far from a haven of peace: there have also been attacks on mosques and Hindu temples, bombings and shootings there. And Kattankudy obviously has no monopoly on reformist ideas about Islam and efforts towards Islamisation: the dynamic of Muslim anxiety, the preoccupation with identity and ethnic boundaries, and differences between Sufis and Islamic reformers, who have contradictory ideas on how to define these, are equally present in Akkaraipattu (Klem 2011).

Both Sufism and Tabligh are thriving in Akkaraipattu, but the movements for revival and reform have not so far produced overt antagonism. Tablighis and Sufis have not attacked each other, and Tawhid – so dominant in Kattankudy – comprises only a small group with a low-profile mosque.

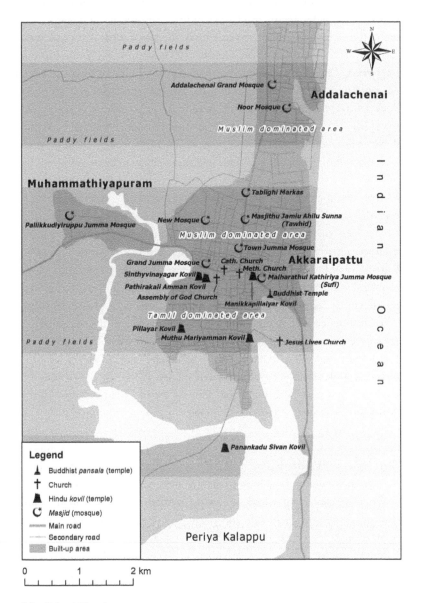

Map 5.2   Akkaraipattu.

Note: Religious buildings are not displayed exhaustively; a selection was made of those most relevant to this book.

Tablighis in Akkaraipattu do not encourage saint worship, but they avoid confrontation with Sufism and retain some respect for Sufi mysticism. Crucially, Tablighis see themselves as radically apolitical. They emphasise piety, the simple everyday requirements of Islamic life that everyone can fulfil (Van der Veer 1992; Metcalf 1993; Sikand 2007). During our interviews, Tablighis would never tire of emphasising that their teachings are pure and simple, while evading theological questions and stressing their cordial relations with the Sufi community. They would go to lengths to explain why they distance themselves from politics and would even play down major Muslim grievances – such as the 1990 expulsion from Jaffna – as the will of Allah. Rather than retaliating against the perpetrators (in this case, the LTTE), or working towards a peaceful political framework, a better world could only come about, they argued, by practising simple, everyday activities in an Islamic way.

The case of Akkaraipattu thus shows that the war heightened the need to demarcate and preserve boundaries and identities (as we saw in Kattankudy), but did not induce violent intra-Muslim strife. The 'ethnic problem' as the vernacular has it, is not the only game in town and it does not inevitably lead to clashes among Muslims. It does not help us explain a key difference: the rise of Tawhid in one place and its near absence elsewhere. Why did a large number of people embrace its doctrine in Kattankudy and not in Akkaraipattu? To answer that question, we need to take a look at who the people involved are. Although the divides are obviously not absolute, there are patterns in the membership of the different Muslim sects. Sufism is associated with the traditional local elites of the towns. Historically, mosque organisations are in fact very similar to the organisations of Hindu temples in the Tamil community: prominent clans (*kudi*) will tend to have a strong say in prestigious temples or mosques. Reform movements, Tawhid in particular, have a different profile.

When we take a closer look at Tawhid membership, especially the hard core of active members, we find particular segments of Kattankudy's population have joined. Most obviously, most Tawhid mosques and their followers are located in what is known as New Kattankudy, this is the eastern part of town that grew due to in-migration and 'internal' fertility in the 1980s and 1990s. The people of New Kattankudy are generally less prosperous, land pressure is especially high, and the location is more physically vulnerable (as became clear in the 2004 tsunami). The old elite of the town lives in Old Kattankudy (west of the main road), which is also where we find Sufi supporters and their mosques.

In addition to spatial distribution, there is also a story about the labour history. Many Tawhid leaders, and a significant part of their followers, have been abroad. They were part of the wave of Sri Lankan labour migration that followed the liberalisation of the economy and easing of travel restrictions in the late 1970s. Along with migrants from other parts of Sri Lanka, they signed up with agencies that arranged their stay in the Middle East, where they spent several years working as drivers, mechanics, cleaners and factory workers. Among Tamil and Sinhala communities many women migrated to work as housemaids, but in Kattankudy and other Muslim towns, labour migrants were almost exclusively male. Labour migration peaked in the late 1980s, but has become gradually less attractive financially in recent years due to increased competition from other labour-supplying countries. The height of this transnational movement thus correlated with both the war and the rise of Islamic reform movements in Sri Lanka. Many of those who presently support Tawhid went to Saudi Arabia, and this is one factor that seems to have shaped their religious orientation. The connection to Saudi Arabia persisted after their return to New Kattankudy. This is reflected in the Islamic charity funds from the Middle East that enable Tawhid groups to construct wells for their followers, or fulfil other material needs. Initially, the spread of Tawhid's doctrine took place through Islamic laymen who coincidentally encountered these ideas in the Middle East. Subsequently, Kattankudy *madrasas* also sent people to Islamic universities in Medina and elsewhere to study. Dedicated Tawhid *madrasas* started to mushroom, and more and more people thus became familiar with Tawhid's teaching of vigorous adherence to Quran and *hadith* and the rejection of 'pagan' Sufi practices.

That brings us to the third and last characteristic of Tawhid's make-up: most of the younger members were educated at *madrasas* rather than government schools. They often pride themselves on their ability to speak and write Arabic. *Madrasa* education has a long tradition in Kattankudy – for decades, even devout families from elsewhere sent their children to Kattankudy Sufi and non-Sufi *madrasas* – but this tendency was reinforced in recent years. Moreover, many of the new *madrasas* have a reformist allegiance: two-thirds of them are Tawhid-oriented. Altogether, among Tawhid followers we thus find a large proportion of *madrasa*-educated people, who live in New Kattankudy and worked in the Middle East.

The significance of this constituency becomes clear when we look at Akkaraipattu, precisely because it is largely absent. We do not find a densely populated zone that is disconnected from the agricultural hinterland, labour migration has been less common and *madrasa* education is less popular. Whereas the war more or less cut off Kattankudy from the rich paddy fields across the lagoon, Akkaraipattu agriculturalists continued to farm despite the dangers of military and paramilitary activity. And when we scrutinise the socio-economic profile of Tabligh, the main reform movement in Akkaraipattu, we find a constituency that – put very generally – lies somewhere between Tawhid and the Sufis. Agriculturalists and white-collar workers are well represented among the active cadres of Tabligh. The movement is mainly propagated by people who are relatively well to do (unlike Tawhid), do not necessarily belong to the old elite (unlike Sufism), but aspire to climb the socio-economic ladder through higher education or economic success.

Many of Tabligh's prominent members in Akkaraipattu have office jobs – others are businessmen – and attended government schools, and a significant proportion of the leadership speaks English. They thus fulfil the rudimentary standards of worldly success, as defined by rural Sri Lankan communities. Their status is complemented by the ownership of paddy land. As is common in most peripheral Sri Lankan towns – but not in Kattankudy, which has become increasingly cut off from its hinterland – office clerks and shop owners supplement their income with rice cultivation. They typically hire wage labourers for the planting and harvesting, while they themselves try to visit their fields on a regular basis to inspect the work, feed their animals and so on. Tabligh's doctrine of simplicity, and the recurring assertion that power and wealth are transient and thus meaningless for the afterlife, is sufficiently fluid to be combined with some level of economic success. During interviews, leaders would extol the simple virtues of Tabligh and present themselves as respectable people, both morally and materially: God-fearing, dedicated and well-regarded citizens. While refraining from direct criticism of Tawhid – let alone a theological critique – some would occasionally hint at the 'extremism' and Saudi infiltration of this movement and they would denounce the violence in Kattankudy. They would also contrast themselves with the exclusivist stance of Tawhid by emphasising the unity of Islam and their cordial relations with Sufis.

When we look beyond the activist core of the different sects, the contrast presented here becomes more diffuse. Sufism, Tabligh and Tawhid all have followings among marginalised uneducated wage labourers or fishermen. In addition, there are of course exceptions to the overall profiles sketched above. The contrast between the Tablighi stereotype of a white-collar worker with a plot of paddy land, and the urbanised, *madrasa*-educated follower of Tawhid is striking though, because it maps directly on to the key difference between Kattankudy and Akkaraipattu.

Akkaraipattu is a paddy town. It is a relatively compact settlement of 60,000 inhabitants surrounded by irrigated rice fields. Although it lies directly on the ocean, it has no significant fishery sector. The *kudi* (clan) system still plays a pivotal role in the organisation of society. This mechanism regulates dowries and inheritance (and thus land ownership) as well as religious institutions (temple and mosque trustee boards). In eastern Sri Lanka, the *kudi* system is matrilineal (McGilvray 2008). While the importance and rigidity of this clan system appears to be declining, it became clear from interviews and observations in Akkaraipattu that *kudi* continues to play a significant role in local social order.

The difference with Kattankudy is striking. There *kudi* no longer dictates marriage and mosque organisation; it is considered a merely symbolic or historic remnant. In part, this is related to the decline of the agricultural sector. The *kudi* system after all derives much of its importance from regulating landownership and inheritance. Farming has disappeared almost entirely in Kattankudy. The town has long been a trading hub and this trend was bolstered by the war. The town's farmlands used to be situated across the lagoon and became inaccessible when the LTTE established their regional stronghold there in the 1990s. The town was thus cut off from the limited agricultural hinterland that it had, and came to rely almost exclusively on 'urban' livelihoods, such as small-scale manufacturing. Kattankudy sarongs are famous and desired (although Indian imports after Sri Lanka's liberalisation in the 1980s have affected demand) and we find large numbers of people involved in producing garments, jewellery, mats, masonry, carpentry and welding. Elaborate trade links stretch out to Colombo and elsewhere across the country. Kattankudy families now own some of the highest profile clothing shops in Sri Lanka. Some of these features are not entirely absent in Akkaraipattu. We also find shops, rice mills, a sawmill and home-based *beedi* (local cigarette) production in Akkaraipattu, but these activities employ only a fraction of the population. They are dwarfed by the agricultural sector, in which almost every family is somehow involved.

Education is a second point of difference between the two towns. *Madrasas* never were firmly established in Akkaraipattu. Though the oldest *madrasa* of the region is situated in the neighbouring town of Addalachenai (East Ceylon Arabic College), it has not expanded significantly (about 100 students at the time of our field research). Akkaraipattu used to have a small *madrasa*, but it closed due to a lack of students. (Apparently, another one has opened more recently.) The marginality of *madrasas* stands in striking contrast with the prospering education sector as a whole. Education, in fact, is a highly valued commodity and parents make great sacrifice to secure enrolment at the most prestigious schools. *Madrasas* and their associated job prospects (religious teacher, *maulavi*) are thus trumped by the more alluring prospect of advanced degrees, university enrolment and careers as engineers or doctors. Akkaraipattu houses 24 state schools with over 18,000 students (from a population of 60,000). Both the Tamil and the Muslim parts of town have a 'national' school (the highest standard in the Sri Lankan public education system), which teaches partially in English: Ramakrishna College and Central College, respectively. The town has earned a name as an emerging regional centre of education and it cherishes the list of successful alumni from its schools.

In line with the relative success of the education sector and associated white-collar employment, labour migration has attracted fewer people from Akkaraipattu, though accurate statistics are difficult to come by. As in Kattankudy, many in fact have gone abroad to earn money, and some of them returned with new kinds of religious enthusiasm. The emergence of one Tawhid mosque and a nascent Jamaat-i-Islami group bear witness to this. The numbers of these organisations are small though, and new *madrasas* have altogether failed to emerge. (Possibly, the choice of labour destination may be a factor here, as a larger proportion seem to have travelled to countries other than Saudi Arabia.)

For the sake of clarity (and at the risk of over-simplification), we can summarise the main differences between the two towns. Put simply, we find the contrast between an agro-town with traditional clan structures (Akkaraipattu), and a more urbanised, trading hub (Kattankudy). The contrast matches the socio-economic profiles of Tabligh and Tawhid, respectively. Tawhid thus established itself in the trading town, which already had a strong tradition of *madrasa* education, and where people move around more, including after the 1970s to Saudi Arabia. Akkaraipattu, on the other hand, houses a community that revolves around agriculture and professional education, and where the traditional social organisation (*kudi*) remains largely intact. This has proved a fertile home for a piety movement like Tabligh, but much less so for a more radical and demanding movement like Tawhid. The antagonism and violence towards Sufism that we found in Kattankudy can thus be attributed to two key factors: its gradual disconnection from agriculture (with all that has subsequently ensued in terms of educational and employment patterns); and its situation as the most confined and densest Muslim enclave along a coastline dotted with similar urban Muslim enclaves. The two factors, of course, are not discrete – the disconnection from the paddy-producing hinterland is at once a cause and a consequence of Kattankudy's status as enclave *par excellence*.

Intra-Islamic contestation and violence is not just a spin-off of the ethnic conflict in the country or a mere side effect of globalisation. It is the outcome of a highly localised interaction of these and other processes. We can distinguish three developments in eastern Sri Lanka. First, we see religious dynamism. New Sufi leaders and Islamic reform movements have sprung up in the area, and differences between them at times have led to tension or controversy. In itself, that is not a new phenomenon, but we have seen an intensification and fragmentation in recent decades. Second, the conflict that evolved between the separatist LTTE and the government engulfed the region. This resulted in a hardening of ethnic faultlines and the emergence of ethnic enclaves. Identity issues became of central concern, not least for the Muslim minority, which found itself trapped between Sinhala and Tamil nationalist formations. Third, there is a cluster of socio-economic changes. Improved educational opportunities and trade entered the region. The liberalisation of the Sri Lankan economy in the late 1970s reinforced these developments and cleared the way for labour migration to the Middle East.

There is also a contextual factor relating to political geography: Akkaraipattu is located in a district (Ampara), where Muslims are the majority ethnicity and, although the highest government officer historically has been Sinhala, Muslims hold many administrative portfolios and are well represented in the Parliament with their own politicians. Tamils are only a smaller minority in Ampara District and politically the weakest of the three communities. Also, the LTTE's grip on these territories was much weaker than in Batticaloa District. Kattankudy, in turn, was an enclave surrounded by Tamil settlements, in a district with a strong Tamil majority and a Tamil-dominated administration, as well as a strong LTTE presence during the war years (before the split). This enclave and frontier mentality in Kattankudy possibly made the quest for unity even stronger and those who defected from the true course of Islam were therefore branded as traitors from this course.

These sets of developments and contexts each have their own distinct causes and dynamics. There are, however, also many connections between them. The armed conflict hardened boundaries and put the spotlight on identity issues, which in turn added weight to contesting religious claims on Muslimness. The war also disabled some parts of the local economy – most notably agriculture in Kattankudy – that gave extra impetus to the tendency to seek employment abroad. Labour migration in turn resulted in the import of new religious ideas. There is thus a complex web of interactions. Rather than connecting these factors into a grand theory, our empirical material calls for a more contingent and localised approach. The way these global, national and regional factors interact with each other is highly context dependent. The two towns we discussed – Akkaraipattu and Kattankudy – are remarkably similar. To a large extent they have the same 'grand ingredients', but the way they mix and the results they produce are quite different. These differences are important for scholarly analysis, but also have very real consequences for the people living in the towns: religious skirmishes and a destroyed prayer house in Kattankudy and relative quiet in Akkaraipattu.

What, though, of the bigger picture? If we think purely in terms of our analysis of two Muslim towns, the obvious gain from our approach is a sense of complexity and a concomitant avoidance of premature generalisation. There is not a singular story to be told about Muslims and conflict in eastern Sri Lanka. We have found at least two, but there are still others to be told. With complexity comes a sense of the limits of our study. Our comparison remains schematic and really begs for fuller study in each locality. Our conclusions as often as not take the form of further questions, and these can only be answered with more work in particular places. So this collaborative ethnography is not a simple replacement for, or improvement on, other kinds of ethnographic approach.

In the previous chapter, we analysed a long-running dispute between Buddhists and Muslims about developments in and around the Buddhist site of Dighavapi. That story also provides examples of mimetic contestation across religious boundaries. Faced with the Buddhist use of archaeology to support their own claims to territory, Muslims respond by establishing their own archaeological museum with evidence of their presence in the area. Conscious of what they see as their own structural weakness as a politically divided community, Buddhist leaders organise themselves into a district-wide body quite clearly modelled on the area's successful mosque federations. The institutional structure of local Islam and local Buddhism provides a kind of armature on which other parts of our story may hang. Dialogical contestation, like that between Muslims and Buddhists about their claims on land, valorises some kinds of religious practice (saints' tombs for example) over others. Muslims, seemingly, have to choose between intensely local and intensely translocal versions of Muslimness.

The Dighavapi dispute allowed for a symmetrical story, tacking back and forth between Buddhists and Muslims. Other relations are less symmetrical. Members of the Kattankudy Mosque Federation complain about their difficulty in locating equivalent figures to act as representatives for their Tamil neighbours. The difference here is at once structural (Hindu temples in the east simply don't provide 'leaders' quite so obviously) *and* contingent (anyone who put themselves forward as a leader of the Hindu community in the years of war became a potential target for both the army and the LTTE). The Catholic Church, on the other hand, provides a disproportionate number of leaders who try to act as protectors and intermediaries for the wider Tamil community: this is an organisation that has seen more than its fair share of civil wars in its long history. If a certain kind of 'leadership' is inherent in its hierarchical structures, the Church's teaching on its social mission since the 1960s emboldens a new generation of priests to stand up for their parishioners (not unlike their equivalents working under similar pressures in parts of Latin America). This story will unfold at greater length in the chapter that follows.

Throughout, we encounter new movements and styles of religiosity, some (like the female oracles studied by Patricia Lawrence in the 1990s) very much a product of the war, but others, such as Tawhid or the new Pentecostal Churches that have grown in the region in recent years, as much a part of some bigger, more global story. The closest equivalents to the Kattankudy events described here, at least in terms of violent outcomes, are probably the attacks by Buddhists on Pentecostal Churches in and around Colombo in the past decade. We will return to the Pentecostals and their place in the post-war religious landscape in Chapter 7.

6

Boundary Politics, Religion and Peace-Building

Deadly Boundaries

Christmas Eve 2005. In St Mary's cathedral, Batticaloa town, the Catholic Bishop Kingsley Swampillai was presiding over the midnight mass ceremony with a packed congregation. At 1.10 in the morning, the 71-year-old Tamil parliamentarian Joseph Pararajasingham was returning to his pew, alongside his wife, after receiving communion, when two men emerged from the congregation and shot the MP dead, injuring his wife and seven others.

Even in Batticaloa, with its long history of violence, this killing seemed to be a particularly shocking and transgressive act; it occurred during a stuttering peace process, over the Christmas period, in a sacred space and

Figure 6.1   Calvary church, Veeramanagar, 2010 (photo by Bart Klem).

in front of the Bishop. As the well-known Tamil commentator D.B.S. Jeyaraj wrote at the time:

> The brutal manner of Joseph being killed in church after partaking of communion within full view of the Congregation in the presence of the Bishop demonstrates the depths of depravity. Whatever his politics Joseph Pararajasingham did not deserve to die or be killed in this manner.[1]

Pararajasingham, although born in Jaffna, had grown up in Batticaloa and spent most of this adult life there. He was part of the Catholic elite – he attended St Michael's College, became a government civil servant, and worked as a journalist before becoming a prominent TULF politician, first entering Parliament in 1990. Ironically, he survived the most violent and turbulent years of Batticaloa's history, even though by then he had become a high-profile figure, an advocate of the Tamil cause and, in the eyes of many, too closely linked to the LTTE. In 2001, he joined the TNA, an LTTE-organised alliance of Tamil political parties. But in 2004, the emergence of the LTTE breakaway faction led by eastern commander Colonel Karuna (and supported by the Sri Lankan government) threw Tamil politics into disarray. Tamil leaders were faced with a deadly choice; should they align themselves with the LTTE under the banner of Tamil unity, or should they support Karuna, who was protected by the government, and presented himself as an advocate for eastern Tamils? The assassination of Pararajasingham was interpreted by most commentators as the outcome of this deadly intra-Tamil conflict. Because of his long-standing connections with the LTTE leadership, he had become a marked man following the split. St Mary's cathedral was in a highly securitised area, surrounded by military camps. Pararajasingham had armed bodyguards outside the cathedral who did not fire a shot at the assassins. Most interpreted the murder as a state-sanctioned killing, at the hands of the Karuna faction.

This distressing incident illustrates a theme explored in this chapter – the complexities and dangers of contested boundaries in a period of turbulent transition. Being able to 'read', navigate, and negotiate boundaries and borders can, quite literally, make the difference between life and death. As Pararajasingham's assassination shows, violent acts simultaneously transgress and inscribe boundaries. The fact that it occurred in the Catholic cathedral, breaking down the protective barrier dividing the sacred from the profane, religion from politics, was especially shocking. This happened despite the 'boundary-work' of religious figures, who attempt to maintain a clear line between the Church and the dirty world of politics. Religious ceremonies and rituals, the creation of sacred spaces and separate institutional structures, can all be understood as, among other things, attempts to erect protective barriers, and to some extent the Catholic Church has been successful in creating a safe space for itself, one outside the politics of the conflict. The clearest example of this is perhaps the pilgrimage site of Madhu, in the heart of the Vanni, which became the focus of very public concern from all sides as the final wave of fighting swept past it in late 2008 and early 2009.[2] Yet as the murder of Pararajasingham shows, the ability of the Church to stand above or beyond the political fray is always provisional, and the boundary between religion and politics is a tenuous and permeable one: there are complex entanglements between the religious and political fields.

To some extent, members of the Catholic Church in the east have played an active role in constructing these entanglements: by cultivating an image of purity while systematically drawing on the Church's institutional base and material resources, they have built a powerful platform for the Church to create a new role for itself as a significant social and humanitarian actor in the east. As already noted in Chapter 2, this stands in contrast to Stirrat's (1992) account of the Church's declining confidence and relevance in the Sinhala parts of the country in the 1970s and 1980s. The back-story behind this incident is therefore more complicated than simply the Church's failure to keep politics out. In many ways, Catholic figures have actively invited politics in, by seeking to engage with the world 'out there', as humanitarians and social workers, but also in more explicitly political roles, for example as advocates for the Tamil cause, or as mediators between political and military groups. In the south of the country some of the more public engagements by (mostly Tamil) Catholic leaders have invited predictable nationalist responses, in which Catholic leaders can be dismissed as pro-LTTE, or as 'white tigers'.

By entering the political arena, the Church came to be regarded by some, not as a neutral onlooker or commentator, but as an active player. Even so, to reinforce the earlier point, people were still shocked by the brazen, almost sacrilegious nature of Pararajasingham's killing. Even the LTTE had tended to respect the autonomy and religious sensibilities of the mainline churches. Yet this killing reinforces the point that the most violently contested boundaries are the internal ones: it is consistent with a long-running history of brutal intra-Tamil violence involving the identification and eradication of traitors (Thiranagama 2010). Violence in this sense is performative – it is meant to communicate a message to a particular audience, and in this case it was probably the very crude one of warning pro-LTTE Tamils that there was nowhere to hide, nowhere was safe, not even the sacred ground of the cathedral. In this case, the message was primarily targeted at Tamils who had assumed positions of leadership, thus illustrating the dangers of taking on such a role, especially during moments of transition when the new rules are being negotiated and new boundaries established. For most of Pararajasingham's political career, his close links with the LTTE were a source of protection in the east, but with the emergence of the Karuna split, they became a fatal liability. Other, less overtly political leadership roles were also affected; for example, although it may not have been the perpetrators' primary intention, Bishop Swampillai was profoundly shaken by the killing, and many felt that it had a noticeable effect on his subsequent role as a Church leader in the east, influencing his willingness to take risks, to speak out and to engage explicitly with politics. This in turn contributed to tensions between a local Batticaloa clergy, many of whom had been radicalised by the war, and a Jaffna-born Bishop, who had been appointed by the Catholic hierarchy in Colombo.

The assassination of Joseph Pararajasingham was of course a tragedy, like countless other killings during the course of the long and brutal war in the east. In this respect, it constitutes another sad story in an extended history of violence. Yet it is also a powerful example of the many ways in which individuals and groups in the east have attempted – and often failed – to navigate, affirm or negotiate different kinds of boundaries – spatial, institutional, political and religious. We focus in this chapter in particular, on how the Catholic Church has been shaped by, and in turn, itself further shaped, the boundary politics of the east during successive periods of war, no-war, no-peace and post-war.

The Church in Time of War

Batticaloa is a town of just under 100,000 people. With the terminus of the rail line from Colombo and the west, an imposing fort, a public library and an anthropologically famous Readers' Circle (Whitaker 2007), Batticaloa is the administrative, political and cultural hub of the southern half of the east coast. It was also, of course, the government's security hub during the long years of war. Although Catholics now only make up around 20 per cent of the town's population, they often seem disproportionately visible in local affairs. St Michael's College has been the pre-eminent school in the region, educating the sons of the landowning class that emerged in the years of colonial improvement in the late nineteenth and early twentieth century (Chapter 3). St Michael's was founded by French Jesuits in the late nineteenth century, and the Jesuits have been particularly prominent within local affairs ever since.

In Chapter 2 we briefly reviewed Stirrat's (1992) account of Sinhala Catholicism up to the 1980s, a period in which the combined forces of an ascendant Buddhist nationalism, and internal reforms in the post-Vatican II Church, seemed to have tipped the Church into terminal decline as a political force. We also noted Deborah Johnson's (2012) more recent work on Catholics in the north, where the war gave priests precisely the kind of public role that Sinhala Catholics had been forced to abandon in the south. Nineteenth-century missionaries saw their role as mediators between man and God and between Catholics and the state. But with the rise of mass politics, this second role declined, and in 'the post-Vatican II world the role of priests has shifted from being a mediator between man and God to being something closer to a social worker, salvation being defined as something to be gained through the brotherhood of man rather than spiritual activities' (Stirrat 1984: 202). As a result of these shifts, the Catholic Church's ability to tackle questions related to power and peace has been highly circumscribed. As Stirrat put it in an overview of the Church's role at the very start of the civil war:

> If the Church attempts a mediating role, then it throws itself open to attack from the Sinhalese Buddhists. If it continues its present policy of accommodation with the government, then the split between Sinhalese and Tamil Catholics will only become more extreme. Racism recognizes no religious frontiers. (Stirrat 1984: 212)

However, this does not mean that the mainline churches were inherently conservative or always avoided taking difficult positions, even in areas dominated by the forces of Sinhala Buddhist nationalism. Since at least the 1960s, there have been on-going tensions between more conservative and more radical elements within all the churches. A case like the Batticaloa Council of Religions shows that the driving force for a more active approach to peace-building has often come from the north and east, but there has also been a history of progressive politics emerging from church groups in the south. Priests influenced by Vatican II began to work for oppressed sections of society such as the estate Tamils, while outspoken figures such as Father Tissa Balasuriya and Father Paul Caspersz were actively involved in left-wing politics: 'Although never very numerous, these radical priests were well organised and highly articulate Western-educated intellectuals whose aim was to produce a "contextual theology" relevant to the particular situation in which Catholics found themselves in Sri Lanka' (Stirrat 1992: 48). They helped to catalyse the emergence of a number of organisations and networks that shaped debates on justice, human rights and the ethnic question, including the Movement for Inter-Racial Justice and Equality (MIRJE), Satyodaya, the Centre for Society and Religion, People's Action for Free and Fair Elections (PAFFREL) and the Free Media Movement. Some activists from these organisations were also linked to the Student Christian Movement, which had strong north–south connections, because of the involvement of university students from the north-east. At a time when donor-funded civil society had yet to emerge, the churches were one of the few sources of funding for such non-governmental forms of public action. For example, the Catholic Church provided land for new buildings for organisations like MIRJE and the Centre for Society and Religion, and new specialist institutions concerned with economic and social 'upliftment' such as SEDEC (Social and Economic and Development Centre) were formed.

These groups and their international allies adopted leftist positions on a range of issues. The churches continued to play the role of spawning and promoting progressive organisations – partly because some priests had been frustrated by the internal conservatism of the Church and partly because organisational proliferation reduces the exposure of the Church's formal institutional structure. But to a great extent NGOs are still seen by their nationalist critics as part of a 'Christian mafia'. The National Peace Council (NPC) for example was formed by SEDEC and the National Council of Churches (NCC) because they found that a Christian identity was a limitation for expanding the peace constituency. The result was a secular organisation which continues to have strong participation from religious people.

Johnson (2012) describes the prominent role of the Catholic Church in Tamil-speaking areas during the years of conflict, drawing on its institutional and social base, the background and education of its leadership, and its ideological position and rituals. This introduces another contrast within Christian organisations in the east – between the so-called 'mainline' churches (including Methodists and the Church of South India) and the new Pentecostal churches. While the latter have, on the whole, flourished and grown since the 1980s, they are very conspicuously absent from the sorts of public engagement associated with the mainline churches, and the Catholics and Jesuits in particular.

From the 1980s onwards, in the north and east the Tamil political field was in a sense over-determined because of the overweening influence of the LTTE. After the outbreak of war, there was virtually no space for autonomous public action, except – to a very limited degree – in the non-governmental sector (Goodhand and Lewer 1999). Tamil political leadership, at every level from village development committees to national political representatives, became scarcer and less visible with each year of war. Few wanted to put their head above the parapet – 'you only open your mouth to eat' – and those who did often paid the price. By their own account, Tamils had virtually no political voice or representation.

As other forms of leadership atrophied, the social authority of the churches, particularly the Catholic Church, increased in the east. Religion was one arena in which leadership might be exerted without being automatically targeted by the LTTE or other paramilitary groups. This authority derived from several sources. First, in Batticaloa town, Catholics are a substantial presence (one informant estimated there were 80,000 Catholics in the east overall) and the laity are strongly represented within the town elite. Most of this elite were educated at St Michael's, are members of the influential Old Boys Association (OBA), which has branches in Colombo, UK, US, Canada and Australia, as well as Batticaloa itself, and hold, or have held, senior positions in the government service, the university, the law and other professions.[3] But this does not mean there are no divisions within the Catholic laity – for instance within the OBA during our fieldwork there were divisions between supporters of the LTTE and Karuna's TMVP. The case of Joseph Pararajasingham, murdered in the symbolic centre of the Catholic community, highlights these divisions. Second, the moral authority of the priests is enhanced by the fact that they are English speakers, with high levels of education and training – the Jesuits being paradigmatic in this respect. What Stirrat says of priests and administrators during the colonial era resonates with contemporary Batticaloa:

> Missionary and administrator needed each other. For the administrators, the missionaries acted as unpaid assistants, settling local disputes not just between Catholic and non-Catholics. A word from a Government Agent (GA) to a priest was often enough to solve a problem, the power of the missionary being something the administrator frequently envied. (Stirrat 1992: 17)[4]

The attenuation of the power of the Church which Stirrat describes so convincingly in the south, has not occurred in the east – the local administration (both the state and the shadow LTTE administration) and the lay population (Catholic and non-Catholic) still viewed the Church as an important force politically and socially. In the words of one Catholic priest:

> There is a tradition of respect amongst the authorities for the priest … Priests are able to provide protection to the people. They come here to feel protected – in the church there's always a priest attached to it. And we have the institutional structures – local, national, regional, international, which the Hindus don't have, nor the Muslims.

However, playing a mediating role has involved a fine balance, as conflict dynamics and political shifts redefine what is considered to be legitimate political action, and institutional structures have a limited capacity to protect (as the assassination of Pararajasingham was to show). Many priests were forced to leave the country, either temporarily or permanently, because of the conflict and some, like Chandra Fernando in 1988, were killed. But because of the war, the consequent hardening of boundaries and the denuding of Tamil leadership, there are few figures beyond the Church who have been able and willing to cross communal or political boundaries without losing their legitimacy. In fact boundary-crossing has increased the legitimacy of Church figures: as one informant noted, 'The Bishop's standing has increased during the conflict as he's been able to act as a mediator.' The diplomatic skills and personal charisma of the Bishop have clearly also been a factor. Although what Stirrat describes as 'indigenisation' (1992: 45–6) and the ethnic conflict have accentuated Tamil–Sinhala divisions within the Church, the fact remains that networks and linkages under the institutional umbrella of the Church continue to span the divide. And these networks and relationships constitute a significant source of social capital that can be drawn upon for mediation and peace-building at both the macro and micro levels. For instance, it is reported that the churches (particularly the Bishop of Mannar) were responsible for the opening up of back-channel negotiations between the LTTE and the Kumaratunga government in 2000, which led in part to the 2002–3 peace talks. At the micro level, priests were often able to gain privileged access to army commanders who were Christian. The Catholic NGO, EHED, for example was able to get banned items such as concrete into the uncleared area of Vakarai during the 1990s, by exploiting such contacts, while other NGOs were powerless.[5]

Paradoxically, religious leaders' legitimacy comes from their apparent distance from the dirty world of politics, yet this in turn gives them a degree of moral authority to act in the political realm. But becoming too enmeshed in politics and becoming too vocal an advocate, may undermine one's ability to be a broker or mediator. Some priests appear to have irrevocably stepped over the political line – becoming either too close to the LTTE, or to a specific political party (such as the TULF), or too outspoken a government critic. Therefore, priests are positioned differently in relation to different kinds of boundaries and these differences, though a source of tension, can sometimes also be useful. As one Jesuit noted: 'To play a role as a mediator you have to be neutral, but people like Father J. [a priest alleged at one time to have had sympathies for the militants] who are not perceived to be neutral may be useful intermediaries.' However, because religious leaders' authority is primarily based upon a constituency within one religiously bounded group, their ability to address wider political problems may sometimes be limited.

The churches are wealthy institutions and they have a strong organisational base at the international, regional, national and local levels. Batticaloa diocese (which incorporates Batticaloa and Trincomalee) is one of 13 dioceses island-wide. Until recently, Batticaloa had only one Bishop (Bishop Joseph Kingsley Swampillai), but an Auxiliary Bishop was appointed in 2008. There is a total of 50 priests, plus some 20 Jesuits, and a small number of Oblates of Mary Immaculate (OMI), an order based in France whose members work in and around Trincomalee. Since the nineteenth century, the Jesuit presence has been especially important in the east. French Jesuits established a presence at the end of the nineteenth century, and they were followed by a large number of American Jesuits from New Orleans who arrived around the time of Independence. One of these, Father Harry Miller, has achieved some national fame as a flinty witness to the years of war. He arrived in Batticaloa at the age of 23 in 1948 and, apart from a brief experiment at retirement in New Orleans in 2009, has remained there ever since. Links with India have always been important, particularly in relation to the indigenisation process, and many priests still go to India (and the Philippines) for training.[6] Regional linkages are also significant and Sri Lanka is part of the Federation of Asian Bishops Conference that has 38 member countries.

At the national level the National Bishop's Conference is the primary decision-making body, which is composed of Bishops from the 13 dioceses.

Furthermore, there are several national structures formed specifically to support peace-building, dialogue or social welfare activities. These include the National Peace Programme, the National Commission for Dialogue, the National Laity Commission and SEDEC (renamed Caritas Sri Lanka in 2003). There are ten seminaries with two major ones in Jaffna and Kandy. Bishops are appointed by Rome, though people from the diocese are consulted. All Tamil Bishops in Batticaloa have come from Jaffna, and this has been a source of resentment among the priesthood and laity. The appointment of an Auxiliary Bishop from Batticaloa can be understood in part as an attempt to address local dissatisfaction on this issue.

The Batticaloa diocese gets an annual subsidy from Rome. In addition, resources are raised locally, drawing upon Church assets, for example revenue raised through its coconut estates, the renting out of church halls and the sale of land for church construction. Individual donors, both local and from overseas, provide money on occasion for particular projects such as church construction. The parish raises money through local donations in addition to a stipend from the Bishop that varies according to the wealth of the parish. Only three to four parishes in Batticaloa are wealthy enough to be self-sustaining. Parish priests have a strong organisational base in society through a multitude of grassroots organisations. In any one parish there is likely to be a St Vincent de Paul society, an Anbiam Society (prayer group), a Pius Association, a Catechist society, a Catholic Youth Association, a Holy Childhood Movement, the Legion of Mary and a Parish Council. Finally, the Catholic priests are involved with and support a range of important organisations in Batticaloa, including EHED, St Michael's, a retreat called 'Mandresa', the Butterfly Garden, a counselling centre, Eastern University and the Jesuit Relief Services.

In some respects, the Church's institutional base provides the priesthood with a springboard to engage in political or social activities. Conversely, vested interests connected to these institutions may act as a brake on such activities. Because the Catholic Church is bigger in size and has a higher profile than the Protestant Churches, it has more to lose and consequently tends to be more risk averse than the Protestants: 'When an organisation is bigger, their survival becomes more important than their mission.' Catholic Bishops in the south have therefore sometimes been wary about taking controversial positions so as not to endanger their flocks in remote areas where they are a minority.

Post-Vatican II teachings, particularly liberation theology, found a receptive audience in the east as the war unfolded, particularly from an increasingly radicalised priesthood. This accentuated tensions between a politically careful and risk-averse centre and a radicalised, politically more engaged and exposed periphery.

> The [Catholic] Church feels isolated from Colombo. We are not getting enough support as Colombo identifies with the Sinhala community and Batticaloa with the Tamil community.

> The Christians in the south didn't speak out when Joseph Pararajasingham was killed in Batti.

Although within the Bishops' Conference there is a Peace Task Force, 'The Church has taken a moral or ethical position rather than a rights or justice position':

> Religion is supposed to play the overriding role for us – it should be above ethnicity, but this is not possible because of racism. People are taken for granted. If we organise a protest against the High Security Zone in Trinco, there's no one to speak on our behalf within the Church.

> They [Bishops in the south] play politics – they want to curry favours with the powers that be and they look after their own Church's interests.

Political action can be legitimated by the teachings of the Church. As already mentioned, Vatican II marked a transformation in the stance of the Catholic Church and had a major impact on the Catholic community in Sri Lanka (Stirrat 1992: 43). First, it marked a shift in the official attitude of the Church to other religions. The councils encouraged the view that other religions, instead of being simply dismissed as 'heresies', enshrined different ways of approaching God. This allowed priests to take a more expansive view of the community they served. As one priest told us, 'The priest is there for the whole flock, not just the Roman Catholics.' Another pointed out that 'The Catholic Church has taken a lead in the ecumenical movement which is stronger on the east coast than elsewhere.'

The Protestant churches have also been strong supporters of ecumenicalism – in the 1950s, for example, the Methodists started an ecumenical centre and the NCC is linked to the South Asia ecumenical programme. Therefore, local organisations, like the Council of Religions and the Inter Religious Organisation for Peace (IROP) in Batticaloa, are reflections of a wider trend towards ecumenicalism. To some extent the trend towards stronger inter-church collaboration is logical in the postcolonial context, given that Christians felt increasingly under threat and pushed on the defensive. In many respects it can be seen as a risk-spreading strategy.

Vatican II also instituted major changes to the liturgy. Pre-Vatican II services were held in Latin and post-Vatican II in the vernacular. Other changes included the priest saying mass facing the congregation and the encouragement of indigenous customs in the liturgy. Vatican II redefined the nature of the priesthood and in so doing made it more legitimate for the Church to engage in political and social work:

> In the pre-Vatican II Church, the priest had been the mediator between man and God, the channel through which grace flowed. In the new vision of the priesthood he became not the mediator but the exemplar. Grace comes not through such sacramental channels, but rather through individual action. (Stirrat 1992: 44)

This view was echoed by a Batticaloa Jesuit:

> Social activities and conflict resolution activities are political activities … Man cannot keep quiet. You have to be politically involved as politics changes social structures, and structures can become just, not sinful … The Catholic lay people must be involved politically. Communicating through the media is a way of communicating the message of God … Nothing is outside the purview of the Church.

There are, then, three important factors that shaped the Church's capacity for public action in the war years. One is an organisational structure that has historical depth, transnational capacities and no small amount of material wealth. A second is a theological shift that allowed the clergy to reimagine themselves as part of a community considerably larger than their own Catholic flock. And the third was the redefinition of the role of the priesthood itself, which provided a template for young radical priests searching for a mission through which to realise their own aspirations for justice and radical change.

The Church's Public Engagement

There is a long history of religious and non-religious public action in the east, especially in the spheres of humanitarian action, development and peace-building. For example, in Batticaloa town in the 1960s, a Christian discussion group was formed to promote better relationships between the different church schools. This was subsequently broadened out to become the Council of Religions, which included 'outstanding figures' from Batticaloa, including the Catholic Bishop and representatives from the Anglicans, Methodists, Buddhists and Hindus (the Ramakrishna Mission was a member) as well as a number of lay people. With a mandate to mediate conflicts between and within religions, the organisation survived for 20 years until the beginning of the war in the 1980s. By the mid 1980s the Batticaloa Council of Religions, which had been founded by the Bishop, had stopped functioning, and during the period of the Indian Peace Keeping Force (IPKF) a Citizens Committee was formed in response to a different set of challenges. This was reflected in a different mandate and focus, which was largely concerned with addressing human rights abuses (primarily for Tamils) at the hands of the military. The Citizens Committee then became the Peace Committee. During the IPKF period, it became very difficult to operate as they were threatened by both the IPKF and Tamil militants. The head of the Citizens Committee, Father Chandra Fernando was killed in 1988, probably by one of the armed groups connected to the army.

Following the withdrawal of the IPKF there was a brief hiatus, when the LTTE moved into the power vacuum. This was followed by the advance of the Sri Lankan Army (SLA) into Batticaloa. Shifts from one phase of the conflict to another have usually been accompanied by an intensification of the violence as new positions and regimes of control are established. The SLA advance led to widespread displacement, killing and destruction of property and infrastructure. Also, during these periods of flux, when boundaries are being reconfigured, the importance of mediators and protectors within civil society rises to the fore. This was the period when Ben Bavinck started driving his trucks of supplies to church projects in the north and east (Chapter 3). His diaries from this period provide an especially vivid account of the unpredictable ebb and flow of violence, the work of church groups trying to distribute relief supplies to the displaced, and the lonely figures seeking to document the atrocities mounting up and around them. An excerpt from November 1990, which describes a 'solidarity visit' to the east from the World Council of Churches, under Bavinck's guidance, gives a sense of the times:

> Trinco seemed much more normal. The Methodist pastor had arranged a program, which also included meetings with police officers and Buddhist monks, who all spoke in very positive terms about the situation ... When we continued our journey and went to Batticaloa the

next day, it was very sad to see the totally deserted Tamil areas between Valaichennai and Eravur, and again between Eravur and Batticaloa town. All the Tamils had fled, their houses stood deserted with the doors opened … In Batticaloa we had some good meetings with local church groups. In a combined meeting, surprisingly critical comments about the role of the Tigers were made. (Bavinck 2011: 152)

This was also the period when other foreign peace activists started to appear sporadically in places like Batticaloa. Often particular figures had first come to the country because of an interest in Buddhism, and had only then become involved in relief work for those affected by the war. Particularly important individuals moved between organisations, often ending up with Quaker Peace and Service, which established an office in the town in 1991, or Peace Brigade International, which was active for a brief period around the same time. Occasional Colombo-based activists, both Sinhala and Tamil, joined in the Batticaloa activity. Foreign Quakers started training locals in non-violent conflict resolution, and many of those who underwent this initial training in hard-pressed Batticaloa in the early 1990s went on to careers elsewhere in the island and beyond as peace activists.

Patricia Lawrence provides a powerful description from this period, of the self-conscious way in which activists used the 'safe' space of religious activity to reclaim a public voice in the face of atrocity:

On September 5 1996, the sixth anniversary of the 'disappearances' [the abduction of 158 Tamil refugees from their temporary shelter at Eastern University in 1990] 175 people held an hour-long vigil at the Vantharamulai camp. Three family members of the 'disappeared' spoke before the gathered collectivity and a group meditation was held. The public event, organized by families of the 'disappeared' was described as a 'prayer.' Such events of collective, non-violent public expression of loss have seldom been organized in this region, and as the use of the term 'prayer' indicates, the people involved were anxious that the gathering should be described in apolitical terms – a reasonable stance at a time when 'disappearances' continue to occur in the Vantharamulai area. (Lawrence 1997: 123)

Often religious leaders were less concerned with delivering goods and services than acting as brokers, communicators and protectors. Their comparative advantage in relation to other local organisations was their ability to mediate between the national and local levels – to gain access to actors in the international and national spheres, to cross frontlines and to make connections with the local level. At the local level, we were frequently told stories that stressed the importance of religious institutions and actors as agents of protection, mediators and advocates. When violent incidents occurred people would seek shelter in religious buildings or would go to religious figures for support and protection. When young men were abducted by the army or militant groups, people immediately went to the priest, pastor or mosque federation leader.

The IROP is the most recent in a chain of organisations created to support and protect the local population, squeezed as it was between often oppressive state security forces, and dangerous and capricious paramilitary forces. IROP was founded in 2004 to address the 'absence of leadership' at the local level to mediate and address inter- and intra-community conflicts. The main catalyst behind its formation was the Bishop, who called together representatives from all four religions to form the organisation, and the Catholic Church continues to be the driving force behind IROP. The Bishop has been a central actor for all significant interventions, and other members of the Catholic clergy have been active participants.

Like its predecessors, including the Council of Religions, the Citizen's Committee and the Peace Committee, IROP's members tend to be from the elderly English-speaking professional classes, but the organisation is structured to ensure representation from all religions. In 2008, the Chair was Bishop Kingsley Swampillai, underneath which there is a Secretary General (Mr Ganeshan), two secretaries, who are Christian (Mr Jebarajah, an accountant for World Vision) and Muslim, and three Deputy Chairs who are Muslim, Hindu and Buddhist. In addition there is a Coordinator (Mr Selvarajah, a retired TULF MP), an administrative officer, plus clerks and peons. There are 30 people in all in the formal organisation. The Catholic Church is IROP's main financial supporter. At the time of our fieldwork they were receiving funding for administration from EHED. Other sources of money included support from a diaspora group called the Batticaloa Development Society, plus money from Germany and Canada, directed to them via the Bishop. Following the tsunami, they received funding from some INGOs, as well as support to implement livelihood programmes from Jesuit Relief Services (JRS). IROP also had links to Catholic institutions at the national level including the National Commission for Dialogue.

When the tsunami hit in December 2004, IROP, like other peace organisations in the area, immediately got involved in the humanitarian response, and similarly, following the military operations and displacement with the reopening of the war in 2006, they implemented humanitarian projects for IDPs. The additional funding that came through this work was used to increase the number of paid workers, as previously they had relied on volunteers. Besides their humanitarian work, IROP's activities can broadly be divided into conflict mediation and advocacy. Their mediation work is by definition reactive and ad hoc, and to some extent it is difficult to distinguish between interventions by individuals and by the organisation. It is clear that for high-level interventions, the Bishop must be involved and IROP needs the Bishop more than the Bishop needs IROP.

Mediation in Post-Election Violence

In this section, we focus on one post-election incident on the border with Kattankudy, in order to provide a snapshot of the complex boundary politics in the east and the potential and limitations of religious public action, and specifically of organisations such as IROP, to address conflict dynamics. Three points are crucial to understanding this case. First, villages on the frontline between different ethnic enclaves have become zones of high conflict potential. In Batticaloa District, one can identify three such zones – Kattankudy–Arayampathy, Eravur and Valachchenai–Oddamavadi – and violent incidents in one zone may frequently generate copycat or revenge attacks in another. Second, there is something like a continuum of conflict, in which distinct categories of violence – individual, interpersonal, communal and political – may become fused with one another as the conflict takes on a life of its own. Third, the 'peace' that followed the government takeover of the east involved an inherently unstable coalition of politico-military groups. In 2008, the government hoped to legitimise the new political dispensation through elections and the delivery of a peace dividend in the form of a donor-funded reconstruction programme.[7] By doing so, they also aimed to consolidate the controversial de-merger of the Northern and Eastern Provinces. To this end local council elections were held in March followed by Provincial Council elections on 10 May. The elections were hailed as a watershed that delivered 'a people's mandate for democracy over terrorism' (cited in International Crisis Group 2008: 9).

The May 2008 Provincial Council elections saw a rise in tension, especially between Muslims and Tamils in the communities in and around Batticaloa town. The March elections were won decisively by the TMVP's new regional leader, Pillayan. The 10 May elections pitted the United People's Freedom Alliance (UPFA) composed of the SLFP, TMVP, and a range of smaller Muslim parties, against the UNP, running in coalition with the SLMC. President Rajapaksa, in order to undermine the SLMC vote bank, at the last hour persuaded Hizbullah, the key Muslim SLMC MP from Kattankudy (see Chapter 5), to switch sides. The President is said to have promised the Chief Minister position to either Hizbullah or Pillayan depending upon who gained the most votes. This turned the elections into a direct inter-ethnic competition, with each community voting, not necessarily out of support for a candidate, but to prevent a Tamil or Muslim from becoming the Chief Minister. With the TNA boycotting the elections, and no well-known Tamil candidates on the UNP ticket, Tamil voters wanting a strong voice in the Provincial Council had no choice other than the TMVP (International Crisis Group 2008: 11). Polling was affected by violence and intimidation of candidates. Government thugs were brought in so that it was virtually impossible for opposition candidates to campaign. The TMVP remained armed throughout the campaign, and the consensus from international observers was that there was a range of serious malpractices. The TMVP intimidated opposition voters and party workers, impersonated voters and took over polling stations to stuff ballot boxes (International Crisis Group 2008: 11).

Ultimately, the UPFA coalition won 52 per cent of the vote and 20 seats in the 35-seat council (International Crisis Group 2008: 10). Although more Muslim candidates were elected in the Provincial Council than TMVP candidates, Pillayan was appointed Chief Minister. This angered the Muslims and accentuated animosities that had been building up during the election period.

On the Kattankudy–Arayampathy faultline, these animosities spilled over into violence. It started on 22 May, when the TMVP leader for Arayampathy, Shantan and his bodyguard were killed in Kattankudy by two men on a motorcycle. Shantan had established several TMVP offices in the Tamil village of Arayampathy and had reportedly been stirring up inter-communal passions during the election campaign. Many interpreted the assassination as a payback for this by militant young Muslims. However there were at least two other theories about the attack. First, given the mode of attack and its skilled execution, it might have been an LTTE pistol gang. Second, it might have been the result of the growing struggle within the TMVP between factions loyal to Karuna and factions loyal to Pillayan. But most people interpreted the event as an attack by Muslims on Tamils and it triggered an immediate retaliation. On the same day, as soon as TMVP cadres heard the news they came out of their offices in Arayampathy and fired randomly on Muslims. Three were killed on the spot.

This was followed on the same day by the kidnapping and killing of two Muslims from the town of Eravur, 14 km north-east of Batticaloa, who were travelling to Batticaloa to pay their electricity bills. The police called a two-day curfew, and Muslim leaders called a *hartal*. Transportation routes with Colombo were blocked. There were rumours that Muslims were planning to attack the Tamils bordering Eravur, which prompted the displacement of around 2000 Tamils in Eravur who, fearing retaliation, sheltered in a school and Catholic church to the south. Muslims organised a protest march in Eravur that spilled over into violence and led to the security forces shooting into the crowd and killing a Muslim woman. Finally, another Muslim from Eravur was killed when he left town to sell vegetables.

The precise details of the negotiations that followed these killings are hard to ascertain. But most accounts appear to agree on the following. A high-level meeting was held which involved direct talks between Pillayan's personal secretary, Ragu, the Superintendent of Police, and representatives of the Kattankudy Mosque Federation. External facilitators of this process were reported to be the Bishop, IROP, EHED and the Non-Violent Peace Force (NVPF, a prominent INGO active in Batticaloa at the time). According to one account, the Muslims first approached International Committee of the Red Cross (ICRC) representatives for help in transporting the three Muslim bodies back to Kattankudy from Batticaloa town for burial, which they were unable to do because of the curfew. Because this fell outside of ICRC's mandate, they approached the Bishop instead. In any event, the meeting occurred with the support of IROP – 'when the conflicting parties came together they talked directly and we stood behind' – and an agreement was made about transporting the bodies. Both sides agreed to a joint statement which emphasised peaceful coexistence and this was subsequently disseminated in both Batticaloa and Kattankudy.

It also appears that negotiations with community leaders in Eravur were going on from 23 May onwards and a high-level meeting involving the Muslim leader Mir Ali and Pillayan was also held. The TMVP were very actively involved with the displaced Tamils from Eravur, providing them with lunch packs and evidently trying to exploit the situation to generate political capital for themselves. NVPF workers talked about being actively involved in negotiations with the two communities and attempting to prevent rumours from spreading. On 24 May, with negotiations concluded, the displaced Tamils were able to move back to their homes.

To some extent, the intervention by IROP and others helped to prevent the conflict from escalating, and allowed a new equilibrium to emerge. At the time of our fieldwork in late 2008, a detente of sorts had developed between Pillayan and Hizbullah, but the situation remained inherently unstable. Tensions between Karuna and Pillayan appeared to be growing – a grenade attack on a newly created TMVP office linked to Karuna's faction in Batticaloa town was symptomatic. Karuna appeared to be increasingly flexing his muscles and there were rumours of imminent defections from the Pillayan camp. Furthermore, LTTE infiltration in the east was said to be growing, with stories of a TMVP office being taken over temporarily by LTTE cadres. In this dizzyingly complex and unpredictable context, the IROP intervention helped to dampen the immediate conflict dynamics temporarily, but did little to transform the structures and incentives underlying it.

Such 'low-intensity' conflict is clearly not random, and for powerful actors it fulfils important functions. For the state, 'top-down' violence can be an instrument of governance – a level of instability helps to prevent the emergence of powerful coalitions that might have challenged its particular brand of state-building in the east. The means of violence are franchised out to non-state actors to evade accountability, but these actors are never allowed to become too powerful. One interviewee, perhaps taking the functionality argument too far, even argued that the government's own Special Task Force (STF) were responsible for stoking up violence in the east to avoid being posted to the north. For local actors, 'bottom-up' violence is a means of hardening in-group/out-group boundaries; extending their control; or extracting resources, both locally and from the centre. Violence often tends to have its own rhythms and patterns and in a sense is choreographed – it can be understood as a dramatic production, part of an on-going 'conversation' between competing military and political actors.

Just as conflict can be seen as functional, so too can conflict management processes which keep conflicts within certain bounds but do not transform them. Peace-building organisations may inadvertently be useful allies for those seeking to benefit from conflict. Resolving conflict once and for all would undermine the power base of many actors who rely on violence or the threat of violence. Therefore, organisations like IROP may be useful, because of their ability to mediate across boundaries without actually challenging those boundaries. Paradoxically, with its quota system of religious representation, IROP may play a role in reproducing and reinforcing the boundary politics of the conflict itself. The organisations that make up the patchwork of IROP, such as the mosque federations and the Catholic Church, are hardly indifferent to the policing of their own boundaries. Religious groups that are more genuinely indifferent to the social origins of their membership – the new churches, demotic Hindu and Muslim healers – are conspicuous by their absence.

However, IROP had established a niche in the complex ecology of violence and conflict management in the east at the time of our fieldwork for the following reasons. First, its religious base means it has some authority and legitimacy, as it is seen to be separated from the dirty world of politics. Second, members of IROP are, generally, elderly and retired, and as such are non-threatening to more overtly political figures. Their age and background gives them a level of authority within their own constituencies that makes them useful to the politically engaged. Third, the authority of the organisation depends to a large extent on the Bishop: 'The Bishop had the authority to call the TMVP, which we didn't have.' Fourth, although the Catholic Church is the pivotal player within IROP, from the Church's point of view, the larger organisation plays a useful role in diluting the risks of being solely involved in such sensitive processes. As one member commented about another intervention process which involved talking to the armed forces: 'There are 18 of us, which gives us some protection.'

In short, IROP has been involved in a series of *ad hoc* interventions, which are primarily aimed at preventing conflict from escalating rather than transforming the bases of conflict. The members of IROP are not naive about this and are keenly aware of the limitations of their work: 'Religious leaders have a role in dealing with tensions but without political support they can't do anything ... and the leadership are using mediation to generate good publicity for themselves.'

After the War

The military victory in the east in 2007 transformed the political landscape for peace-building. Initially, the military prevented human rights and peace organisations from gaining access to newly cleared areas and international staff working for these organisations experienced problems getting their visas renewed. There was a great deal of pressure on NGOs (and donors) to support the government resettlement and reconstruction programme. Peace and human rights organisations were seen as an irritant, which might slow down or obstruct the government's efforts to pacify the east.

In the new political context, conflict resolution organisations also found it difficult to operate because their old contacts with the LTTE were no longer relevant, and the Pillayan–Karuna split within the newly all-powerful TMVP made it difficult to know who to negotiate with. In such a fluid context, in which the boundaries between political violence and criminal violence, including robbery and kidnappings, became increasingly blurred, and with the reappearance of white vans (the pre-eminent symbol of state-supported 'disappearances'), it was far more difficult to mediate between sides in order to dampen conflict or protect the population. A 2007 evaluation of the hitherto highly successful early warning programme, set up by the Federation for Coexistence (FCE), showed that its effectiveness had been severely circumscribed, because it was no longer able to maintain relationships with key military and political figures (Goodhand and Walton 2007). While the LTTE always had an influence on the NGO sector (especially local NGOs), they were usually conscious of the need for the sector to at least appear to be independent.

After the war, the field of protection and peace-building was therefore much smaller and less powerful than it had been earlier. The Peace Committee had continued, with Catholics playing a central role, with Father Miller as President and Mr Mutt of EHED as Secretary. But it had limited leverage. The key institutional innovation of the Norwegian brokered ceasefire, the Sri Lanka Monitoring Mission (created to oversee the truce), had been disbanded and the Human Rights Commission was powerless. The Muslim Peace Secretariat remained and there was talk of establishing a new TMVP-aligned Peace Secretariat. ICRC, UN Human Rights Council, UNICEF, Norwegian Church Aid (NCA) and NVPF were the main international agencies with a protection role and mandate in Batticaloa, but there were divisions between them about how best to respond. On the one hand, UNHCR had been a strong proponent of the need to support the government resettlement programme and to shift into longer-term developmental programmes. On the other hand, NCA argued that it was not a conducive environment for development, and there was a need for more robust advocacy on human rights and protection issues. 'It's especially precarious right now ... The humanitarian community have deprioritized the east as it's no longer seen to be an active conflict.'

On the government side there appeared to have been a subtle shift in position. On the one hand, the government sought to marginalise human rights groups or critics of government policy in the east – for instance, the President's powerful brother Basil Rajapaksa refused to extend the visa of the UNOCHA (UN Office for the Coordination of Humanitarian

Affairs) coordinator when she was critical of the human rights situation at a meeting with him in Batticaloa. But the government seemed to have taken a different tack in relation to conflict resolution organisations, some of which, including IROP and NVPF, worked alongside military and government officials in order to prevent conflicts from escalating. Conflict resolution organisations might have a longer-term role in stabilising the 'peace' in the east, so long as they seek to dampen conflict dynamics, working within the paradigm set by the government. The Colombo-based Consortium for Humanitarian Agencies (CHA) for instance initiated a programme funded by UNHCR called the Confidence-Building and Stabilisation Measures (CBSM) programme, which essentially was focused on forging more cooperative civil–military relationships. So long as civil society agencies are supportive of hegemonic actors and do not question the foundations upon which peace is to be built, they are seen to be useful partners in the pacification process.

This chapter has brought out the dialectical nature of the relationship between religion on the one hand, and peace and conflict on the other. To a great extent the most interesting and pertinent questions concern the ways in which religion itself may be transformed by conflict. And we need to be able to go some way towards answering these questions before addressing the more obvious and instrumental question of how religious figures and organisations may or may not be able to build peace (or fuel conflict).

Yet again, our story makes clear that there are significant differences both between and within different religious traditions and institutions, especially in styles of public engagement. The Catholic Church, with its long history and robust transnational institutions, emerges as a major participant in the attenuated space for public action that was available during and immediately after the war. Muslims, stereotypically regarded as 'well organised' and 'united' by other religious communities (but not so much by themselves), are not far behind, with their political parties and their mosque federations. But the leaders who emerge from these institutional structures are as often as not concerned to police the boundaries of their own religious community. Dialogue is possible, but only if premised on the idea of a dialogue between discrete, well-bounded religious communities in the first place. Other religious specialists – charismatic healers from all communities, for example – seem far more open to the movement of devotees across conventional boundaries, but do not themselves emerge as major actors in the public arena. This is a world of healers and leaders, but the healers are rarely leaders, and the leaders are less enthusiastic about the charismatic gift of healing. At an early meeting with representatives from IROP, we asked about the kinds of religious figure so vividly described by Lawrence in the 1990s. Ah yes, we were told by an evidently embarrassed Catholic priest, there are such people in the area. But, he said brightening up, for 'trauma' we prefer 'counselling'.

Religious practices and institutions look very different when viewed from only slightly different political and geographical circumstances. Stirrat's account of a decline in the standing and authority of the Catholic Church may be true in the south, but out in the east the reverse has been the case, with priests finding new roles and relevance in the maelstrom of the war. These differences are very obvious to the actors themselves: Tamil Catholics are only too aware of the limitations of the Colombo hierarchy, just as Buddhist monks in border villages are eager to distance themselves from their more inflammatory colleagues who live far from the consequences of their actions in Colombo and Kandy.

This chapter has also illustrated the dynamic and complex relationship between religion and boundaries. On the one hand, religion, and religious institutions in particular, seems to provide a safe, bounded space, a form of protection from the vicissitudes of the war: 'In my daily life I don't have control so I grab it back in religion.' On the other hand, religious leaders gain their legitimacy precisely because of their ability to transgress boundaries. Religious figures have to an extent been able to engage in the very political act of boundary transgression because they can pretend to be apolitical, or above the world of dirty politics. But this then creates its own limitations, as overtly political engagement can only reduce the protective mantle provided by claims to religious authority.

Finally, as the IROP case shows, religious public action does not represent a magic bullet for transforming violent conflict, particularly in a context where religious actors are often themselves divided and politically marginal. This is not to say that religious actors and organisations have not been an important part of the story of how people survive, cope and sometimes flourish in a context of chronic conflict. Whether it is by providing a story to tell the grieving about where their disappeared family have gone, as Lawrence's oracles have done for years now, or taking his motorbike on the ferry across the lagoon to talk to the LTTE in their territory, as one of our informants used to do routinely during the years of war, religious figures can do much to make the war endurable. But they cannot, it seems, do a great deal by themselves to make it stop or to change the political mechanisms that keep it going.

7

Afterword: War's End

The outskirts of Trincomalee, the historical harbour town to the north of our main research area, used to be a contested borderland during the war. Along the coastal road to the north, one would arrive at Sambaltivu lagoon, a muddy backwater with a small checkpoint on the causeway. From this point on, the eroded gravel road traverses a sparsely populated coastline, subject to navy surveillance. Watch posts along the road were never far apart. The scrubby forest in the interior was known to provide shelter for LTTE cadres and the vast forested area to the north and east, known as the Vanni, was the LTTE's main stronghold. After dusk, cadres moved around relatively freely through the Tamil and Muslim settlements along the coastal belt. After dawn, in turn, navy sailors would patrol the road to clear it of possible ambushes. This alternating cycle of control, infiltration and surveillance routinely repeated itself, everyday again and again.

Travelling the same road after the defeat of the LTTE in 2009 was a different experience. The shore that had marked the beginning of a scrubby and insecure forest was now home to Trincomalee's biggest Hindu temple complex, its golden roof visible from far away. This display of prosperity stood in stark contrast to the impoverished state of most Hindu settlements in the area. The man behind the Sri Lakshimi Perumal shrine, our Hindu interlocutors whispered to us, was one of Trincomalee's most successful Tamil businessmen, who also owned some of the newly refurbished tourist infrastructure in Trincomalee town. Significantly, he had accumulated his capital thanks to – rather than despite of – the war. Notwithstanding the apparently impure antecedents of its funds, many Tamil visitors witnessed the Krishna temple with awe, and the stalls at the entrance were gradually expanding.

The temple presented a number of paradoxes. Not only did it seem to connect, for some at least, spiritual devotion and the war and its associated world of smuggling, bribery and military connections, it also comprised an audacious demarcation of Tamil Hindu space in a post-war landscape that was otherwise seen to be shaped by Sinhala Buddhist triumphalism.

Right behind the Krishna temple, a new road known as the Outer Circular Road had been constructed. More than anything else, it was a security measure: it was built by the army and it put a military ring around the strategic navy town of Trincomalee. Just beyond that road, lay the Vilgam Vihara, a newly rejuvenated shrine that catered to busloads of tourists and pilgrims. Vilgam Vihara has had a contested history with mixed Tamil–Sinhala influence, but the government triumph over the Tamil insurgency has been the impetus for a very public reassertion of Buddhist claims to the site (cf. Kemper 1991: 150).

An impressive new Hindu temple, new army roads, refurbished religious sites, crowds of tourists and pilgrims – all in a formerly military borderland. Our book was not expected to be about the end of the war in Sri Lanka. When we started our fieldwork, the Norwegian-facilitated peace process was falling apart and armed hostilities were in full force. In the months that followed, government forces ousted the LTTE from the east. In the north, the war continued with widespread anticipation that it would come back to the east coast in due course. The LTTE had staged many comebacks in the past. But as the frontlines moved and the losses kept rising, it started to become clear that this time such a reversal was not on the cards. Government forces cornered the LTTE and a final battle ensued, in which the LTTE were finally and comprehensively defeated in May 2009.

Building on new research in Trincomalee District, just north of the other sites discussed in this book, this chapter tries to do two things. First, we aim to get a sense of changes and continuities after the end of the war. If the war created a common predicament that enabled us to explore diverse religious traditions from a single vantage point, as argued in Chapter 2, are there equivalent shared post-war predicaments? Second, what do post-war observations tell us about the recent past? What changes have taken place, what has become possible or impossible, what forms of leadership have emerged – or disappeared?

A Post-War Frontier

'I am here to cultivate and contribute to the nation.' The speaker was a Sinhala agricultural labourer, recently settled in a rather modest dwelling along a newly constructed dirt road in the south of Trincomalee District. For poor rural families with limited access to land, the prospect of a free plot in the newly 'liberated' east coast (along with seeds and dry rations) promised the start of a better life. Until very recently, the soil on which they settled had been a scrubby jungle, an uncultivated place where wild elephants and boar roamed freely. More importantly, their new habitat used to mark the boundary of what had been LTTE-controlled territory during the war. After the insurgents were driven out, the army had constructed a new road, straight through the forest, connecting Seruvila and surrounding peasant towns with the Sinhala interior and the 'ancient city' of Polonnaruwa, while passing the isolated Buddhist temple at Somawathie on the way. The prime purpose of the road was to enable pilgrims to travel between these different religious sites. But the journey was rough. The uninhabited area had no facilities and wild animals posed a threat, particularly after dark. That is why the chief monk of the Seruvila temple had invited landless labourers from elsewhere to settle here, 'to protect the pilgrims'. All settlers along this new road had personally registered with this monk. 'Contributing to the nation' thus not only meant taming the jungle by making it productive for agriculture, it also meant settling a Buddhist population around a network of Buddhist sites.

The Seruvila temple has a history as a Sinhala outpost in predominantly Tamil and Muslim territory reaching back to the 1920s, but intensifying with the involvement of a hardline nationalist politician, Cyril Mathew in the 1970s and 1980s (Kemper 1991: 148–60). (Mathew's name is frequently cited in allegations of government involvement in the 1983 Black July riots.) During the war, Seruvila was surrounded by Tamil–Muslim towns (Mutur, Thoppur) and LTTE-controlled territory (Sampur, Verugal). The defeat of the LTTE made it possible to build roads to Buddhist sites that had been inaccessible before. Following the improvised signposts directing travellers through what was once de facto Tamil Eelam, visitors arrive at Lankapatuna (Kemper 1991: 155). This natural anchorage within view of the Seruvila stupa is believed to be the place where the Buddha's tooth-relic was brought ashore in 301 CE. A plaque at the site explains that Lankapatuna was subsequently controlled by the 'terrorists'. The strategic location – a rock at the mouth of the lagoon – was well suited for a gun-post, not least because its archaeological significance would deter hostile attack. Following recapture by the army in 2006, the site has now become a popular destination for pilgrims and tourists. The military retains a small checkpoint at the entrance of the site and a large camp with permanent housing structures right next to it.

Six kilometres to the south, at a place known as Kallady (not to be confused with the Kallady in Batticaloa District discussed in Chapter 2) there is another Archaeology Department information board, which refers to 2,000-year-old inscriptions from a Buddhist temple. The site's most obvious feature – a tall metal mast – belongs to a more recent past: the Voice of Tigers (the LTTE radio station) used to broadcast from here. After the LTTE defeat, the antenna was put to new use; it now forms the base for a golden Buddha statue, sitting on its top. The transmission room, housed in a shipping container, has been converted into a home for the newly arrived monk. Born in Ratnapura, in the south, and trained as a medical doctor in Kolkata (he proudly recalls meeting Mother Theresa), the monk was only recently ordained. He decided to do so because of the war. He was working as a doctor in Saudi Arabia, when he learnt that a temple that he felt particularly close to had been attacked by the LTTE: 'I decided to come back and become a monk. I wanted to change my life and help the poor people.' He helped to refurbish that temple, and when it was finished, came to Kallady to do the same thing. While the soldiers of the neighbouring camp are helping with the construction of a visitor centre, he uses his medical knowledge to run a small dispensary. This is mostly frequented by Sinhala people, but he does not mind helping Tamils. 'I don't make a difference. All can come here. I will help anyone.' Having learnt Tamil when he worked in the Hill Country, he complains that most *bhikkhus* do not know the language. 'Then it is a problem to work here.' Because he prioritised making a practical contribution, he explains, 'I never had the chance to properly learn the prayers and other religious activities. I have to take a course at one of the main temples.' Meanwhile, more help is needed in this area, he continues, for the people and for the temple, but the government has not been forthcoming. 'This is only a small site, but we have to preserve it for the future generation. I want to do some more work here and then go to Singapore. There's a temple there [to go to].'

A casual observer might conclude that the creation of new shrines and sites is a purely Buddhist activity. That is far from the truth. The Krishna temple described at the beginning of this chapter provides us with a Hindu equivalent, and, in simple material terms, a much bigger one at that. New churches, to which we will turn in a minute, are probably the most visible new structures in the post-war landscape. And Muslims have built new mosques, and expanded existing ones, often as part of the growth of movements like Tawhid and Tablighi Jamaat. But other Muslim sites seem to combine devotion and leisure rather like the development at Lankapatuna. Just outside Akkaraipattu, on the road to Ampara and not far from Dighavapi, a new Sufi site has sprung up. People visit the site for devotion and to present their problems to the resident sheikh. In addition, visiting families enjoy the day out in the nicely landscaped exterior, where they have picnics, play games and take snapshots. As much as a centre of spiritualism, devotion and mysticism, the site is a public attraction, a stage for performing good family life, a fact that is also reflected in the entry fees that are levied. Until very recently, Cegu Issadeen had been one of Akkaraipattu's most prominent politicians. Having been outmanoeuvred by the town's current MP, Issadeen decided to turn his back on politics and put his leadership skills to new use. He declared himself a Sufi and created this public space for consultation, devotion and leisure (cf. McGilvray 2011: 58–9).

New Muslim, Christian and Hindu sites attract attention and sometimes controversy, but not on the scale of Buddhist sites in the east. Buddhist sites invoke controversy among the Tamil and Muslim community because of the larger political history of Sri Lanka's north-eastern frontier (Korf 2009). In the twentieth century, government-sponsored irrigation schemes converted unruly forest into orderly paddy land. They also involved large-scale movement of people, dramatically altering the ethnic composition of the east, and they came accompanied by dense allusions to the glorious past of a hydraulic society of Sinhala Buddhist kingdoms (see Chapter 3). All this was perceived as 'colonisation' by many Tamils and Muslims. The restoration of Buddhist sites is interpreted as the religious component of a resumed 'colonisation', which also involves settlement processes, military infrastructure, patriotic monuments like war memorials and increased centralisation of government power. The east, in short, is seen to be increasingly integrated into a 'Sinhala kind of geography' (Korf 2009) and sacred sites are part of that process. As our farmer put it, they 'contribute to the nation'.

New Churches

The case of Cegu Issadeen, Akkaraipattu's politician turned Sufi, illustrates the remarkable fluidity of leadership in eastern Sri Lanka. In the mixed Tamil–Muslim town of Mutur, during the war, a respected Muslim citizen and civil servant explained to us:

> The mosques had the power to control everything … It's important to control the people. The mosque would control the youngsters. When they were drunk, or doing bad things like theft. The mosque federation would punish them.

But only two years after the defeat of the LTTE, the federation's authority seemed to be eroding: 'They can't exercise punishments any more. People go to the police. And the courts have resumed functioning as well. If there is a problem, people can complain everywhere.' Movement and freedom from one sort of surveillance, could lead into other forms of surveillance. When the LTTE was still there, people could not just go anywhere, he explained. This made possible an everyday form of surveillance by fathers and religious leaders, and, by extension, the mosque federation. 'But now, the youngsters are free to go. People are thinking to work individually.'

As something more like 'normal' politics returned to war-affected areas (Klem 2014a), we might expect the space for religious public action to shrink. At the same time, the scope for circulation increased after the war, particularly in formerly LTTE-controlled areas. Everyday movement in eastern Sri Lanka had long been problematic because of the dilapidated infrastructure and checkpoints, but this had not prevented the creation or arrival of new religious movements and mutations. Tawhid Jamaat, new Sufi sects, Pentecostal churches and Amman temples took root in the region over the decades of war. With the defeat of the LTTE, new churches mushroomed in areas like Verugal, Vakarai and the interior of Batticaloa District, and they attracted Hindus and mainline Christians alike. 'They are troublesome, but they are now the majority,' one Catholic priest claimed: 'There are now 260 different churches in Batticaloa and Ampara District.'

Along with two other new churches, the Assembly of God arrived in one village after the LTTE was ousted from the area. A year later, about half the village was said to have joined these churches. While the musical element of their service might have provided a welcome change to the more scripture- and sermon-oriented services of the mainline churches, it was their healing power that had the greatest appeal. A Hindu woman explained:

> They cure people's sickness and then people join. They tell people don't smoke, don't drink alcohol, don't do this and that. But people were really cured. It was no trick. That is their faith. Then one person joins, and then their mother, and so on.

From the early 1990s onwards, proselytisation by non-mainline churches has become an increasingly common phenomenon, and chanting and the miraculous treatment of illnesses have always been part of the equation. The female priest leading a 'Jesus Lives' church near Akkaraipattu explained to us that she used to be a Methodist.

My body was full of rashes. I went to Jesus Lives and I was cured. ~
forty days, I took one meal a day only. My father had tuberculosis. It
went the same way. My sister's son missed a kidney. He was very sick.
The same way, he was cured.

She handed us the latest church periodical, an English-language booklet
containing pages and pages of letters bearing testimony to the miracles
the church had made possible: blind people regain their vision, asthmatics
start to breathe properly, cancer patients fully recover and demons are
driven out. Through these activities, they show that they are different from
Catholics and Methodists: 'We really believe the word of the Bible. We
actually cure the people.'

The rise of the new churches has caused some concern. 'Church
planting' occasionally met resistance from the neighbours, sometimes
violent, as well as more subtle forms of disapproval. Hindus and mainline
Christians alike complained about the 'noise'. Particularly in towns, where
the new churches had powerful loudspeakers, regular late-night chanting
and screaming was not appreciated. Catholic leaders were critical of the
unsanctioned 'pagan' influences. While Catholic priests tended to reject the
approach of these churches with some firmness, the Methodist Church
appeared torn between concern and admiration. 'These new churches are
not always wise, but extremely zealous,' a prominent Methodist pastor in
Colombo observed:

Not all their pastors are theologically competent to handle the
scriptures. But what they lack in depth and understanding, they make
up for with zeal. And people listen to them. Many people join them
because of miracles.

His use of the word 'miracle' was significant. Other priests that we
interviewed – Catholics in particular – resorted to more derogatory terms.
When we asked him about this he said: 'Some of these miracles, I think,
are authentic. But certainly not all of what is reported. They do work
with charms and demons.' For him, this was in no contradiction with
Christian theology. 'I accept the existence of demons. They are not behind
every bush, as some people seem to think, but I think the devil manifests
himself in different ways in different societies.' He continued:

To us, it is very real. People come with cases of possession. Some of
these may have been psychologically induced. Charismatic churches go

to town on this. They see demons in every home and place. For the people, their capacities are a sign of God's power. I wouldn't know what to do with these charms. All I could do is pray.

By now there was an element of awe in his voice, which was precisely what bothered some of his Catholic colleagues. As a Catholic priest in Batticaloa put it: 'The Methodist Church has completely fallen into the grip of evangelical churches. They have become like a Pentecostal church.' And indeed, some of the Methodist priests that we interviewed in the east admitted they were adapting their services to avoid losing more 'flock'. There was more 'singing, clapping, shouting, praising', a pastor from Akkaraipattu said. 'I don't like it, but the people do.'

The post-war expansion of new Christian churches in the north and east of the country is an important enough development to deserve much fuller investigation than we can give here. In the Sinhala areas of the south, Buddhist attacks on so-called 'unethical' conversion have continued through the later years of the war and after (Mahadev 2013). New – or allegedly new – churches (and mosques) in some cases have been physically attacked by crowds accompanied by Buddhist monks. There is little sign of such overt hostility to the new churches in the north and east, which is an indication in itself of persistent differences in the space for public action between predominantly Tamil and Muslim areas and predominantly Sinhala areas. Although there is still little sign of figures from the new churches taking on the kinds of public leadership role we discussed in the previous chapter, there are signs that the more ambitious churches are beginning to move into more or less developmental activity in areas like housing and, in some cases, income generation.

Moral Disturbance

In 2011, Kattankudy briefly became the object of a story in the international news media. On 28 June, the BBC reported an attack on two young women in the town, who were accused by a group of young men of visiting an internet café in order to watch pornography. A day later, it was reported that local mosques had been forced to broadcast an apology to the girls following legal intervention by their parents.[1] Kattankudy is, as we have explained, an ethnic enclave par excellence, while internet cafes have become a convenient symbol for the moral danger created by the end of the war and the consequent opening up of the enclave.

Mutur is a similar enclave. Surrounded by LTTE-controlled jungle on one side, and the sea on the other, in the war years the only route in and out of town was either by a highly unreliable ferry to Trincomalee, or a long and circuitous road through the forest that was inaccessible after dark and during most of the monsoon period. Few outsiders would visit Mutur, and internet access and mobile phone coverage were patchy at best. That is not to say, of course, that the Tamil and Muslim communities – that inhabited different parts of the town – were completely cut off. Many Tamil families had relatives in the diaspora and not a few Muslims went to the Middle East to work from the late 1970s onwards.

The following transcript of an interview with a senior citizen illustrates a local sense of moral stability in the face of political collapse:

> For us the main thing is Islam. Police and army and all may be there, but what really guides us is the Quran. Our ladies wear black dresses that cover their face. That way, we can't see whether she's ugly or not. Then, there is never a misunderstanding. Also, a thief can't see whether she's wearing jewellery. Men also have this desire for sex. If a lady goes alone and she's half dressed, showing part of her body, men are attracted and sex is coming. Then rape may happen, that could happen to me. That's why Muhammad gave us guidance.

Our Muslim interlocutor in fact had an unshakable belief in the durability of Muslim community values, despite his awareness of post-war changes in the town:

> Change may happen, but our religion will not change. It is always under Muhammad. The community will not accept change. If I drink, the people will not respect me. If I take interest on a loan, the people will not respect me. We have to do everything in an Islamic way. When I come home, I have to say *salaam*. After all, the woman may be sleeping and her clothing might be open or something. And in the family we all eat from one plate. The boy tells the father, 'You take first,' and vice versa.

Not everybody shared this man's confidence in the resilience of the community's traditions, piety and chasteness, however. New people were coming to Mutur, the town's inhabitants could move around, and more and more people have mobile phones. 'Young people are taking alcohol,' one of Mutur's respected Muslim government officers observed. 'They are even smoking. Because they are connected to the other areas. People are worried about this, but we can't control that.' There were unexpected new influences also. China Harbour, a Chinese construction company, was contracted to construct the main road passing Mutur. The Chinese staff who now frequented the town left distinct traces: 'Fried chicken used to be a rare dish, now we can get it anytime. The disadvantage is the effect on our culture. Like the Chinese, most people start drinking, smoking and so on.'

When the LTTE was there, people could not just go to the next town:

People were with their families. So children were under close control of their father. Now, the youngsters are free to go. People are thinking to work individually, the social organisation can't be controlled so easily.

The LTTE used to control Tamil society, in particular. For example, they effectively forbade alcohol consumption:

Nobody could drink. Nowadays, they don't control the Tamil community. Everybody does their own hobbies. Now, people from here go to the Tamil places to do these things. How can we control the good way if people have the intent to do these things? I can't control my son not to use the internet. I teach him to use it for his future. But when he goes out, I don't know what kind of internet he's using. What kind of pages he is watching. In Tamil we say, we can't see the other side of the wall. We are thinking, maybe that is better. However, we are trying to see what is on the other side. Muslim youth may also want to see what's on the next page. Gradually, it will increase. The sale of alcohol is high. The selling of cigarettes is high. People's use of public places, also very high. They think, after freedom, we need entertainment. They go here and there for picnics. That affects all kinds of cultural and religious things.

These signs of post-war moral disturbance were not only heard among Muslims. We were told very similar stories by Sinhala and Tamils. The general sense of a traditional society of chaste and dignified people being engulfed in a world of impure influences could be found across all ethnic and religious groups. The opening up of the region after years of wartime closure has, it seems, created a common predicament.

There were positive sides to the changes, of course: increased mobility, the ability to travel at night, visits to unfamiliar places, access to higher-quality education in schools that were further away, stable phone networks, and cable television. There was a regained sense of freedom, we were told in a conversation with a Sinhala school principal and a Buddhist monk at one of the small temples near Mullipotana (near Trincomalee). 'After the war, we are blossoming,' said the former.

> Yes [confirmed the monk], the people are enjoying. The young ones in particular. [The problem was, though], they are also enjoying liquor. We are trying to stop that. Illicit liquor in particular. The open market also brings drugs and internet and mobile phones. Unnecessary things come. We are closer to the world. So those things are also closer to us. That is a challenge. People used to read books, now they sit in front of the television. The new technology is a challenge.

Most of these concerns, of course, sound awfully familiar – to anyone, frankly, who has ever been young and subject to parental scrutiny. Clearly one does not need to travel to erstwhile war zones to hear people lamenting the decay of traditional values, the vices of youth, the corruption of sexual morality, and the steady erosion of piety. What is interesting in this particular context, though, is that we might expect people to have more pressing concerns when they are picking up the pieces of their battered lives after nearly three decades of war. But looseness and movement have long been central antagonists of purification and place-making, with movement viewed as a threat to purity and – by the same token – migration a source of moral disorder (Gamburd 2000; Spencer 2003).

Demons and Disorientation

The pervasive sense of moral vulnerability in the east crystallised unexpectedly in a few months in 2011. In July, police arrested two men after a series of murders of elderly women in Ratnapura District in the south. The murders, it was rumoured, were the work of a 'grease devil' (*grease yaka* in Sinhala). The grease devil is a long-established presence in the island's folklore: a thief who strips to his underwear and covers himself with grease in order to evade capture.[2] In some versions, the grease devil steals women's underwear and physically attacks unprotected women. By the middle of August, rumours of grease devil sightings were sweeping the island, and reports of injuries and deaths in vigilante attacks started to accumulate. Initially, sightings were confined to the southern and central parts of the island, then, after the killing of two strangers on an Up Country tea estate near Haputale on 11 August, the rumours spread to the east.

As rumours spread up and down the east coast, angry protesters targeted the security forces, either for failing to protect the women of the community or, for many, because it was believed the grease devils were members of the police, army or navy, or at the very least were operating with their active collusion. In the earlier attacks in Sinhala areas, a slightly different interpretation prevailed – not active members of the security forces, but roaming deserters, unattached and dangerous men, were believed to be responsible. Many argued that the government was responsible; government spokesmen in turn sought to blame leftist critics, anti-national forces and the pro-LTTE Tamil diaspora. As they did so, relations between the security forces – still present in massive numbers in the Tamil areas of the north and east – and local communities became increasingly fraught. Two police officers were attacked and chased in Sammanthurai, then the naval base close to Kinniya, near Trincomalee, was surrounded by an angry crowd. The sightings moved to the Tamil heartland of the Jaffna peninsula, where again the security forces were accused of complicity. Then on 21 August, the most serious incident yet saw the killing of a police officer by angry crowds in Puttalam on the north-west coast. Press conferences were called. The powerful Secretary to the Ministry of Defence, the President's brother Gotabaya Rajapaksa, summoned the mosque federation leaders of the north and east to a meeting. He told them: 'Allegations being levelled against the government and security forces were baseless and the harassment of Muslims in the Eastern Province and Puttalam, was the work of certain bad elements living in the respective areas, who wanted to create chaos and stall the development process.'[3]

And then? And then – nothing. The rumours and attacks petered out just as mysteriously as they had first appeared. By the end of 2011, the excitement had been almost forgotten.

One striking feature of the grease devil panic was the proliferation of public interpretation. Whether it was the government, the opposition, the army, the navy, deserters, anti-national elements, everyone seemed to agree that someone had to be responsible for what was happening. The status of the grease devils themselves was the subject of much confusion – were they men disguised as devils, figments of people's fevered imaginings, or 'real' devils, accepted members of the popular cosmology of gods, ghosts and demons widely believed to be ever interfering in people's lives? Despite the surface confusion, there were at least three surprisingly consistent strands in the grease devil talk. One was the emphasis on the physical and sexual vulnerability of women. A second was the way in which the grease devil seemed to give shape and substance to anxieties about the military which otherwise lacked a means of public expression: in the south the focus was on military deserters, the murky underside of the public celebrations of heroism and victory; in the north and east, the focus was on more visible manifestations of the security order, real military men in their bases and manning their checkpoints. The third, which has gone almost entirely unremarked, is the way in which rumours effortlessly crossed religious and ethnic boundaries – in stark contrast to the circulation of rumours in times of earlier collective violence, for example, when their circulation is tightly bound to the groups whose stereotypes they most closely correspond to (Spencer 2000).

The fact that the grease devil panic occurred at a time of drastic political change, raises some interesting questions. After all, the conjunction of demons and supernaturally oriented violence and fundamental political transformation is not without precedent in anthropology. Among many possible examples, we could point to James Siegel's (2006) fascinating work on the sudden spree of witch hunts in East Java, which occurred alongside Suharto's downfall in 1998. While this part of Indonesia has a historic reputation for witchcraft and sorcery, these cases were different, mainly because of the numbers involved (Siegel counted 120 witch hunts with many people killed in three months in one area), but also because the witchcraft allegations seemed to escape the level of individual malevolence and brought into play forces that were beyond the traditional world of Javanese spirits (Siegel 2006: 131). The occurrence of these violent outbursts at the moment of abrupt collapse of a dictatorship that had firmly ruled the country for over three decades was clearly not coincidental.

In the east (but not in the south of the island) irrespective of the occult and magical elements that were often woven in, accounts of the grease *yaka* would invariably point to the government, more specifically the military, as the orchestrator of disturbance. Increasingly, incidents were reported of the grease man running away to an army camp to hide. In other cases, the culprit was said to have been caught with an army identity tag around their neck, and there were versions of the story where the police or armed forces would make sure the offender was either not caught or released after capture.

A Muslim government servant told us about the Kinniya incident:

There was an incident at the navy camp near our town. They saw a group of young girls, shouting. They had seen someone come into their yard. The people tried to catch him. He ran. They followed. He entered the navy camp. People demanded the man was handed over to them. The navy denied there was anyone. There was a small crisis. The navy opened fire and three were injured, two of which were admitted to the Kandy hospital and are still in critical condition. That night, there was a lot of tension. Afterwards, the army established checkpoints everywhere.

This was considered quite ironic, and it fuelled suspicions of ulterior government motives. After all, Kinniya – an almost exclusively Muslim town – had not had many checkpoints during the war, but following the grease *yaka*, the army was on the streets and the whole town was under surveillance. 'Ya, the grease man … is it rumour or fact?' a local politician from Kinniya asked himself during an interview. Either way, he went on, 'It is good timing for the government … Maybe it has to do with the lifting of the emergency laws.' This was in fact a quite common explanation among suspicious political commentators. The government was under international pressure to end emergency rule and this might deprive the security establishment of a whole range of privileges and powers. The military could be thought to have an interest in subtle forms of unrest.

But if people believed that the military was behind the whole thing, was the grease *yaka* even a demon? 'No, he's not a demon,' an old Tamil man in a newly built relocation village told us, as if we had made a silly suggestion. 'He's a man!' 'In fact', he went on, 'He's a party man!' A government operative in other words. His neighbour told us an anecdote that illustrated just how closely related the grease devil and the military were in people's minds. 'One day', he said, 'we saw a man coming from the sky. We thought the grease man was going to land here with a parachute. But it was the air force … It was a training, but we were scared, because we thought it was the grease man.'

After the War

In this chapter, we have expanded our argument in both time and space. Many of the examples come from Klem's fieldwork in and around Trincomalee in 2010 and 2011 (Klem 2014a, 2014b), two years after the final victory over the LTTE in May 2009. Our subtitle for this book is 'A Collaborative Ethnography of War and Peace', and this chapter provides an opportunity to restate our general scepticism about the existence of two straightforward conditions, 'war' and 'peace'. We began our research in a period characterised by some as one of 'war and no-war', a period of official truce, but a period characterised by persistent violent episodes from all sides. The official chronology reinforces our sense of incoherence: 'victory' was declared in the east in 2007, but 'war' only officially restarted with the formal abrogation of the 2002 ceasefire the following year in 2008. Overall victory over the LTTE in May 2009 was much more unambiguous, in the sense that the organisation seems to have been entirely destroyed in Sri Lanka itself, and there has been not the slightest evidence of renewed operations in its name in the years since. But many of those in the north and the east, living with a heavy military presence and a sense of constant surveillance, would contest any casual use of the word 'peace' to describe their post-2009 condition.

The government has focused its attention on infrastructure development in the years since the end of the war. Travel to Batticaloa, and along the coast to the north and south, has been transformed by new highways that were swiftly built after the fighting stopped. Checkpoints on the road to the east have also disappeared (although not on the main road to the north). A few sites like Passekudah to the north of Batticaloa, have been appropriated for intense tourist development. There seems to be a house building boom in progress in towns like Batticaloa.

Politically, though, the government has not been able to move so decisively. In the previous chapter, we described the flurry of violence around the first post-war elections in the east, those for the Eastern Provincial Council in 2008. Those elections were boycotted by the main Tamil party, the Tamil National Alliance (TNA), which allowed the TMVP, the remains of the LTTE faction, which defected to the government side under the eastern commander Karuna in 2004, to emerge as the government's key political partner in the region. But in national elections in 2010, which were contested by the main Tamil parties, the TMVP vote collapsed to less than 10 per cent, stripping the party of whatever shred of legitimacy it clung to from its success in the turbulent 2008 campaign. A similar pattern emerged in 2013 when Provincial Council elections were held for the first time ever in the north: the government alliance, heavily dependent on the Eelam People's Democratic Party (another party with roots in a paramilitary faction), took less than 20 per cent of the vote, and the TNA won a convincing victory. In both the north and the east, the Provincial Councils have had to operate under tight constraints, every action subject to possible veto by a centrally appointed Governor, with the military insisting on a final say on many initiatives.

Crucially for the story we are telling, we have yet to see a new generation of political leaders emerge in the Tamil community of the north and east. Although the LTTE no longer poses the same threat it did in the years of its dominance, politics remains a dangerous game for anyone challenging the powers that be. In this respect it is perhaps not surprising to see collective aspirations being invested so heavily in the new churches (as well as the thriving Hindu temples) of the east, institutions that remain happy to operate beneath the political radar, but which still provide some scope for collective activity and a glimmer of hope for the future.

What, though, of the widespread lamentations about imminent moral collapse? Why should the end of a war, which, at its worst moments, seeped into every aspect of life (Walker 2013), be followed by such a strong shared sense of cultural and moral insecurity? There is a simple explanation, but it does, however, require a single counter-intuitive move on the part of the reader: that we learn to see the war not primarily as a source of disorder, but instead as a source of order every bit as encompassing and durable in its way as Suharto's New Order had seemed to the people whose lives are documented in Siegel's work. Indeed, something like this was put very directly to us at a meeting in Jaffna with 'civil society' leaders in early 2012. When asked what was the biggest challenge facing Jaffna society, the talk was much less of the aftermath of the war and continuing military occupation. Instead, we were told about teenage pregnancies, rising crime levels and a general sense of imminent moral danger. Eventually a student leader explained the problem succinctly: 'Until three years ago [i.e. until the defeat of the LTTE] there was at least a proper source of order and discipline in this society.'

8

Reflections

In this final chapter we return to some of the issues we raised at the start of this book. We begin with the theoretical and methodological challenge of a plural religious field. We then return to the theme of public action, and specifically to the question of something that might be described as distinctively 'religious' public action. Finally, we return to the question of religion and politics, arguing that there is a need to devote more attention, theoretically and empirically, to the problem of the political, rather than simply problematising the concept of religion and the religious. We start, though, with the problem of pluralism.

The project on which this book is based was born, in part, of a sense of mild dissatisfaction with academic writing on Sri Lanka. As the war gained its slow momentum in the late 1980s and early 1990s, one discipline – anthropology – took the lead in early analyses of the crisis (Uyangoda 1997: 8–9). But the great strength of classic anthropological fieldwork is its close focus on very specific local detail; understanding the war, as it developed and matured, would seem to demand a very different scale. To take an obvious example, Trawick's book on the LTTE in Batticaloa, is so trapped by its own close focus, that it completely fails to grasp any bigger picture, even in the immediate area of the study (Trawick 2007; cf. Das 2008; De Alwis 2014). The richest and most nuanced anthropological work on the war in Sri Lanka has been written, perhaps not surprisingly, by Sri Lankan anthropologists. Both Valentine Daniel's *Charred Lullabies* (1996) and Sharika Thiranagama's *In my Mother's House* (2011) engage with the dispersed effects of the war by building a composite narrative out of very disparate materials – an interview with a torture survivor, the story of a Muslim family forced to flee Jaffna by the LTTE in 1990, and so on. The individual components of their carefully crafted books bring a certain intensity to the narrative, while the deployment of differently located points of view, among other things, successfully undermines the otherwise inescapable teleologies of nationalist historiography. Individuality is central to the analyses in both books, because as Thiranagama herself explains, the mode of operation of movements like the LTTE forces us to think about the ways in which the war changes the very conditions of possibility for processes of individuation (Thiranagama 2011: 36–40).

Our project is not intended as a challenge to this kind of work, but more as a complement, and, as such, our focus is rather different. In this book, we have looked at alternative forms of public action that have developed, and in some cases blossomed, during the war years – alternative, that is, to the claims of the militant movements like the LTTE and mainstream Sinhala Buddhist nationalism. The question we have asked is how much, and in what ways, does 'religion' provide a point of departure, a tactical ground if you will, for these emerging forms. Individuality is part of our picture too, in so far as leadership emerged as an important part of our story. But we have tried to think about leadership in terms of the conditions of possibility that have enabled some kinds of people to emerge as public figures in circumstances of extreme danger, and, as often as not, those conditions of possibility seem to be institutional. This is most obviously evident in the changing role of the Catholic priesthood during the course of the war. But, as we explained at the start of our book, some of the institutional preconditions that made Catholic priests so prominent in a place like Batticaloa – the protection afforded by a strong transnational institutional structure and the model offered by post-Vatican II visions of a more socially engaged priesthood – had rendered otherwise similar priests increasingly marginal in the south of the island (Stirrat 1992). In other words, the factors we have discussed are conditions, not determinants. What actually happened in particular places at particular times is not reducible to a simple causal story about religion in general, or about specific religious traditions in particular.

Somehow we needed to find a way of working that would hold fast to the immediacy of the best ethnographic reporting, while also allowing us to take tentative steps towards the construction of a bigger and more systemic picture. Of course, not all big pictures are equal, and big pictures constructed from the comfortable distance of Colombo (or often even further) are less valuable than bigger pictures built, as it were, from the ground up. Or so we think. In this closing set of reflections, we will try to assess the gains, and in some cases, losses that resulted from the decision to research and write a collaborative ethnography.

One point of departure might be the issues of space and scale. As Chapters 4, 5 and to some extent 6, illustrate, in our analysis space becomes at once a token for religious identification – and thus a potential source of tension (e.g. Buddhist sacred sites such as Dighavapi) – and a zone of possibility for protective public action (the compound of the church or temple). At the same time, the spatial qualities of the east, which is not made of separate territorial blocks, but is rather a jigsaw of different religious sites and spaces, side by side and folding into each other, makes conflict an everyday experience, even as it makes cooperation a necessity to make civic life possible.

Veena Das (2013) suggests four scales in which we can ask questions about religious pluralism: theological reflection, statecraft, circulation and mediation between communities, and intimacy and subject formation. Our book concentrates on the second and third of these. We have shown that religious actors have filled spaces in political mechanisms that the conflict has created – mosque federations, Catholic priests, IROP. Religious actors have also fostered an 'intensification of politics', in the sense of deepening the friend–enemy boundary between friend and enemy, us and them, in more sustained ways. In Dighavapi, for example, religious actors sometimes bridge communities, as with the early Buddhist monks who settled there, and sometimes drive them apart, as in the case of Soma and his successors, while politicians under certain circumstances can also build links between communities, as Ashraff tried to do with his support for the Dighavapi temple. We have certainly worked on circulation and mediation between and within religious communities, within a single community in the Kattankudy case, between Muslim and Buddhist communities in Dighavapi. We have had less to say on what Das calls 'theological puzzles', although we have sketched in some of the specifically religious background to public action among both Catholics and Muslims. And if our fieldwork strategy was most successful in uncovering issues of statecraft and mediation, it was necessarily much less illuminating on issues of intimacy and subject formation. For these, we have to defer to other ethnographers and their compelling accounts (Lawrence 1997; Thiranagama 2011; Walker 2013).

A Single Religious Field?

Can eastern Sri Lanka be coherently thought of as constituting a single religious field? This was our premise at the start of the book and the time has come to take a reckoning of what might be gained, and what might be lost, as a result. First, though, a very obvious caveat. Our use of the idea of a field is heuristic and no more. It allows us to scale up above the level of the village study, without collapsing into the obvious alternative, which is to treat the nation-state as the object of study. There are, in fact, some quite good grounds for thinking of the east as a unity: we believe that there is potentially a single story to be told about the ways people have made a living in this landscape of paddy fields and coastal settlements. The ecology and political economy reviewed in Chapter 3 do constitute an important source of shared history and economic interdependence, a centripetal counter-force to the centrifugal forces of mass politics and their divisions along ethnic and religious lines. People have moved in to the area, for example on government settlement projects in the 1950s, and products – surplus rice to feed the north and the workers on the central tea estates – have long been exported. In political-economic terms, a coherent tale can be told.

So too with the idea of a religious field. A very high proportion of the institutional apparatus of the religious traditions we encountered – the Catholic hierarchy, the Buddhist *sangha* – has obvious roots outside Sri Lanka, let alone outside eastern Sri Lanka. Many of the new religious phenomena are more or less global in their scope: Pentecostal churches have grown rapidly in Latin America and Africa; Islamic reform currents are as ubiquitous in Southeast Asia and Africa as they are across South Asia. A purely local explanation of their trajectories of change in some quite specific setting is in clear danger of missing the global point. So our religious field is not in any sense a bounded, discrete entity – rather it is something dynamic and rapidly changing, in which the movement of people, practices and ideas, both in and out of the particular geographic setting, is an especially important part of what we have to study. Movement generates disturbance, and this in turn invites attempts to manage, contain or deflect its effects. This can be seen most obviously in the work that goes into making and maintaining boundaries, work which has been one of the most persistent themes in our analysis.

If we begin with the idea of the boundary, we can start with something so simple and obvious that it almost goes unremarked, but something that provides an early vindication of our commitment to the idea of a single field. This is the tacit agreement to respect existing boundaries and to refrain from overly public attempts to convert members of one religious community into another. What, of course, made this otherwise hidden norm explicit was the disturbance occasioned by the arrival of the new Pentecostal churches. Unlike the Catholic Church, or indeed Muslim reform groups like Tablighi Jamaat, for the new churches proselytisation and conversion are axiomatic activities, completely fundamental to their entire religious project. The effect of their arrival has been to generate a surprisingly unanimous disdain among religious leaders from all the other traditions in the area. Of course, we have not attempted any sustained empirical test of the claim that no one attempted conversion in the past, and clearly the claim has to be of quite recent provenance, but even a shared *pretence* of non-conversion is worthy of note.

Our second point is almost as obvious, but still needs restating: institutions matter. Catholicism is pre-structured to produce leaders. Immediate circumstances – the LTTE's closing off of alternative spaces for more overtly political leadership – gave Catholic priests the opportunity to take on the mantle of social engagement many of them had been trained for in the post-Vatican II Church. Not all Catholic priests responded to these circumstances in the same way: some tried to keep out of dangerous public engagements, and some identified themselves more wholeheartedly with the militants of the LTTE. Buddhist monks in the border villages often assumed a more service-oriented role than their counterparts elsewhere in the island, but here the causality is more complex, as it is often the attractions of such a role that brought the monks to these out-of-the-way villages in the first place. The Muslim community had institutions in the form of mosques, and they had would-be leaders of various sorts, but the old mosque leadership had lost authority in the 1960s and 1970s, and the new circumstances of the war prompted them to create new institutional structures to provide vehicles for their leaders: a new political party, the SLMC, and the new mosque federations.

The most visible and enduring – by their own reckoning at least – religious institutions in the east are the big Hindu *kovils*. Although reports of their seemingly paradoxical flourishing at the peak of the war (Whitaker 1999) helped us frame our research from the start, it was not long before we noticed their relative invisibility in a lot of our fieldwork. The reason was partly empirical and partly methodological. Our research focused on public religion, in the sense of religious engagement in civil life broadly understood, and our fieldwork often started with the most visible and engaged religious leaders. Few of those we encountered were based in the big *kovils*, a point sometimes commented on by members of other religious communities. The Kattankudy Mosque Federation members, for example, lamented the difficulties they experienced finding appropriate interlocutors in neighbouring Hindu villages, while Catholic priests often became de facto representatives for Hindu and Catholic Tamils alike. Important religious *figures* emerged in Tamil society in the war years – figures like Lawrence's friend Saktirani (Chapter 2) – but these were often women, and much of their efficacy as healers and seers depended on their ability to operate, in Timmo Gaasbeek's phrase, 'below the radar'

(Gaasbeek 2013). Again, with our focus on visible public engagement, figures like Saktirani often passed below our radar too.

Why were there so few Hindu leaders involved with organisations like IROP (Chapter 6)? One answer might be institutional – the key political figures in and around the *kovils* are not the priests, but the chief trustees. But we know that political leaders can use temples as their personal political vehicles at other times and in other places, not least in the Sri Lankan Tamil diaspora (Maunaguru and Spencer 2012). Class and education might explain some of the relative pre-eminence of Catholic priests as local leaders, at least compared to Hindu priests themselves. But the trustees of the big *kovils*, who in other contexts routinely use the temples as political platforms (Mines and Gourishankar 1990: 763), usually come from exactly the same elite sections of local society as the Catholic priesthood. This leaves the other, painfully obvious, explanation: the physical threat from all sides – army, LTTE, other paramilitary groups – experienced by anyone who put themselves forward as a leader in the Tamil community. In this case, then, and in contrast to the situation of some of the Catholic priesthood, grim political reality trumped the possibilities offered by other local religious institutions. Those institutions, the *kovils*, flourished through it all, but in a curiously involuted way, their backs half turned on local politics.

The example of the *kovils*, and of charismatic healers like Saktirani, can help us think our way into a more systematic mapping of the religious field. To be a little more precise, it can help us start to map the religious field of the east, as it has emerged and unfolded in the course of the war. A similar exercise in, say, the 1970s, before the war took off, would have been perfectly feasible, but it is unlikely that it would have highlighted exactly the same dimensions of similarity and difference. We suggest that the religious field, as we encountered it, can be imagined as operating in terms of two contrasting styles of religiosity and religious leadership, one founded in hierarchy, the other in healing. The first, exemplified by Catholic priests, *bhikkhu*s, and mosque federation leaders, is based in strong institutional structures and provides a ground for visible, and sometimes very effective, public action. The other, exemplified by ecstatic healers like Saktirani and many of the new Pentecostal churches, and also by new kinds of Sufi leader like Payilvan, is much less dependent on institutional structure – what structure there is, whether it be a new shrine to a deity, a new church, or a breakaway from an existing church, tends to be built around an individual figure who has established themselves as possessed of special gifts which can help those dealing with the trauma of war. We are likely to encounter women as much as men in this second category, but, as we have seen throughout this book, we are far less likely to find people from this background coming forward as mediators in flashpoint situations, or as formal members of citizen's committees and inter-religious groups. The new churches and the ecstatic healers from other traditions address the most experientially immediate consequences of war, but they do this through the register of the body and healing, rather than through more conventional public engagement.

When we turn to the issue of boundaries, and the idea of a religious community, the contrast becomes more interesting. Where leaders from our strong institutional pole can self-consciously 'cross' the boundaries between one group and another, our less institutional healers and ecstatics often seem simply indifferent to the same boundaries. Healing shrines attract supplicants from all communities, and new churches, in principle at least, convert from all communities. The mosque federations, though, are accused by others (like Payilvan's followers) of policing the boundaries of the community and encouraging the violent expulsion of those who would transgress its internal rules of purity. Catholic priests, it goes without saying, are quite familiar with the need to police the boundaries of their flock. In other words, seen through the lens of boundary-work, we have a contrast between the actually existing pluralism of demotic religious practice, often focused on healing and solace, and a rather different pluralism, in which certain leaders can mediate between separate and bounded religious or ethnic communities, but only because their very position is predicated on the idea of a world of discrete and tightly bounded religious communities in the first place.

In this contrast between everyday pluralism, usually lived below the radar, and self-conscious public pluralism, predicated on a landscape of precise divisions between groups, we may also find one of the many reasons why it is hard to imagine a scaling up of the sort of interventions we explored in this research. To fully understand the limits of religious interventions, we need to think through two other issues: one is the issue of public action, and specifically whether or not we can posit something describable as specifically religious public action. The other is the issue of politics and the political.

Non-Governmental Public Action

Is there anything to be gained by trying to bring together the different phenomena we have discussed under a single rubric? Before we discuss the coherence of the 'religious' as a binding theme, it might help to return to the term under which we started – non-governmental public action – and ask what it might do to clarify the distinctive features we encountered. We may start with the idea of the 'non-governmental', as we found it in eastern Sri Lanka, before asking what 'public' might connote in that setting.

Before rehearsing the history of the idea of the non-governmental in Sri Lanka, it may be wise briefly to consider its antonym, the governmental. When INGOs poured into the country after the 2004 tsunami, veteran disaster workers were often slow to realise that, in most important respects, Sri Lanka did not correspond to the standard expectations of a 'failed state'. Behind the narrow strip of devastation along the coastline, post offices, schools and hospitals functioned well enough, as they had done through the war years. Civil servants carried on with the everyday workings of a postcolonial bureaucracy, even in areas under the control of the LTTE (Klem 2012). What was at stake in many areas was not so much an absence of the institutional structures of the state, but an excess of such structures, especially in those periods, such as the late 1990s and the post-ceasefire years, when the LTTE was keenest to exhibit its own state-like capacities to the world. What differentiated and separated different spaces was not governmentality as such, but violence. Violence was the currency in which claims to sovereignty were made and contested, and the quantity and style of violence varied with the degree of contestation in any particular place at any particular time. For ordinary people negotiating their way through these times, typical dilemmas might be, for example, whether everyday disputes should be taken to the police or to the LTTE, or in Muslim areas, to the mosque federation? Each of these could be seen as attempting to constitute its own sovereignty through its deployment of violence in a particular territory (see Hansen 2005).

Conventional non-governmental activity was above all shaped and conditioned by the pattern of violence, and here we need to acknowledge the specificity of the circumstances of our fieldwork. Writing in the late 1990s, Goodhand and Lewer (1999) mapped the effects of the war on the organisational landscape in a range of villages in the east. Not surprisingly, they found a correlation between relative stability – which might often mean a stable pattern of LTTE control – and the relative health of local organisations. External NGOs were active in the region, but were already the object of criticism, for their failure to attend to local concerns and for their lack of coordination. Despite this, they also noted the opportunities NGO work offered for ambitious people who might otherwise – otherwise than the war and the dangers it posed – have been drawn into political careers in the area. The period after the 2002 ceasefire saw a marked increase in NGO activity, fuelled by donor support for peace-building projects in particular. In some cases, the 2004 tsunami response built on organisational capacity that had grown in response to the ceasefire. In other cases, incoming INGOs, hungry for functioning local partners, diverted, or even undermined, the work of small local organisations (Hasbullah and Korf 2009). Some sense of the cumulative impact of this activity can be gleaned from an incident in 2006, when rumours swept the towns of the east about the distribution of pornographic DVDs, made by INGO staff with the participation of local young women (Gaasbeek 2010b: 140). It remains unclear if there was ever any basis for these stories, but, as ever with rumour, the speed with which they circulated demonstrated only too clearly an emerging consensus that external NGOs might be best understood as morally threatening outsiders.

Of course, in many cases, local religious leaders were also necessarily involved with both local and foreign NGOs, but, we were told, their capacities as leaders derived from their institutional support within a particular religious community, rather than from their NGO connections. Whatever the sources of their legitimacy as leaders, they all had to operate in an environment in which the very idea of 'the public' was at best unstable and shifting. The word 'public' conjoins two overlapping connotations: the public is a space where things are visible, and, in normative terms, where argument is open and accessible, and the public is a collection of people, the audience that sees and hears whatever happens in that space. The two senses are strongly interdependent, and it is easy to see why and how the war rendered both problematic. The idea of the public as collectivity – both subject and object of 'public action' – is an early victim of civil war, and much of our ethnography can be read as evidence of attempts to remake a public, often partial and incomplete, but always necessary for the possibility of public action.[1] Other observers' favourite metaphors speak for themselves: 'flying under the radar', 'putting one's head above the parapet'. In the conditions that we encountered in the east, conditions of war, not-war, and dangerous peace, visibility is equivalent to vulnerability, and what one says is necessarily guarded or mute. Nowhere is completely safe, but some spaces are less dangerous than others; the 'public' as conventionally understood, is inherently dangerous, so alternative spaces have to be made and that process, in turn, requires people to do the making. Think back to Lawrence's description, cited in Chapter 2, of the way that the priestess Saktirani, 'counters the landscape of danger by reconstituting her domestic space at home as a public space' (Lawrence 1997: 106). Saktirani's house, or the shrine she frequents on the edge of Batticaloa town, are instances where we can see this work of making safe (or we can see it through Lawrence's eyes). So too with the mosque federations, while other spaces of lesser danger – the big *kovils* and Catholic churches – pre-date the war and, to some extent, come ready-made for their new purpose.

Religion, Politics and Toleration

When we visited the Kattankudy Mosque Federation in 2008, one of the first things we were told was that when local politicians wanted to do anything, the first thing they would do is visit the federation for advice, guidance and approval. A couple of hours further into the same conversation, we were told that one of the secrets of the federation's enduring success was simple: it kept the politicians completely out of its affairs (cf. Spencer 2012). Of course, the situation is much more convoluted, and the way in which the space of the federation was kept clean from the dirty world of politics, while not excluding politicians completely, continues to change. In most periods, politicians were 'kept out' as politicians, but not as individuals or as representatives of NGOs. So, most influential local politicians took part in the meetings of the mosque federation, but not in their official function as politicians. Similarly, mosque federation leaders campaigned for politicians, or stood as candidates themselves (Hasbullah and Korf 2013). The line separating religion and politics is subtle and fragile, context-specific and time-specific.

In Chapter 4, we recounted our meeting with a celebrated forest monk, who had only recently taken up robes after a long career as a senior military commander. He explained lucidly why it was not the duty (*dhamma*) of the *sangha* to get involved in politics, yet in another room of the same monastery, we found photo after photo of famous politicians – including Presidents and Prime Ministers – visiting the monastery in pursuit of ostentatious demonstrations of public piety. We were also given a pamphlet outlining the history of the monastery – written by a leading member of the ultra-nationalist party, the JHU. On another occasion, we visited a Buddhist temple a few miles on the other side of Ampara. The annual ceremony to mark the end of the rainy-season retreat (*kathina pinkama*) was coming to an end and a group of monks were preparing to leave. One disengaged himself from his fellow monks and introduced himself as a representative of the *bhikkhu* Federation of the North and East, and a 'spiritual adviser' to the local security forces. He told us animatedly about his actions to thwart attempted conversions by new Christian churches. His body language was aggressive and, in our eyes, unlike the demeanour usually associated with a monk. After he left, we had a long, and radically different, conversation with the incumbent of this temple. He had worked extensively with Tamil villagers since the tsunami, and also spoke warmly of his relations with the late Muslim leader Ashraff, when he was a political force in the area. He also spoke of the big Sinhala politicians, including J.R. Jayewardene and Premadasa, with whom he had worked. His views on the ethnic issue, and on the role for Buddhists, echoed those of the earlier priest at the forest hermitage: Buddhism does not discriminate between races and ethnic groups. We are all human beings. That is the principle.

Two religious figures participating in the same event, one the archetypal potentate, patrolling the boundaries of his community with all the zeal he could muster, the other a traveller, moving back and forth across religious and ethnic borders – and across the border between religion and politics. Apparent contradictions abound. Our book is nearly done: it is time to return to the vexed relationship between religious institutions and the political. In these closing remarks, we draw on these examples and suggest that there may yet be useful life in the concept of secularisation, and that a careful deployment of the term might shed more light on our dilemmas than the blunter and more encompassing 'secularism'. We do this by way of Jose Casanova's forensic analysis of the secularisation debate in (predominantly European and American) sociology. We also draw on Michael Walzer's notion of 'regimes of toleration' (1997), rather than the more diffuse notion of 'tolerance'. Secularism and tolerance are complex words, infused with normative expectation, yet also somehow supposed to be usable in simple descriptive terms: tolerance is something we should self-evidently recognise when we encounter it. A shift from 'tolerance' to 'toleration' as the focus of concern, Walzer points out, is a shift from 'attitude' to 'practice'. So too, just possibly, with a shift from 'secularism' to 'secularisation', our attention moves from a putative condition, or a value, to a process, or possibly a further set of practices.

Walzer, in what is essentially a very American reflection on toleration and difference, argues for the need for 'a historical and contextual account of toleration and coexistence, one that examines the different forms that these have actually taken and the norms of everyday life appropriate to each' (1997: 3). So, rather schematically, in our work in eastern Sri Lanka we might minimally identify two regimes of toleration at work. Toleration 1 is best exemplified by the mediation work carried out by religious leaders to lower tensions, deflect confrontations and generally manage relations between pre-defined religious or ethnic communities during a period of extended crisis. Toleration 1 is predicated on strong institutions, and privileges those leaders with the most developed hierarchical structures. It is not for nothing that the Jesuits took on such prominent public roles during the war. Toleration 2 is the zone of quotidian religiosity, a zone in which men and women may cross community boundaries in pursuit of some kind of solace to heal the personal wounds of war. For Toleration 2, leadership is self-evidently charismatic, and hierarchies are usually shallow. The promise of healing – of whatever sort – is central to the practices of Toleration 2. But healing brings with it the possibility of conversion, and Toleration 2 is also, for some at least, a space of potential proselytisation. Toleration 1 is the toleration of formal initiatives for inter-faith dialogue, and is closely related to that kind of official multiculturalism that takes the existence of separate and clearly bounded cultures as axiomatic and necessary. In that same spirit, the toleration of proponents of Toleration 1 rarely extends to the practices of Toleration 2. Toleration 1 is characterised by a specific hostility to proselytisation, and a more general hostility to what are seen as the impure and unbounded practices of Toleration 2.

Two notes in passing. First, comparative attention to different regimes of toleration almost certainly requires an equivalent attention to different regimes of *non*-toleration. Second, at this level of abstraction, the link between secularism, or secularisation, and practices of toleration seems contingent rather than necessary.

Casanova's attempt to shift the terms of argument around the concept of secularisation were first laid out in his 1994 book *Public Religion in the Modern World*. We turned to these arguments midway through our analysis of the eastern Sri Lanka fieldwork. That turn was itself a response to a sense of mounting frustration with the intellectual equipment at hand for dealing with the problematic relationship of religion and politics. Talal Asad's (2003) critical genealogy of secularism dominates these recent arguments, at least in anthropology (Cannell 2010), and for all its stimulating properties, it seemed oddly unilluminating when confronted with the actually existing practices of religion-politics in Sri Lanka. Instead Casanova seemed more helpful.

Casanova summarises his key points at the start of a (not especially fruitful) exchange with Asad in a *festschrift* edited by two of Asad's former students:

The main point of my reformulation of the thesis of secularization was to disaggregate what usually passes for a single theory of secularization into three separate propositions, which in my view need to be treated differently: 1) secularization as a differentiation of the secular spheres from religious institutions and norms, 2) secularization as a decline of religious beliefs and practices, and 3) secularization as a marginalization of religion to a privatized sphere. (Casanova 2006: 13).

Casanova's central argument is that the second and third of these propositions are demonstrably untrue: religious decline is a peculiarly European phenomenon (rendered universal by the myopia of European social theorists); and the 'privatisation' of religious expression is much more empirically limited than theorists have claimed. This leaves us with the first proposition as the only defensible component of the secularisation thesis: the modern differentiation of the religious sphere from other spheres – politics, science, the economy. This differentiation, for Casanova, is a central requirement of modern social and political arrangements. Asad's response is that Casanova's attempted disaggregation of the different arguments about secularisation is impossible – if religious conviction can continue to operate in public argument, despite apparent attempts to differentiate a separate sphere for religion, it will produce hybrids where there should ideally be boundaries: Casanova's proposition 1 is so tightly bound to proposition 3, that it cannot survive without it (Asad 2003: 182–3). Casanova's counter to this is that his idea of differentiation is 'neither as fixed nor as rigid' (2006: 14) as Asad implies; religious actors enter the public sphere not least to 'participate in the very struggles to define and set the modern boundaries' (Casanova 1994: 6). Casanova's version of differentiation is broad enough to include arguments against the very idea of differentiation itself – which of course makes it hard to imagine any evidence which might conclusively refute it. Despite this methodological limitation, it has the very real virtue of mapping directly on to the material we have assembled in this book.

The exchange between Asad and Casanova, which has gone through two rounds over the decades, is oddly inconclusive. At times it looks as if both men entirely agree; at other times they seem to be determinedly talking past each other. But it does provide us with a much clearer sense of what we might find empirically interesting: not a condition or an ideal called 'secularism', but an on-going, often bumpy or contradictory process we might call 'secularisation'. In this version, secularisation might denote the attempt to bound and contain religion as a sphere of life separate from the economic or the political, but it could also denote the push-back, the arguments to justify the presence of religious values in political discourse, or even religious actors in political institutions, or the attempts to engender forms of economic practice – Islamic finance, ethical investment - that align with agreed religious values. If the second and third propositions – religious decline and a privatisation of religion – seem absurdly inapplicable in South Asian contexts, the first, construed as constant argument about the proper boundaries between religion and other areas of life, looks much more empirically familiar than that rather implausible object we have come to call 'secularism'.

That is why secularisation could yet be an interesting idea to reflect on in the Sri Lankan context. In contrast to India, where the possibilities and impossibilities of secularism have been warmly debated for the past three decades (Nandy 1990; Madan 1997; Needham and Sunder Rajan 2007), in Sri Lanka 'secularism' as such has been oddly unexplored in public argument. The state is heavily involved in religious matters through a separate Ministry of Buddha Sasana and Religious Affairs. The title reflects the constitutional position since 1972, when Buddhism was granted the 'foremost place' among the island's religions, and the state was enjoined to 'protect and foster' Buddhism while ensuring the religious rights of all communities (Schonthal 2012). To some extent too, the state is heavily implicated in the reproduction of clear religious boundaries – for example in the provision not merely of separate schools but also, in some parts of the east, separate health facilities for Muslims. Obviously, this aspect of state engagement is most conspicuous in those cases where religious boundaries align with the categories of official ethnicity. But, as in India, the state also has a deep history of entanglements with religious institutions through the courts and the law.

The best-documented points of tension in modern Sri Lankan history do not concern the relationship of 'religion in general' to politics and the political. They concern the relationship of very specific religious actors – members of the Buddhist *sangha* – to modern political activity. The story of this difficult relationship has been well documented, especially by Seneviratne (1999) and Abeysekera (2002), but there are two specific aspects we would draw attention to. One is the longevity of the tension: almost from the start of modern mass politics in the early 1930s, the question of participation by the *sangha* was an issue. So, in 1939, the young J.R. Jayewardene published an essay which started with what was presented as the authoritative position: 'It is said that the Buddha advised members of the Buddhist Sangha not to take part in politics. No one can say that he exhorted politicians not to study or follow his teaching' (Jayewardene 1957 [1939]: 41). And Jayewardene's political opponents, the radical *bhikkhu*s associated with the Reverend Walpola Rahula, put the case for a necessary engagement with politics in the 1946 Vidyalankara Declaration:

> We believe that politics today embraces all fields of human activity directed towards the public weal. No one will dispute that the work for the promotion of the religion is the duty of the *bhikkhu*. It is clear that the welfare of the religion depends on the welfare of the people who profess that religion ... We, therefore, declare that it is nothing but fitting for *bhikkhus* to identify themselves with activities conducive to the welfare of our people – whether these activities be labelled politics or not – as long as they do not constitute an impediment to the religious life of a *bhikkhu*. (Rahula 1974 [1946]: 132)

The second point, which has generally gone unremarked, is that the religion-politics 'problem' is not the classic liberal one – that religious certainties will corrupt the rational deliberation required in a liberal polity. It is the reverse – that the political will infect and corrupt the religious. Jayewardene welcomed an infusion of Buddhist values into political debate; it was Buddhist monks he wanted kept clear of it.

This particular problem is also presented in terms of the 'duty' of the monk, which is of course exactly how it was described to us by the forest monk we quoted earlier. Observers of an earlier generation in South Asia had already noticed the easy affinity between modern expectations of differentiation, described, for example, in terms of 'compartmentalisation' between religious commitments and economic considerations, and much older Indian ideas of differentiation – by caste, religion, region, language, and age, each of which has its own specific expectations in terms of *dharma* or duty (Singer 1972: 323). In this respect, the idea of a distinct, and vigorously delimited, ethic for Buddhist monks has deep historical roots. An historical sociology of Casanova's Secularisation 1, therefore, has to avoid the assumption that all efforts at ethical differentiation are necessarily the products of colonial or postcolonial modernity.

If differentiation as such is not a novelty in the long historical run, what then is new? The easy answer is modern mass politics. Politics – or, to be precise, the practices and rhetoric routinely identified as political – are the object of convergence between the different religious traditions in Sri Lanka, the final common dilemma. For some, like the Muslims, politics has directly followed the contours of religious community, attempting to mobilise Muslims as Muslims. But here, the recurring complaint is of division, and of the new ruptures in the community created within the corrosive world of the political. A similar complaint is heard on the Sinhala side. For Tamils, the story has been somewhat different: in claiming to be the sole voice of the Tamil people, the LTTE suppressed all alternatives, but the results were hardly harmonious and hardly peaceful. With the demise of the LTTE during the period of our fieldwork, their successors, the TMVP, also split, and also continued the cycle of purification by violent death. A folk sociology of non-toleration in Sri Lanka would start and end in one place: the political. Again and again we were told that ordinary people have no problem living alongside each other, it's only the politicians that create the divisions for their own purposes. And while this interpretation conveniently ignores the degree of enthusiastic buy-in politicians receive from their supporters, it is not entirely false either.

The version of the political that animates this interpretation also provides the ground for what we might call tactical secularisation: the self-conscious invocation of religious boundaries as a kind of protection against the corrosive effects of the political. This is what is happening when the mosque federation leaders assert that their organisation works because it keeps politicians out, or when the Buddhist monk tells us it is not his duty to engage in public politics. In both these cases it is quite easy to show that the boundary being defended is rather more rhetorical than actual. Politicians queue up to patronise the monk's temple, mosque federation leaders are also active in local politics. If the idea of a boundary can be productive, even at the level of rhetoric, in other cases, like the Hindu temples during the war, the boundary seems to have been rather more tangible. It allowed the middle-class men of Whitaker's Mandur to pursue their interminable arguments about honour and precedence (1999), ignoring the war raging around them, but it also provided a space for Saktirani and her followers to gather together and speak about the otherwise unspeakable.

Of course, an insistence on the need to separate religion from the political cuts both ways. Bracketing off everything that is bad and divisive and calling it politics is in the end a strategy of self-containment. This is why it is hard to imagine scaling up the mediating work of religious leaders to address the political causes of the war. If our examples suggest there could be merit in trying to keep the vices of the political out of the space of religion, they also reveal a disturbing lack of virtue in the practice of politics. In that bleak vision of a politics without virtue, religious or otherwise, lies the longer tragedy. In the stories we heard of the men and women who not merely endured the long years of war, but used whatever means they could find to make those years more endurable for the people around them, we can yet see the glimmer of hope.

Notes

Chapter 1

1. By the time of our research, the JVP had long since been identified as a hard-line Sinhala nationalist party first and foremost, although since 2009 it has retreated from this position to occupy a more straightforwardly oppositional position on the left of the (increasingly nationalistic) government (Venugopal 2010).

Chapter 4

1. This rock inscription is said to have been discovered in the Dighavapi site by the Reverend Bandigode Nigrodha Buddharakkita, also from the Bibile temple, sometime in the 1840s. A copy of the *sannasa* is available with the Government Agent of Ampara, but the original inscription has reportedly been displaced since then.
2. The story of Muslim villagers removing bricks from the Dighavapi site appears to be a more recent construction rather than an actual event the Reverend Rewatha witnessed when he first came.
3. It must be noted that Ashraff also supported a number of temple expansion projects in Buddhist temples in Ampara town.
4. Digamadulla is a Sinhala name for Ampara District.
5. All quotations are taken from the Supreme Court judgment SC FR 178/08, 1 June 2009. We are grateful to Benjamin Schonthal for providing us with a copy of this document.
6. 'Sri Lanka Buddhist monks destroy Muslim shrine'. BBC News South Asia, 15 September 2011. http://www.bbc.co.uk/news/world-south-asia-14926002, accessed 12 November 2012.

Chapter 6

1. D.B.S. Jeyaraj, 'The benign parliamentarian from Batticaloa', http://transcurrents.com/tamiliana/page/4?s=pararajasingham, accessed 29 July 2013.
2. Ruki, 'Madhu Shrine: the struggle to preserve the sanctity of a sacred shrine and humanitarian space', *Groundviews* 7 April 2008, http://groundviews.org/2008/04/07/madhu-shrine-the-struggle-to-preserve-the-sanctity-of-a-sacred-shrine-and-humanitarian-space/?doing_wp_cron=1375114859.586013 0786895751953125, accessed 29 July 2013.

3. Writing about Catholic networks in the south, Stirrat (1992: 19) notes that: 'The success of Catholics in obtaining powerful and prestigious jobs was not just a matter of their education: it was also a matter of the close-knit networks of contacts which developed within the small community. Catholics were expected to help each other.'

4. There is some evidence that Tamil civil servants also retained more status and authority during the years of LTTE dominance than their equivalents in Sinhala areas, who found their powers eclipsed by local politicians (Klem 2012).

5. Though working on the frontline was still risky. A priest working for EHED for example was arrested and accused of being an LTTE supporter when he went to Colombo for a workshop.

6. At least one priest wanted in connection with militant activities was successfully 'transferred' to the Philippines in the early days of the conflict, returning some years later when the authorities had lost interest in his case.

7. This parallels in many respects the attempt by the People's Alliance (PA) government in 1996 to mobilise donor support for a Jaffna rehabilitation programme following the military takeover of the peninsula.

Chapter 7

1. 'Sri Lankan police investigate attack on Muslim girls', BBC South Asia, 28 June 2011, http://www.bbc.co.uk/news/world-south-asia-13948979, accessed 2 August 2013; 'Sri Lanka mosques exonerate pornography girls', BBC South Asia, 29 June 2011, http://www.bbc.co.uk/news/world-south-asia-13959901, accessed 2 August 2013.

2. There is a fine description of the process in Michael Ondaatje's *Cat's Table*, a novel first published in August 2011. The figure of the grease devil also appears in popular culture in other parts of Southeast Asia (e.g. Malaysia).

3. *Island*, 24 August 2011, http://www.island.lk/index.php?page_cat=article-details&page=article-details&code_title=33125, accessed 12 February 2014.

Chapter 8

1. In some sense, mobilisation and participation in the war is self-evidently also a form of public action, but the sense of 'public' at work in these cases is drastically attenuated.

Bibliography

Abeysekara, A. (2002) *Colors of the robe: religion, identity, and difference.* Columbia, SC: University of South Carolina Press.

Ahmad, M. (1991) Islamic fundamentalism in South Asia: the Jamaat-i-Islami and the Tablighi Jamaat of South Asia. In: M. Marty and R.S. Appleby (eds) *Fundamentalisms observed.* Chicago: University of Chicago Press, pp. 457–530.

Asad, T. (1986) *The idea of an anthropology of Islam.* Occasional paper series. Washington, DC: Center for Contemporary Arab Studies, Georgetown University.

Asad, T. (1993) *Genealogies of religion: discipline and reasons of power in Christianity and Islam.* Baltimore, MD: Johns Hopkins University Press.

Asad, T. (2003) *Formations of the secular: Christianity, Islam, modernity.* Palo Alto, CA: Stanford University Press.

Baumann, G. (1996) *Contesting culture: discourses of identity in multi-ethnic London.* Cambridge: Cambridge University Press.

Bavinck, B. (2011) *Of Tamils and Tigers: a journey through Sri Lanka's war years.* Colombo: Vijitha Yapa Press.

Bayat, A. (2007) *Making Islam democratic: social movements and the post-Islamist turn.* Palo Alto, CA: Stanford University Press.

Berkwitz, S. (2008) Resisting the global in Buddhist nationalism: Venerable Soma's discourse of decline and reform. *Journal of Asian Studies,* 67(1): 73–106.

Bohle, H.G. (2007) Geographies of violence and vulnerability: an actor-oriented analysis of the civil war in Sri Lanka. *Erdkunde,* 61(2): 129–46.

Bohle, H.G. and H. Fünfgeld (2007) The political ecology of violence: contested entitlements and politicised livelihoods in eastern Sri Lanka. *Development and Change,* 38(4): 665–87.

Brass, P. (1997) *Theft of an idol: text and context in the representation of collective violence.* Princeton, NJ: Princeton University Press.

Brohier, R. (1935) *Ancient irrigation works in Ceylon: Part 3 – Western, southern and the eastern areas of the island.* Colombo: Ceylon Government Press.

Brubaker, R. (1994) *Nationalism reframed: nationhood and the national question in the new Europe.* Cambridge: Cambridge University Press.

Brubaker, R. (2004) In the name of the nation: reflections on nationalism and patriotism. *Citizenship Studies,* 8(2): 115–27.

Canagaratnam, S. (1921) *Monograph of the Batticaloa District of the Eastern Province, Ceylon.* Colombo: Government Printer.

Cannell, F. (ed.) (2006) *The anthropology of Christianity.* Durham, NC: Duke University Press.

Cannell, F. (2010) The anthropology of secularism. *Annual Review of Anthropology,* 39: 85–100.

Casanova, J. (1994) *Public religions in the modern world.* Chicago: University of Chicago Press.

Casanova, J. (2006) Secularization revisited: a reply to Talal Asad. In: D. Scott and C. Hirschkind (eds) *Powers of the secular modern: Talal Asad and his interlocutors.* Stanford, CA: Stanford University Press.

Centre for Policy Alternatives (2012) *Brief note: legal framework governing places of religious worship in Sri Lanka.* Colombo: Centre for Policy Alternatives.

Clarke, G. (2006) Faith matters: faith-based organisations, civil society and international development. *Journal of International Development,* 18(6): 835–48.

Curtis, J. and J. Spencer (2012) Anthropology and the political. In: R. Fardon et al. (eds) *The Sage handbook of social anthropology,* vol. 1. London: Sage, pp. 168–82.

Daily News (2008) Editorial – A commendable decision, 22 February, http://archives.dailynews.lk/2008/02/22/main_Editorial.asp, accessed 13 March 2014.

Daniel, E.V. (1996) *Charred lullabies.* Princeton, NJ: Princeton University Press.

Das, V. (2008) Violence, gender and subjectivity. *Annual Review of Anthropology,* 37: 283–99.

Das, V. (2013) Cohabiting an inter-religious milieu: reflections on religious diversity. In: J. Boddy and M. Lambek (eds) *A companion to the anthropology of religion.* Oxford: Wiley.

De Alwis, M. (2014) Review of M. Trawick, *Enemy lines: warfare, childhood and play in Batticaloa. Contributions to Indian Sociology,* 48(1): 151–3.

Deegalle, M. (2004) Politics of the Jathika Hela Urumaya Monks: Buddhism and ethnicity in contemporary Sri Lanka. *Contemporary Buddhism,* 5(2): 83–103.

Denham, E. (1912) *Ceylon at the census of 1911.* Colombo: Government Printer.

Dunham, D. (1982) Politics and land settlement schemes: the case of Sri Lanka. *Development and Change,* 13(1): 43–61.

Eickelman, D.F. and J.P. Piscatori (1996) *Muslim politics.* Princeton, NJ: Princeton University Press.

Farmer, B. (1957) *Pioneer peasant colonization in Ceylon: a study in Asian agrarian problems.* Oxford: Oxford University Press.

Feher, M. (ed.) (2007) *Non-governmental politics.* Cambridge, MA: Zone/MIT Press.

Frydenlund, I. (2003) Kataragama in a time of national crisis: diversity and exclusion in a sacred place in Sri Lanka. MA Dissertation, University of Oslo.

Frydenlund, I. (2011) Canonical ambiguity and differential practices: Buddhist monks in wartime Sri Lanka. PhD Dissertation, University of Oslo.

Gaasbeek, T. (2010a) Bridging troubled waters? Everyday inter-ethnic interaction in a context of violent conflict in Kottiyar Pattu, Trincomalee, Sri Lanka. PhD Dissertation, Wageningen University.

Gaasbeek, T. (2010b) Actors in a *masala* movie: fieldnotes on the NGO tsunami response in eastern Sri Lanka. In: D. McGilvray and M. Gamburd (eds) *Tsunami recovery in Sri Lanka: ethnic and regional dimensions.* London: Routledge, pp. 125–42.

Gaasbeek, T. (2013) Flying below the radar: inter-ethnic marriages in Sri Lanka's war zone. In: D. Hilhorst (ed.) *Disaster, conflict and society in crisis: everyday politics of crisis response.* London: Routledge, pp. 167–84.

Gamburd, M. (2000) *The kitchen spoon's handle: transnationalism and Sri Lanka's migrant housemaids.* Ithaca, NY: Cornell University Press.

Geiger, W. (ed. and trans.) (1912) *The Mahavamsa or the great chronicle of Ceylon.* London: Pali Text Society.

Gombrich, R. and G. Obeyesekere (1988) *Buddhism transformed: religious change in Sri Lanka.* Princeton, NJ: Princeton University Press.

Goodhand, J. and N. Lewer (1999) Sri Lanka: NGOs and peace-building in complex political emergencies. *Third World Quarterly*, 20(1): 69–87.

Goodhand, J. and B. Klem, with D. Fonseka, S.I. Keethaponcalan, D. Sardesai and S. Sardesai (2005) *Conflict, aid and peacebuilding in Sri Lanka, 2000–2005.* Washington, DC: Asia Foundation.

Goodhand, J. and O. Walton (2007) *Assessment of Norwegian economic support to Foundation for Co-existence (FCE), Sri Lanka.* Oslo: NORAD.

Goodhand, J., D. Hulme and N. Lewer (2000) Social capital and the political economy of violence: a case study of Sri Lanka. *Disasters*, 24(4): 390–406.

Goodhand, J., B. Klem and B. Korf (2009) Religion, conflict and boundary politics in Sri Lanka. *European Journal for Development Research*, 21(5): 679–98.

Goodhand, J., B. Klem and G. Sørbø (2011) *Pawns of peace: evaluation of Norway's peace efforts in Sri Lanka, 1997–2009.* Oslo: NORAD.

Goonatilake, S. (2006) *Recolonisation: foreign-funded NGOs in Sri Lanka.* New Delhi: Sage.

Hansen, T. (2001) *Wages of violence: naming and identity in postcolonial Bombay.* Princeton, NJ: Princeton University Press.

Hansen, T. (2005) Sovereigns beyond the state: on legality and authority in urban India. In: T. Hansen and F. Stepputat (eds) *Sovereign bodies: citizens, migrants, and states in the postcolonial world.* Princeton, NJ: Princeton University Press, pp. 169–91.

Harischandra, B. (1908) *The Sacred City of Anuradhapura.* Colombo: published by the author.

Hasbullah, S. (2001) *Muslim refugees, the forgotten people in Sri Lanka's ethnic conflict.* Nuracholai: Research and Action Forum for International Development.

Hasbullah, S. and B. Korf (2009) Muslim geographies and the politics of purification in Sri Lanka after the 2004 Tsunami. *Singapore Journal of Tropical Geography* 30(2): 248–64.

Hasbullah, S. and B. Korf (2013) Muslim geographies, violence and the politics of community in eastern Sri Lanka. *Geographical Journal*, 179(1): 32–43.

Hefner, R. (2000) *Civil Islam: Muslims and democratization in Indonesia.* Princeton, NJ: Princeton University Press.

Herring, R. (1972) The forgotten 1953 Paddy Lands Act in Ceylon: ideology, capacity and response. *Modern Ceylon Studies*, 3(2): 99–124.

Heslop, L. (2014) On sacred ground: the political performance of religious responsibility. *Contemporary South Asia* 22(1): 21–36.

Hoole, R. (2001) *Sri Lanka: the arrogance of power: myths, decadence and murder.* Colombo: University Teachers for Human Rights (Jaffna).

Human Rights Watch (2006) *Human Rights Watch world report 2006 – Sri Lanka*, 18 January 2006, available at: http://www.refworld.org/docid/43cfaea725.html, accessed 25 February 2014.

Hyndman, J. and M. de Alwis (2004) Bodies, shrines, and roads: violence, (im)mobility, and displacement in Sri Lanka. *Gender, Place and Culture*, 11(4): 535–57.

International Crisis Group (2008) *Sri Lanka's Eastern Province: land, development, conflict*, Asia Report 159. Brussels: International Crisis Group.

Ismail, Q. (1995) Unmooring identity: the antinomies of elite Muslim self-representation in modern Sri Lanka. In: P. Jeganathan and Q. Ismail (eds) *Unmaking the nation: the politics of identity and history in modern Sri Lanka*. Colombo: SSA: pp. 55–105.

Ismail, M., R. Abdullah and M.M. Fazil (2004) *Dealing with diversity: Sri Lankan discourses on peace and conflict*. The Hague: Netherlands Institute of International Relations (Clingendael).

Jasani, R. (2007) Violence, reconstruction and Islamic reform – stories from the Muslim 'ghetto'. *Modern Asian Studies*, 42(2/3): 431–56.

Jayewardene, J. (1957 [1939]) Buddhism and politics. In: J. Jayewardene, *Buddhism and Marxism*. London: East and West, pp. 41–44.

Johnson, D. (2012) Sri Lanka – a divided church in a divided polity: the brokerage of a struggling institution. *Contemporary South Asia*, 20(1): 77–90.

Kemper, S. (1991) *The presence of the past: chronicles, politics and culture in Sinhala life*. Ithaca, NY: Cornell University Press.

Klem, B. (2011) Islam, politics and violence in eastern Sri Lanka. *Journal of Asian Studies*, 70(3): 1–24.

Klem, B. (2012) In the eye of the storm: Sri Lanka's front-line civil servants in transition. *Development and Change*, 43(3): 695–717.

Klem, B. (2014a) Showing one's colours: the political work of elections in post-war Sri Lanka. *Modern Asian Studies*, online.

Klem, B. (2014b) The political geography of war's end: territorialisation, circulation, and moral anxiety in Trincomalee, Sri Lanka. *Political Geography*, 38(1): 33–45.

Klingensmith, D. (2003) Building India's 'modern temples': Indians and Americans in the Damodar Valley Corporation. In: K. Sivaramakrishnan and A. Agrawal (eds) *Regional modernities: the cultural politics of development in India*. Stanford, CA: Stanford University Press, pp. 122–42.

Knoezer, S. (1998) Transformations of Muslim political identity. In: M. Tiruchelvam and C. Dattathreya (eds) *Culture and politics of identity in Sri Lanka*. Colombo: International Centre for Ethnic Studies, pp. 136–67.

Korf, B. (2004) War, livelihoods and vulnerability in Sri Lanka. *Development and Change*, 35(2): 275–95.

Korf, B. (2005) Rethinking the greed–grievance nexus: property rights and the political economy of war in Sri Lanka. *Journal of Peace Research*, 42: 201–17.

Korf, B. (2006) Dining with devils? Ethnographic enquiries into the conflict-development nexus in Sri Lanka. *Oxford Development Studies*, 34(1): 47–64.

Korf, B. (2009) Cartographic violence: engaging a Sinhala kind of geography. In: C. Brun and T. Jazeel (eds) *Spatialising politics: culture and geography in postcolonial Sri Lanka*. New Delhi: Sage: pp. 100–21.

Korf, B. and H. Fünfgeld (2006) War and the commons: assessing the changing politics of violence, access and entitlements in Sri Lanka. *Geoforum*, 37: 391–403.

Korf, B., S. Hasbullah, P. Hollenbach and B. Klem (2010) The gift of disaster: the commodification of good intentions in post-tsunami Sri Lanka. *Disasters*, 34(S1): 60–77.

Larkin, B. and B. Meyer (2006) Pentecostalism, Islam and culture: new religious movements in West Africa. In: E. Akyeampong (ed.) *Themes in West African history*. Oxford: James Currey, pp. 286–312.

Lawrence, P. (1997) Work of oracles, silence of terror: notes on the injury of war in eastern Sri Lanka. PhD dissertation, University of Colorado.

Leach, E. (1954) *Political systems of highland Burma: a study of Kachin social structure*. London: Athlone Press.

Lederach, J.P. (1997) *Building peace: sustainable reconciliation in divided societies*. Washington, DC: United States Institute for Peace.

Lewer, N. and M. Ismail (2011) A voice in the political process? Creating political space for a Muslim contribution to peace in Sri Lanka. In: J. Goodhand, B. Korf and J. Spencer (eds) *Conflict and peacebuilding in Sri Lanka*. London: Routledge, pp. 119–31.

Lubkemann, C. (2007) *Culture in chaos: an anthropology of the social condition in war*. Chicago: University of Chicago Press.

MacIntyre, A. (1981) *After virtue*. Notre Dame, IN: University of Notre Dame Press.

Madan T. (1997) *Modern myths, locked minds: secularism and fundamentalism in India*. Delhi: Oxford University Press.

Mahadev, N. (2013) Conversion and anti-conversion in contemporary Sri Lanka: Christian evangelism and the Theravāda Buddhist views of the ethics of religious attraction. In: J. Finucane and M. Feener (eds) *Proselytizing and the limits of religious pluralism in contemporary Asia*. Singapore: ARI Springer Asia.

Manor, J. (ed.) (1984) *Sri Lanka in change and crisis*. London: Croom Helm.

Manor, J. (1989) *The expedient utopian: Bandaranaike and Ceylon*. Cambridge: Cambridge University Press.

Marshall, K. (2005) Religious faith and development: rethinking development debates. Paper presented at the Religious NGOs and International Development Conference, 7 April, Oslo. Available at: www.vanderbilt.edu/csrc/PDFs%20and%20Jpgs/marshall-debates.pdf, accessed 13 March 2014.

Maunaguru, S. and J. Spencer (2012) Tigers, temples and the remaking of Tamil society. *Religion and Society*, 3: 169–76.

McFadden, C. (1954) The Gal Oya project: Ceylon's little TVA. *Geographical Review*, 44(2): 272–81.

McGilvray, D. (1998) Arabs, Moors, and Muslims: Sri Lankan Muslim ethnicity in regional perspective. *Contributions to Indian Sociology*, 32(2): 433–83.

McGilvray, D. (1999) Tamils and Muslims in the shadow of war: schism or continuity? In: S. Gamage and I. Watson (eds) *Conflict and community in Sri Lanka: 'pearl of the east' or 'island of tears'?* Colombo: Vijitha Yapa.

McGilvray, D. (2008) *Crucible of conflict: Tamil and Muslim society on the east coast of Sri Lanka*. Durham, NC: Duke University Press.

McGilvray, D. (2011) Sri Lankan Muslims: between ethno-nationalism and the global ummah. *Nations and Nationalism*, 17(1): 45–64.

McGilvray, D. and M. Raheem (2007) *Muslim perspectives on the Sri Lankan conflict*. Policy Studies 41. Washington, DC: East-West Center.

McGilvray, D. and M. Gamburd (eds) (2010) *Tsunami recovery in Sri Lanka: ethnic and regional dimensions*. London: Routledge.

Medhananda, Revd E. (2005) *The Sinhala Buddhist heritage in the east and north of Shri Lanka*. Colombo: Dayawansa Jayakody.

Metcalf, B. (1982) *Islamic revival in British India, 1860–1900*. Princeton, NJ: Princeton University Press.

Metcalf, B. (1993) Living hadith in the Tablighi Jama'at. *Journal of Asian Studies*, 52(3): 584–608.

Miall, H., O. Ramsbotham and T. Woodhouse (1999) *Contemporary conflict resolution*. Cambridge: Polity.

Mines, M. and V. Gourishankar (1990) Leadership and individuality in South Asia: the case of the south Indian big-man. *Journal of Asian Studies*, 49(4): 761–86.

Moore, M. (1985) *The state and peasant politics in Sri Lanka*. Cambridge: Cambridge University Press.

Moore, M. (1993) Thoroughly modern revolutionaries: the JVP in Sri Lanka. *Modern Asian Studies*, 27(3): 593–642.

Mosse, D. (2012) *The saint in the banyan tree: Christianity and caste society in India*. Berkeley: University of California Press.

Nandy, A. (1990) The politics of secularism and the recovery of religious tolerance. In: V. Das (ed.) *Mirrors of violence: communities, riots and survivors in South Asia*. Delhi: Oxford University Press.

Needham, A. and R. Sunder Rajan (eds) (2007) *The crisis of secularism in India*. Durham, NC: Duke University Press.

Nissan, E. (1985) The sacred city of Anuradhapura: aspects of Sinhalese Buddhism and nationhood. PhD dissertation, London School of Economics and Political Science.

Nissan, E. (1989) History in the making: Anuradhapura and the Sinhala Buddhist nation. *Social Analysis*, 25: 64–77.

Nuhman, M. (2007) *Sri Lankan Muslims: ethnic identity within cultural diversity*. Colombo: International Centre for Ethnic Studies.

O'Hare, G. and H. Barrett (1996) Spatial socio-economic inequalities in Sri Lanka: core–periphery frameworks. *Tijdschrift voor economische en sociale geografie*, 87(2): 113–23.

Obeyesekere, G. (1981) *Medusa's hair: an essay on personal symbols and religious experience*. Chicago: University of Chicago Press.

Obeyesekere, G. (1988) *A meditation on conscience*. Colombo: Social Scientists' Association.

Orjuela, C. (2004) Civil society in civil war: peace work and identity politics in Sri Lanka. PhD dissertation, Göteborg University.

Osella, F. and C. Osella (2008a) Introduction: Islamic reformism in South Asia. *Modern Asian Studies*, 42 (2–3): 247–57.

Osella, F. and C. Osella (2008b) Islamism and social reform in Kerala, south India. *Modern Asian Studies*, 42 (2–3): 317–46.

Peebles, P. (1990) Colonization and ethnic conflict in the Dry Zone of Sri Lanka. *Journal of Asian Studies*, 49(1): 30–55.

Peel, J. (in press) Christianity, Islam and the Oriṣa: comparative studies of three religions in interaction and transformation.

Rahula, W. (1974 [1946]) *The heritage of the bhikkhu: the Buddhist tradition of service*. New York: Grove Press.

Reimann, C. (2004) Assessing the state-of-the-art in conflict transformation. In: A. Austin, M. Fischer and N. Roopers (eds) *Transforming ethnopolitical conflict: the Berghof handbook.* Wiesbaden: VS Verlag, pp. 41–66.

Robbins, J. (2003) What is a Christian? Notes towards an anthropology of Christanity. *Religion,* 33(3): 191–99.

Robinson, F. (2008) Islamic reform and modernities in South Asia. *Modern Asian Studies,* 42(2–3): 259–81.

Rogers, J. (1994) Post-Orientalism and the interpretation of premodern and modern political identities: the case of Sri Lanka. *Journal of Asian Studies,* 53(1): 10–23.

Ruwanpura, K. (2006) *Matrilineal communities, patriarchal realities: a feminist nirvana uncovered.* Colombo: Social Scientists' Association.

Said, E. (1994) Identity, authority, and freedom: the potentate and the traveler. *boundary 2,* 21(3): 1–18.

Sánchez Meertens, A. (2013) Courses of conflict: transmission of knowledge and war's history in eastern Sri Lanka, history and anthropology. *History and Anthropology,* 24(2): 253–73.

Schonthal, B. (2012) Buddhism and the constitution: the historiography and postcolonial politics of Section 6. In: A. Welikala (ed.) *The Sri Lankan Republic at 40: reflections on constitutional history, theory and practice,* vol. 1. Colombo: Centre for Policy Alternatives, pp. 201–18.

Scott, D. (1996) Religion in colonial civil society. *Cultural Dynamics,* 8(1): 7–23.

Scott, D. (1999) *Refashioning futures: criticism after postcoloniality.* Princeton, NJ: Princeton University Press.

Seneviratne, H.L. (1999) *The work of kings.* Chicago, IL: University of Chicago Press.

Sidel, J. (2007) *Riots, pogroms, jihad: religious violence in Indonesia.* Ithaca, NY: Cornell University Press.

Siegel, J. (2006) *Naming the witch.* Stanford, CA: Stanford University Press.

Sikand, Y. (2007) The reformist Sufism of the Tablighi Jamaat. In: M. Hasan (ed.) *Living with secularism: the destiny of India's Muslims.* New Delhi, Manohar, pp. 129–48.

Singer, M. (1972) *When a great tradition modernizes: an anthropological approach to Indian civilization.* Chicago: University of Chicago Press.

Sloterdijk, P. (2013) *Im Schatten des Sinai: Fußnote über Ursprünge und Wandlungen totaler Mitgliedschaft.* Berlin: Suhrkamp Verlag.

Smith, W. (1963) *The meaning and end of religion.* New York: Macmillan.

Spencer, J. (ed.) (1990a) *Sri Lanka: history and roots of the conflict.* London: Routledge.

Spencer, J. (1990b) Collective violence and everyday practice in Sri Lanka. *Modern Asian Studies,* 24(3): 603–23.

Spencer, J. (2000) On not becoming a terrorist: problems of memory, agency and community in the Sri Lankan conflict. In: V. Das et al. (eds) *Violence and subjectivity.* Berkeley: University of California Press, pp. 120–40.

Spencer, J. (2003) A nation 'living in different places': notes on the impossible work of purification in postcolonial Sri Lanka. *Contributions to Indian Sociology,* 37 (1–2): 1–23.

Spencer, J. (2007) *Anthropology, politics, and the state: democracy and violence in South Asia.* Cambridge: Cambridge University Press.

Spencer, J. (2008) A nationalism without politics? The illiberal consequences of liberal institutions in Sri Lanka. *Third World Quarterly,* 29(3): 611–29.

Spencer, J. (2012) Performing democracy and violence, agonism and community, politics and not politics in Sri Lanka. *Geoforum,* 43(4): 725–31.

Stirrat, R. (1984) The riots and the Roman Catholic church in historical perspective. In: J. Manor (ed.) *Sri Lanka in change and crisis.* London: Croom Helm, pp. 196–213.

Stirrat, R. (1992) *Power and religiosity in a post-colonial setting: Sinhala Catholics in contemporary Sri Lanka.* Cambridge: Cambridge University Press.

Stirrat, R. (2006) Competitive humanitarianism: relief and the tsunami in Sri Lanka. *Anthropology Today,* 22(5): 11–16.

Suryanarayana, P. (1998) An Eelam outpost. *Frontline* 15(1), http://www.frontline. in/static/html/fl1501/15010540.htm, accessed 13 March 2014.

Tambiah, S. (1996) *Leveling crowds: ethno-nationalist conflicts and collective violence in South Asia.* Berkeley: University of California Press.

Thangarajah, Y. (2003) Ethnicization of the devolution debate and the militarization of civil society in north-eastern Sri Lanka. In: M. Mayer, D. Rajasingham-Senanayake and Y. Thangarajah (eds) *Building local capacities for peace: rethinking conflict and development in Sri Lanka.* Delhi: Macmillan India, pp. 15–36.

Theyvanayagam, S. (2006) Tantonrisvaram, Kokkatticcolai. In: S. Pathmanathan (ed.) *Hindu temples of Sri Lanka.* Colombo: Kumaran Book House.

Thiranagama, S. (2010) In praise of traitors: intimacy, betrayal, and the Sri Lankan Tamil community. In: S. Thiranagama and T. Kelly (eds) *Traitors: suspicion, intimacy, and the ethics of state-building.* Philadelphia, PA: University of Pennsylvania Press.

Thiranagama, S. (2011) *In my mother's house: civil war in Sri Lanka.* Philadelphia, PA: University of Pennsylvania Press.

Trawick, M. (2007) *Enemy lines: warfare, childhood, and play in Batticaloa.* Berkeley: University of California Press.

Uphoff, N. (1996) *Learning from Gal Oya: possibilities for participatory development and post-Newtonian social science,* 2nd edn. London: Intermediate Technology.

UTHR(J) (1990) *August: A bloody stalemate.* University Teachers for Human Rights (Jaffna), Report no. 5, http://www.uthr.org/Reports/Report5/Report5.htm, accessed 13 March 2014.

UTHR(J) (2006) Terrorism, counterterrorism and challenges to human rights advocacy. University Teachers for Human Rights (Jaffna), Special report no. 20, http://www.uthr.org/SpecialReports/spreport20.htm, accessed 13 March 2014.

Uyangoda, J. (1997) Academic texts on the Sri Lankan ethnic question as biographies of a decaying nation-state. *Nethra,* 1(3): 7–23.

Van der Veer, P. (1992) Playing or praying: a Sufi saint's day in Surat. *Journal of Asian Studies,* 51(3): 545–64.

Venugopal, R. (2009) Cosmopolitan capitalism and sectarian socialism: conflict, development, and the liberal peace in Sri Lanka. PhD dissertation, Oxford University.

Venugopal, R. (2010) Sectarian socialism: the politics of Sri Lanka's Janatha Vimukthi Peramuna (JVP). *Modern Asian Studies*, 44(3): 567–602.

Walker, R. (2013) *Enduring violence: everyday life and conflict in eastern Sri Lanka.* Manchester: Manchester University Press.

Walton, O. (2008) Conflict, peacebuilding and NGO legitimacy: national NGOs in Sri Lanka. *Journal of Conflict, Development and Security*, 8(1): 133–67.

Walton, O. (2012) Peace building without using the word 'peace': national NGOs' reputational management strategies during a peace-to-war transition in Sri Lanka. *Critical Asian Studies*, 44(3): 363–90.

Walton, O. and P. Saravanamuttu (2011) In the balance? Civil society and the peace process, 2002–2008. In: J. Goodhand , J. Spencer and B. Korf (eds) *Conflict and peacebuilding in Sri Lanka: caught in the peace trap?* London: Routledge, pp. 183–200.

Walzer, M. (1997) *On toleration.* New Haven, CT: Yale University Press.

Weiss, G. (2011) *The cage: the fight for Sri Lanka and the last days of the Tamil Tigers.* London: The Bodley Head.

Whitaker, M. (1990) A compound of many histories: the many pasts of an east coast Tamil community. In: J. Spencer (ed.) *Sri Lanka: history and the roots of conflict.* London: Routledge.

Whitaker, M. (1999) Tigers and temples: the politics of nationalist and non-modern violence in Sri Lanka. In: S. Gamage and I. Watson (eds) *Conflict and community in Sri Lanka: 'pearl of the east' or 'island of tears'?* Colombo: Vijitha Yapa.

Whitaker, M. (2007) *Learning politics from Sivaram: the life and death of a revolutionary Tamil journalist in Sri Lanka.* London: Pluto.

Wimmer, A. and N. Glick-Schiller (2002) Methodological nationalism and beyond: nation-state building, migration and the social sciences. *Global Networks* 2(4): 301–34.

Wirz, P. (1966) *Kataragama: the holiest place in Ceylon.* Colombo: Lake House.

Index